BEST DAMN HIP HOP WRITING

THE BOOK OF YOH

TRAVIS "YOH" PHILLIPS

Edited by
Amir Ali Said

Series Editor
Amir Said

Superchamp Books SB

New York

Edited by Amir Ali Said
Arranged and Edited by Amir Said

DESIGNED BY AMIR SAID

Cover, Design, and Layout by Amir Said

Print History:
December 2017: First printing.

Best Damn Hip Hop Writing: The Book of Yoh
/ by Travis "Yoh" Phillips
Edited by Amir Ali Said
Series Editor Amir Said
1. Phillips, Travis "Yoh" 2. Said, Amir Ali 3. Said, Amir 4. Hip Hop Music Criticism 5.
Rap Music Criticism 7. Music Criticism
I. Phillips, Travis "Yoh;" Said, Amir Ali; Said, Amir II. Title

Library of Congress Control Number: 2017963296
ISBN 978-0-9997306-0-7 (Paperback)

As a fellow writer I hope
you understand this being
late was not intentional.

I lose time and get lost in a
sea of words and duties.
For someone who lives by
deadlines I'm bad at them.

I hope this reaches you well.
Thanks again for sending
yours by. Hopefully
we can do something
in the future.

— Yoh

CONTENTS

FOREWORD

About the *Best Damn Writing* Series

There is a lot of good writing happening today. From the explosion of talented essayists to freelance writers to independent authors to DYI poets and more, this era is rapidly producing some of the most engaging and culturally influential writing ever recorded. At the same time, however, much of this writing is being missed by the very readers who would likely appreciate it the most. This is not to say that a lot of the great writing of today is being overlooked, but rather that the number of literary channels — and their outdated publishing methods and often non-inclusive traditions — is insufficient to the growing body of interesting writing that's taking right now. And this is especially the case when it comes to contemporary anthologies.

Anthologies are a great way to discover new writers and a means for further understanding the art and craft of writing. For classic Western literature, the task of assembling an anthology tends to be a foregone conclusion, at least in terms of the writers (nearly all old white men) that readers supposedly *should* know. But I don't believe that contemporary anthologies need to suffer from a similar ideological, non-inclusive fate.

More specifically, the inclusive kind of anthologies — that I believe better serve new voices in writing — do not exist in tall order. Anthologies, which have typically been fashioned by a narrow group of people whose tastes are tuned to an even more narrow corner of writing, are often positioned well outside of the mainstream. Because of this, I think the potential of the anthology, as a pop culture item, is largely unrecognized. That's why I've created the *Best Damn Writing* series. I want to help anthologies become a more recognizable part of pop culture, not something merely for so-called literary types. Moreover, I want to reimagine what the anthology is; how it's shaped, who it's for, and how it works.

To me, anthologies are playlists for readers. And just like music playlists, literary playlists benefit from the specific tastes and backgrounds of its curators. Within this context I believe that there is a premium for curated literature that stands beyond bloated listicles or selection archetypes commonly found among literary elitists. I've cultivated my taste from a broad consumption of literature, music, film, art, and pop culture. Certainly, this is not to say that my taste is superior to anyone else's, but rather it's fine tuned to the areas of culture that I've long had deep interest in and, in many cases, that I have written extensively about. Thus, I want the *Best Damn Writing* series to be an anthology that promotes some of the finest writing in popular culture, specifically in the areas of hip hop, poetry, film, memoir, art, and technology — all of the corners of culture that occupy my deepest interest and exploration.

As to what I believe constitutes the "finest" or "best damn" writing in these areas, well, I base this not so much on personal taste but on what I believe are the three things that anthologies should do. First, I believe an anthology should be about discovery. It should introduce writers to new audiences; and, conversely, it should introduce audiences to emerging and established writers whose work deserves further amplification. Second, I believe that an anthology should offer insight into the craft of writing. That is to say, it should offer a close-up on style and form and the different ways in which themes are developed by writers. Finally, I believe that an anthology should always offer fresh perspectives and insights. The kind that illuminate current cultural moments and shed light on important points from the past.

About the *Best Damn Hip Hop Writing* Series: Documenting Hip Hop Culture and The Rise of Hip Hop Music Criticism and Hip Hop Studies

Hip hop culture has always been a central interest of mine. From my very first book, *The BeatTips Manual,* which explores the history of the art of beatmaking, to my book *The Art of Sampling,* which examines copyright law and music sampling, I've continually aimed to document hip hop culture and demonstrate why it is such a powerful cultural force around the world. Further, since I first began reading *The Source Magazine* as a teenager in the early '90s — my first introduction into hip hop music criticism — I have continued to be impressed by the level of writing being done in this area. Moreover, the academic discipline commonly known as hip hop studies, which has also produced a number of notable works over the past 30 years, has helped inspire my own writing in this field.

But today, hip hop music criticism is a pretty mixed bag; and hip hop studies often feels stuffy and dominated by scholars who seem to be outside of the hip hop community. The freedom of the internet has made it more possible than ever before for individuals to publish their own ideas and observations about music. That bloggers (myself included) have been able to do so as an alternative to what the so-called tastemakers have to publish is particularly liberating. And to be certain, there are some really terrific (highly knowledgeable) hip hop/rap music bloggers. That being said, most hip hop bloggers of today tend to be of three types: (1) Highly subjective fans (of one artist, sound, style) who write glowing write-ups; (2) News writers whose main objective often leans into the world of gossip; and (3) Think-piece writers who carry the analytical skillset and writing chops that you would expect from any good journalist.

The latter type is certainly outnumbered because coverage at many hip hop publications has shifted towards news (often sensationalist gossip) and away from quality analysis. So while the quality of hip hop music criticism has risen in some places, the overall quality hip hop/rap music criticism has become a bit of a crap shoot — a zone where overzealous subjectivity, disconnected analysis, and/or poor writing often drowns out the signal of terrific writing.

As an academic discipline and literary category, hip hop studies is fairly new. Within this space there have been some important works written by various recognized scholars. But the voices, often buried in exhaustive research and dense prose, are often kept inside the walls of academia and are therefore not exposed to pop culture and the people (practitioners) most vested in hip hop culture. In order for hip hop studies to grow, I believe that the walls between academia and pop culture must come down. This point is key because the work of many hip hop scholars is often disconnected from the actual pulse of hip hop culture; likewise, the writing of far too many hip hop music writers demonstrates a serious lack of awareness of the pivotal work that has been published by scholars. Thus, scholars will be better served by more inclusive peer reviews (if you will), and those who engage with hip hop culture primarily from a non-academic paradigm will certainly benefit from a more direct exchange with the work of scholars. In this context, I want the *Best Damn Hip Hop Writing* series to serve as a link between the interrelated worlds of hip hop music criticism and hip hop studies.

Finally, whether it be hip hop music criticism or hip hop studies, the goal of this series is to provide a pathway to a deeper understanding to some of the critical themes in hip hop, while also offering critical observations on some of hip hop's most influential artists.

—Said (Amir Said),
Paris, France
October 30, 2017

Introduction

Today, hip hop music criticism stands as an eclectic mix of think pieces, clickbait, listicles, and gossipy news. So in this current environment, it's difficult to stand out as a writer. But Yoh (Travis Phillips) has been able to achieve much notoriety in just a short period of time. In terms of what I would describe as "outlier" hip hop bloggers — the most intelligible, savvy, and/or creative hip hop writers — Yoh is one of the brightest and most promising. What sets him apart is that he does not follow the routine, formulaic approach to music criticism, nor does he incorporate the hum-drum (often hyperbolic spectacle) found in much of hip hop writing today. He takes chances with his ideas (he often approaches hip hop music criticism through the lens of memoir and short-story writing), and he lays bare his thoughts without pretense, shame, or fear of reprisal.

Thus, what exists in this volume is an examination of hip hop from a broad mix of devices. From artist retrospectives to critical observations about craft and industry to Yoh's personal essays, this collection demonstrates the artistic, economic, and emotional power of hip hop culture. Collectively, *Best Damn Hip Hop Writing: The Book of Yoh* represents the work of a writer who is not quite at the beginning of his career, but peering out from its horizon nonetheless, aiming high for what opportunities will afford his unique talent. It is a moment so rarely captured in a writer's career that the exercise itself benefits readers (especially fellow writers) in innumerable ways. Thus, I hope readers find what I've found in Yoh: A writer whose expertise, knowledge, vulnerability, and raw dedication is so aptly woven together that it reminds you of the flexibility and creativity of hip hop culture itself.

—Said (Amir Said),
Paris, France
October 30, 2017

Part 1
CRITICAL
OBSERVATIONS

Hip Hop and the Spectrum of Summertime

As a child who loathed the colder months, the first kiss of warmth from the season change was nothing short of a hug from heaven. Halloween, Thanksgiving and Christmas are why weather fit for snowmen and penguins, igloos and Coca-Cola bears is endured. When the holidays end, to be warm again is all that's desired.

Spring's arrival is the brief interlude that leads up to summer's dawn, the foreword that you read before diving into your favorite novel. I thought everyone viewed spring through the temporary lens—a transitional period—until I heard Chance The Rapper say, "I heard everybody's dying in the summer, so pray to God for a little more spring."

Death, God and hope for an extended spring aren't words you will find rapped in The Fresh Prince's (Will Smith's) "Summertime." In its three immortal verses, the successful 1991 single paints the imagery of post-spring perfection — the kind of fun, thrilling adventures that can only be had underneath the sun of late May, June and July. "Summertime" was released the year and month of my birth, and every year that followed ushered in my favorite season. I associated that first "drums please" with moon bounce birthday parties and Happy Meal afternoons, long days roller skating and long nights spent shooting a basketball. It was the best of times being soundtracked by a song that encouraged maxing and relaxing.

The Fresh Prince's rap personified what you want to see when you step outside, what you wish every day would resemble when you wake up and school is out. By capturing what it's like being back home in Philadelphia and how it feels once spring takes her very last breath, DJ Jazzy Jeff & The Fresh Prince gave the season a voice, they gave summer a song. It's a musical Kodak moment, but "Summertime" excludes summer's true madness.

Hailing from Chicago, Chance has a vastly different relationship with the hottest season of the calendar year. You can almost smell the stench of gun smoke, the decay of bodies, and the overwhelming fear that radiates from "Paranoia," Chance's most throat-gripping, soul-grabbing song. There's a blunt in his mouth, a gun on his hip, and the looming grim reaper on his mind. Death isn't around the corner, it's all around and his presence is suffocating. Kids are being buried, help is being cried for, and even the sounds of fireworks on the 4th of July can't be enjoyed without the traumatic connection to gunfire. If The Fresh Prince's summer was heaven, Chance's summer was hell.

Cause everybody dies in the summer / Wanna say your goodbyes, tell them while it's spring / I heard everybody's dying in the summer / So pray to God for a little more spring
—Chance The Rapper

Chance once compared heaven to a prison, seeing the gates as a cage keeping loved ones in and not a paradise for souls. The comparison shows a resentment of loss, a pill that never gets any easier to swallow. The above lyric is from "Windows," a song that can be found on Chance's 10 Day mixtape. A few bars prior, he raps, "Some of us is seeing summer, some of us have passed, Some of us ain't seeing summer, some of us have passed," an interesting juxtaposition of passing school classes and friends passing to the other side. This is someone in high school, an adolescent who is celebrating escaping summer school while musing on the kids who couldn't make it to the school year's end.

5

In a 2015 interview with *Chicago Magazine* sometime after the birth of his daughter, Chance said this about life and death in the city that raised him: *"Anywhere past age 13 — 10 if you live in Chicago — you have a relationship with death as you've seen it depicted in media, or around you, if you've watched somebody die."* [1]

"Summer Friends" from Coloring Book touches upon how summer is a season of loss in a subtle manner, much brighter than "Paranoia." Sonically, it sounds like a game of hopscotch in the candy store, but the pain of loss in the summer is still a prevalent theme. Nostalgia is an easy feeling to connect with — and nostalgia is a big part of Chance's artistry — but every memory of summer has to contrast mowing lawns with having to be home early; the first day of camp is followed by the first shooting; friends without fathers and CPD recruiting new officers to handle the impending heat wave. *"Our summer don't get no shine no more, our summer die, our summer time don't got no time no more,"* says it all.

When it gets hot, it gets violent, and often deadly. While the murder rate in Chicago has decreased, history says shootings will increase throughout the summer season. This isn't exclusive to Chicago, though. The heat boils the blood of men and women everywhere. When I interviewed GoldLink earlier this year, collaborator Obii Say explained how the summertime is beautiful, but that it's also when murders and shootings escalate. GoldLink's *At What Cost* is sonically gorgeous, filled with fun and summer anthems, but it's still a story revolving around how quickly things can turn deadly even when you're having the time of your life.

Link's "Meditation" is a summer song that ends with gunshots. One act of violence is all it takes before the entire summer is engulfed in a string of unfortunate acts that can change lives. Vince Staple's debut *Summertime '06* is an album influenced by his adolescence when he was no older than 13. The same year that Young Dro had the world shoulder leaning, Vince was out getting active. The intro starts off with the sound of waves and seagulls, you can close your eyes and envision the beach. At the last second, right before the song ends, a blast shoots through the comfort — summer isn't a time to be comfortable. That's just how the album begins, the rest is a journey through the unforgiving jungle that Vince called home. Both Vince and GoldLink have friends who didn't survive that summer, and they haven't forgotten.

Pop culture has an interesting way of feeding our concept of summer. Movies aren't capturing Chance's paranoia and pain in cinema, summer is still more about lustful flings and careless afternoons, more *Sandlot* than *Hardball*. Spike Lee's *Do The Right Thing* was a film that unapologetically painted the most gruesome picture of how an excruciating heat wave can cause spirits to burn with a vehement fire. On a cooler day maybe Radio Raheem and Sal are calmer; without their minor argument the police don't arrive and choke the very life from Raheem's body. Raheem lives and Mookie doesn't throw that trash can through the window, inciting the riot. *Do The Right Thing* is really a movie that revolves around the hottest day in Brooklyn and how the simmering heat can spiral racial tension to a place of unforgettable proportions. In this context Raheem was just another summer friend who didn't make it to the fall.

The first episode from "The Wire's" fourth season is called Boys Of The Summer and introduces Dukie, Randy, Michael and Namond — four Baltimore students from different backgrounds who we watch walk through their own personal purgatories. One of the most intriguing scenes happens after Dukie is beaten up by a local gang. Of course, boys being boys, they want to react. Michael inquires whether they should get guns, an idea that's not uncommon where they're from. Instead, the boys fill water balloons with piss to throw at their adversaries. Plans fail, they fight, and ice cream is there to cool their bruises. They're young, boyish, and still in that stage where the hellfire on their heels hasn't engulfed their entire beings. I'm pretty sure Chance would relate to Dukie,

Randy, Michael and Namond over "The Fresh Prince of Bel Air" show's Will, Carlton, Ashley and Hilary.

"The show is full of characters who, with few other options, have traveled down self-destructive paths. The audience doesn't often get to see all the factors—internal and external—that have led them astray. But in the fourth season, we're introduced to four black adolescents whose futures are uncertain. The arc unfolds over a semester at a junior high. It's painfully affecting. You're seeing the lives of kids at stake, and that's powerful drama. The Wire was never better than when it was telling their stories." —Ed Burns[2]

"The Wire" doesn't allow the boys' summer to last in innocent bliss. Viewers watch as they slowly get pushed deeper into the fire; the summer friends are thrown into drugs and murder. They aren't product of their environments, they're kids just trying to survive the circumstances they were born into. There's no mercy for the babies, the madness is a hungry hippo and they all are in the belly of the beast. It's why the fourth season of "The Wire" is acclaimed as the series' best, the portrayal of these children and the overall school system is heart-wrenching, yet eye-grabbing. Because you know, deep down, this is reality.

Summer's bliss and summer's madness are two sides of the spectrum, two sides of life. It's what makes all of Chance's songs about summer and death so harrowing; they're all based in reality. GoldLink's reality. Vince's reality. The Fresh Prince wrote "Summertime" from how he remembered summer in Philly but it also feels a bit like a fantasy, like what we long for. Maybe that's why it continues to resonate; we're still dreaming of living that summer.

I've watched countless jaws collide with fists while "Knuck If You Buck" played in the background. I've sat in classrooms in the middle of lessons that abruptly turned into books being thrown and hair being pulled. Watching as teachers stormed out of rooms to get security or assistance wasn't abnormal. My school couldn't have pep rallies because rival schools would sneak over and start fights in the gymnasium. Knives would be brought to homeroom, guns would sit next to books inside backpacks. House parties were shot up so frequently that the news reports became normal.

One of the wildest days of my youth occurred when someone called in a bomb threat to my parents skating rink, and I can still feel the frantic fear and pulsing panic in the air. But never death. Unlike Lil Uzi Vert, all my friends are alive. Sometimes it would come close, as a reminder not to get comfortable, not to forget any second could be the last. I can't imagine knowing death at the age when I'm still trying to know myself, trying to figure out my place in this whirling world.

Kendrick Lamar Has Quietly Become Music's Biggest Christian Rapper

Unlike DMX, who would pray on his albums with a pain-dripping bark that engulfed ears, the boys Kendrick chose to pray on his opening track seem like an insignificant detail once the infamous van begins to roll underneath the Compton street lights. Bible study isn't what has Kendrick Lamar out late with his foot pressed to the pedal; the church is far from his mind as he races to Master Splinter's Daughter.

He's driving through a city where the sinners outnumber the saints, more horns than halos, more darkness than light, through a series of events he plunges listeners into the madness. At the very end of the album, after the rising action has climaxed, right before an act of revenge is carried out, a woman appears standing between a bunch of boys prepared to sin again. Kendrick would later call this woman an angel, for she offered an alternative, a way to battle their hate with love of the Lord. Presenting baptism as an option, having them recite the same Sinner's Prayer from the beginning. Remember this day she said, "The start of a new life, the start of your real life."

In the parking lot of a Food 4 Less, Kendrick was unconventionally baptized by the grandmother of a friend who came across him after a murder. As told on the album, he was saved that day, possibly in more ways than one. It's hard to imagine a man who saw his first murder at five — and second murder at eight — being able to believe in a heaven when hell is all around him. To be a flower buried on the top of a Volcano never knowing when the lava will spill instead of the safe soil can be a heavy burden on the spiritual soul. He raps on the song "Faith," "I opened my Bible in search to be a better Christian. And this from a person that never believed in religion. But shit, my life is so fucked up, man; I can't help but give in."

As the first verse progresses, he's filled with the spirit, but when the Sunday service ends, a phone call of another friend's murder snatches whatever faith was found just moments before. Reality and the circumstances can break any man. The song continues to highlight the difficulties of keeping faith when life doesn't get easier but applies more pressure while you're down. The song may seem more pessimistic than hopeful but in the final verse he states, "But what I do know, is that He's real and He lives forever / So the next time you feel like your world's about to end / I hope you studied because He's testing your faith again."

"Faith" dates back to 2009, when Kendrick first changed his name from K-Dot and released the *Kendrick Lamar EP*. It was a fresh start and an adaptation of a more personal approach to his music and introducing the concept of the good kid. With each album, as he grew into a notable name in the industry, Kendrick's faith has only grown with his acclaim. *Overly Dedicated* has "Heaven & Hell," a brilliant but incomplete perspective of the good and bad based on Kendrick's perspective. It fades away before completing his visions of heaven.

After *Section.80*, he spoke with MTV who asked about his religious upbringing due to the song "Kush & Corinthians." His response was what you'd expect from someone rather young, who is still in the religious stage of asking questions. He goes on to say that he's a sinner who's trying to figure it all out, a mindset that could easily have inspired the hook for "Don't Kill My Vibe." It's not obvious, but "I am a sinner, that's probably going to sin again" is one of the most religious hooks that isn't outwardly Christian to hit the mainstream in some time. You don't even notice when singing along.

I wouldn't say I'm the most religious person, neither were both of my parents. I always do quote-unquote religious songs or whatever you want to call them from the standpoint where I'm trying to find answers. That's the space I speak from and a lot of people can relate because they feel the same way. [I'm] not a person that's putting it in your head — "believe this, believe this, believe this." I'm going through something, I'm a sinner and I'm trying to figure myself out. It never sounds preachy. It sounds like a person who's really confused by what the world has put upon him.[3]

Kendrick is jokingly baptized by Mike Epps in what appears to be a traditional church pool in the "Don't Kill My Vibe" music video except it's a pool full of liquor, a nod to "Swimming Pools." While the mock baptism was good for a chuckle, Kendrick made headlines during the L.A stop on the Yeezus tour when he announced that he was recently baptized while shouting out his Bishop. There's something humorous about Kendrick being on the Yeezus tour with the man that went from singing "Jesus Walks" to bringing him out on stage and deciding that now it's a good time to be saved again. Where was his mind at? To do it while on tour makes the action seem urgent as if he couldn't wait another day.

Three days before the release of *good kid, m.A.A.d city*, Kendrick recorded "The Heart Pt 3," a song where he confronts the pressures of his position, someone not only looked upon as Tupac's successor but a shining beacon of hope for hip-hop's future. "Enough pressure to make you just open the Book of David," he raps toward the end of his first verse, indicating that he sought comfort in the Bible and not worldly vices to deal with all the stress and strains of his upcoming album debut.

Life didn't get easier after the album release, while on the road with Kanye, Kendrick got calls from home that Chad, Braze and Pup were all murdered. Childhood friends that he grew up with, killed in the same mad city that put him on that tour bus, that brought him success in music, that ultimately took him away from them. He mentions them by name on YG's "Really Be," it's an emotional verse with torment and demons suffocating his vocal chords, like it's painful for him to even let the words out. On Fredo Santana's "Jealous," Kendrick goes from boasting about taking private jets for Harold's Chicken and being unable to speak because there's a woman sitting on his face to "I got worry on my brain, I been gone all summer / Just to fly back home and found out y'all done killed my little brother."

In his 2013 *GQ* Rapper Of The Year profile, journalist Steve Marsh begins the article by mentioning how he's unable to locate Kendrick. No one from the either label, TDE and Interscope, knew where he was. He was coping with the death of Chad, the friend he would later mention in the song "u," who was shot and wounded but held on for a month before passing. Kendrick was overseas at the time, the last time they spoke was on Skype. Imagine this burden while in-route to New York City's fall Fashion Week.

Chad Keaton's memorial service was held just before Labor Day weekend; Kendrick attended, then flew straight to a show in Alaska. Next it was on to Vegas to perform at a pool party. He only made it "back to the set" to grieve for a single day, the day we were scheduled to talk. "It can be complicated and confusing," Kendrick says of his life right now, funerals for murdered friends one day, private jets to fashion parties the next.[4]

It takes you back to "Faith," the juxtaposition of feeling near heaven but reality reminds you of the hell that awaits back at home. You can see how these events sparked the survivor's guilt that would be a huge topic on *To Pimp A Butterfly*. His life had changed, he was facing new pressures from inching closer to super-stardom, but bad news was never far, it could've easily pushed him toward a darker solution, but these trials likely brought him closer to God. Which is why his faith plays such a crucial role in *To Pimp A Butterfly*. Kendrick reached a mindset through his beliefs that are soaked into his music but unlike Kanye, he doesn't have a "Jesus Walks" single that commercially and openly displays his beliefs. Kanye was worried about God taking away from his spins, Kendrick doesn't seem to have that kind of doubt, God is the one who brings the spins. Instead of centering his faith into one single, he spread it across the album, wrapped in metaphors and allegories, even without a prayer it's obvious that *To Pimp A Butterfly* was made by a Christian man.

On Halloween, Lamar dressed as Jesus Christ. "If I want to idolize somebody, I'm not going to do a scary monster, I'm not gonna do another artist or a human being – I'm gonna idolize the master, who I feel is the master, and try to walk in his light," he explained. "It's hard, it's something I probably could never do, but I'm gonna try. Not just with the outfit but with everyday life. The outfit is just the imagery, but what's inside me will display longer."[5]

It's done subtly, details so small that they can easily go unnoticed. Instead of saying that Lucifer, the devil that fell from heaven, is the one that's trying to court him, he creates the character Lucy, a woman that has the same purpose but doesn't have the same harsh imagery. You can't make jokes about I Love Lucy with Lucifer, but they are one and the same. Instead of making God into an omnipresent deity that brings him to salvation, Kendrick uses a homeless man to be the figure for the big man that lives beyond the clouds. "How Much Does A Dollar Cost" is done masterfully, the way he transitions from placing judgment on a man he assumes is panhandling for money to being judged by his father in heaven. It's incredible storytelling and artistry; and it's also very Christian. God finds ways to speak to you through others, like the lady from *good kid, m.A.A.d city*, or the homie from "Average Joe" that kicked Kendrick out the car when he was prepared to ride on the bangers that shot at him. His life has been full of angels but he chose a homeless man, someone we see every day to play the role of God.

"It's a true story... These are moments in my life deeper than just handing somebody a dollar. These are actually moments of integrity, actually being able to talk to somebody. Me talking to him was simply a thank you from God. And I felt God speaking through him to get at me." —Kendrick Lamar[6]

The many interviews that came before and after *To Pimp A Butterfly* showed Kendrick speaking more openly about his relationship with God. When he spoke with the *New York Times* he revealed that he considers himself to be the closest thing that some fans have to a preacher, a realization that came while being on the world tour. He explained that he's a vessel for God's work, two very strong statements.[7] Many have cited the music industry as an evil place where souls are lost due to money, fame, and worshiping the material over the spiritual. In Kendrick's case, he underwent a spiritual awakening, an enlightenment that was always there but dormant.

Billboard has listed 17 biblical references that can be found on *Untitled Unmastered*.[8] The first song is Kendrick's illustration of judgment day, The Book of Revelation in rap form. He even walks us through what he's prepared to reply when God asks, "What have you done for me? I made To Pimp a Butterfly for you, Told me to use my vocals to save mankind for you, Say I didn't try for you, say I didn't ride for you, I tithed for you, I pushed the club to the side for you, Who love you like I love you?"

"Whether we was inside a church or not, my mother always kept that faith inside of us. The more I started going through my own things in life, my faith got put to the test, and I had to believe that God is real in my heart, my lord and savior Jesus Christ, and I can't run from that. I'll always put that in my music or it just wouldn't be right. People can take it or leave it, I really don't care, because it's for me to put it on records. And I will continue to put more of a spiritual nature in my music." —Kendrick Lamar[9]

Reading the lyrics, it's a surprise Kendrick hasn't been labeled a Christian rapper. Like all genre labels, there's only one rule that applies to everyone. But neglecting the temptation of radio and club success because you'd rather use your voice to speak for the Lord should be on the list. He basically admits that *To Pimp A Butterfly* was an album he made for God, which connects with the mentality of being a preacher for the fans. When Kanye announced his *The Life of Pablo* as a Gospel album no one knew what to expect. With "Ultralight Beam" as the intro — soulful, choir, Kirk Franklin feature — you assumed that it was the album's blueprint until you hear him rapping about bleached assholes. It's one gospel song, not a gospel album, but that's Kanye, he has to make a big statement. Kendrick doesn't have to scream at us so we realize his faith in God.

I was 19, walking through Atlanta's Lenox Mall, window shopping when a man approached me. He was well dressed and seemingly rather harmless. He asked me what I knew about Jay-Z. I answered as if I had been studying Jigga for Black History Month throughout grade school. I know Jay-Z better than I know myself. I finish, expecting to get free concert tickets or maybe an invitation to a trivia rap game show. Imagine my surprise when he followed up my response with, "So what do you know about Jesus Christ?" I could talk about the Church of Hov all day but the Church of God was a different story, there's a reason why I'm not a gospel music journalist.

If he would've started the conversation about Jesus, I probably would've searched for an immediate way out, but Jay was different, it was a rap discussion, not a religious confrontation. That's what Kendrick does. He just raps and we love it. He doesn't worry about labeling himself or announcing that this album is gangster rap and this album is gospel. That would put him in a box.

LimeWire:
The Wrong That Felt So Right

By the bedside sits a bag full of old compact discs, an early inheritance passed down from my father. On the very top is Makaveli hanging from the cross — bold, black, beautiful, yet gut-wrenching. Underneath him lie albums from Wu-Tang, Slick Rick, MC Lyte, Foxy Brown, Snoop, Jay-Z and other notable names from the late '90s and the early 2000s. I can almost imagine my father walking into Best Buy or f.y.e., or some small record shop and spending his hard-earned cash on all this rap music.

I think about how different our experience with music is, especially since some of the very CDs he has gifted me I've heard but never physically touched. He comes from an age of physical CDs, and I'm from the generation of .mp3s. He's a saint who paid for his music, and I'm a dirty pirate who surfed the internet downloading. He had to leave home to obtain his music, while music reached me by the way of Limewire.

It was around 2004 — I was no older than 13 — that my life revolved around school, the radio, the internet, Toonami and Rap City. I don't remember how we met, or what caused our paths to cross, but it was love at first click. One download and life changed forever; it was the introduction to a new reality. Some doors you walk through and never return. Limewire was that door for me, and there was no going back. Limewire was the definition of simplicity, there was nothing complicated about the software. With no prior knowledge of file sharing, without knowing what peer-to-peer meant and with no real understanding of copyright infringement, I was able to acquire almost any song that came to mind. Just by typing in a title, the files were able to be obtained. My fingers were set ablaze, my mind was racing; I felt like a caveman that just discovered fire. For a kid with a love for music but no money to purchase albums, it was like a cheat code for infinite albums. Limewire didn't bring Christmas early, it gave me Santa's entire gift bag at my fingertips.

What really made Limewire special was the ability to discover. I could type in Lil Wayne's name in search of "Go DJ" and also stumble upon underground music from *The Suffix*, *The Prefix*, and all of the *Sqad Up* mixtapes. The first time I heard Wayne rap over "Ether," "Best Of Me" and "Moment Of Clarity" were all due to curiosity. It was during a Dipset search that I found Roc-A-Fella's version of Queen's "We Are The Champions." Dame's boasting and bragging, Kanye's strong verse, Beanie's Hulk-esque aggression (the tone of his voice when he cuts off Dame showed me that he was a man to be feared), Twista closing with the rapid-fire flow; all things that made it a favorite posse cut. Countless unheard remixes, freestyles, mixtapes and underground releases made Limewire something to spend hours on. It was like a library with shelves of .mp3s instead of books, and I was hungry to hear all that I could. Albums were still bought — 50 Cent's *Get Rich Or Die Trying*, The Game's *The Documentary*, Jeezy's *Thug Motivation 101* and Wayne's *Tha Carter II* were all purchased. Some albums you had to have.

LimeWire wasn't all Eden; there were plenty of snakes in the grass. It was the cause of my first, second and third computer viruses. Each time was like getting food poisoning from your favorite restaurant. After all the vomiting, after swearing to never go back, you still end up walking through the door again asking for a seat by the window. The bad never outweighed the good.

I find it funny how one of the biggest presidential scandals of all time is associated with viruses and Limewire. Everyone loathed downloading a song they really wanted, and being greeted by the voice of Bill Clinton confessing he didn't have sexual relations with that woman. It was a lesson on being aware of file sizes and how not everything that glittered truly wasn't gold. Music, movies, videos, porn — it was all there, it was all accessible, and then it was gone. It only took a few good lawyers and four years of courtroom war to bring down one of the most popular file sharing websites. *The Guardian* reported at the time of termination, over 50 million users were sharing copyrighted files.

In May, Wood found LimeWire liable for widespread copyright infringement. The level of damages faced by the site's New York-based parent company, Lime Group, will be decided in January 2011. The RIAA said LimeWire has cost the music industry hundreds of millions of dollars in revenue. According to figures from the RIAA, U.S. recorded music sales fell to $7.7bn in 2009 from $14.5bn in 1999. The rise to prominence of peer-to-peer filesharing networks is singled out as a primary factor for this decline by the RIAA. The site's popularity is reflected in a survey by NDP Group, which found that LimeWire was used by 58% of people who have downloaded music from a peer-to-peer network in the year from May 2009.[10]

Limewire might've been a gift for the kids growing up on the internet — truly our gateway drug into music — but it was a curse to the music industry. I wasn't aware of how my method of acquiring music was changing the entire infrastructure of a once-thriving system. The music wasn't free; a lot of people were paying for it. Limewire wasn't the first file sharing service to impact the music industry, it was just one of many.

The true forefather that caused a huge ruckus for peer-to-peer music sharing was Napster. One of the biggest, most impactful moments in the internet era was the launch of Napster, a music service that was the big bad wolf that blew the music industry's comfortable house down. Two teenagers, Shawn Fanning and Sean Parker, created a program that made downloading music easier than it had ever been at the time. Launched in 1999 and closed in 2001, with over 50 million users downloading millions of songs in-between. Every revolution begins with a small fire that will eventually engulf the old regime, and Napster was that flame. I wasn't a user—it came and went before a computer was in my household—but millions will never forget. The beginning of album sales dropping, the birth of music being free, and all the other repercussions that came with these two changes cannot be understated.

By now, the heads of the major record labels had gathered for a summit. In the Washington offices of the Record Industry Association of America (RIAA), execs were encouraged to play a game that was informally called Stump the Napster – in other words, try to find at least one of their new singles that wasn't being shared online. All were appropriately horrified and an action was launched against Napster for breach of copyright. The first year of the new millennium was the first to register a dip in global record sales. That scared the labels, and before long individual Napster users were being sued too, some 18,000 all told. Alex Winter told me he met a woman, in the course of making his documentary, who over a decade later was still embroiled in a multi-million-dollar action. She'd once used Napster to download *26* songs.

LimeWire was doomed from the start. It was destined to follow in the same footsteps as Napster. I remember similar, alternative programs born from the demise, but none of them came close to seizing the attention of the masses. The end of Limewire was like the neighborhood kid that had all the Playstation games being forced to move away, and you're left playing Crazy Taxi when just last week you were shooting cops on Grand Theft Auto: Vice City. Napster and Limewire were unjust, against the law, and played a major role in bringing the music industry into its darkest period. They took away the concept of music as a product and made free music our birthright. We were born in this era, and this was our reward. It was wrong, but it felt so right. Downloading music became second nature; what they called piracy became more like breathing to us. All the millions lost, all the lawsuits, all the lives changed; it was all because of the internet.

It was more than just Limewire throughout the years. I lost count of all the albums and mixtapes downloaded thanks to Megaupload, Rapidshare, Sendspace, and Mediafire. They were the file storage systems that I'll always relate to the golden era of the blogs. If you were changing your IP address just so you wouldn't have to wait for the download limit, I tip my hat. When Megaupload was shut down, it was like going to a bar and finding out the friend that gives you all the free drinks was fired for giving out free drinks. Zshare, Bearshare, Hulkshare, Kazaa, Imeem, Frostwire, Demonoid, Piratebay, Isohunt or Mininova... the list goes on. They brought us music, movies, and viruses, and if you were raised on the internet, you are familiar with at least one of these services.

It's hard to fix my lips to speak harshly of the current era of streaming without thinking of how we got here. We got here because of Napster, Limewire and all the music that wasn't bought. The monthly fees we pay today are the cost of years sneaking into Heaven through the backdoor. I have a lot of streaming to do to cleanse my pirate soul for all that I indirectly took. Funny how one man's dream was an entire industry's nightmare. That's the power of change, it affects everyone differently.

My father will be turning 50 in a few days. He still plays his CDs that he has left over, and doesn't care for the streaming services or the streaming war. By the time I'm 50, who knows where the music industry will be? As long as I can pass down my 2016 Apple Music playlist to my son, I probably won't care at 50 either.

From Queensbridge to Compton: Exploring the Duality of the Regional Hip Hop Perspective

Coldness radiates from the piano keys as Mobb Deep's "Survival of the Fittest" begins. Before a single rhyme is rapped, the underworldly piano is leading you somewhere bleak and unforgiving. It's the slow, daunting build up of a roller coaster ascending to the highest point before dropping at the speed of an Acme anvil that makes the seconds unnerving. A strange, almost taunting siren can be heard right before the drums drop, further warning that you've ventured into a place of peril. There are no better words to begin a song that's both thrilling and frightening than "There's a war goin' on outside no man is safe from."

Mood and atmosphere are what Havoc (of Mobb Deep) crafted when he sampled Barry Harris and Al Cohn. When creating based on what's around you, the very sound can be reflective of home. Havoc's home was Queensbridge, New York, the largest public housing development in North America. What the production captures is the chill and ruggedness easily associated with a place that has devoured weaker souls. Mobb Deep's creative approach wouldn't have gravitated toward a sound so dark and merciless if it wasn't for RZA's production blueprint and their surroundings. Queensbridge was the muse that inspired their timeless descent into darkness.

What has always impressed me about Mobb Deep's *The Infamous* is how each beat and rhyme never leaves the underbelly of anguish. LL Cool J was dominating radio with "Doin' It"; fusing soft hip hop with doe-eyed R&B. He won with a crossover worthy of Allen Iverson's applause. Prodigy and Havoc could have attempted some form of replication to achieve similar success, following in the footsteps of the seasoned Queens emcee. They didn't. Commercial influence doesn't exist on *The Infamous*, Mobb Deep's second and most revered album. There's not a touch of glitter or any suggestion that this album was crafted for radio consumption. A realness is buried in the DNA of each of the album's 16 songs, an embedded truth that isn't always apparent in rap but can be found in any courtroom where sworn honesty is the only kind. It's as if Mobb Deep swore they'd be honest, promising every boy and girl in their beloved hood that they would paint their front and backyards with explicit accuracy.

There was a side of New York that wasn't being appropriately represented, a sound that Mobb Deep dared to make its signature. LL was still in New York at the time; Nas was still in New York; and so on and so on — a city overflowing with music and musicians cannot have one face or voice. Within the layers of diversity, identity matters. New York needed Mobb Deep's interpretation of their world the same way it needed A Tribe Called Quest. Both groups leaned heavily on jazz sampling to build their universes, but with vastly different sonic results. When you build a product that's based on the inner world and not the outer world, it births a very distinctive offspring. So many sounds and styles will forever be intertwined with the very men and state that birthed and bred them.

One man can carry a crown and sit upon a throne, but a sole king can not represent a musical kingdom. It was the crown that T.I. and Shawty Lo once beefed over, despite the Atlanta neighborhood of Bankhead needing both of their voices. There was room for "You Don't Know Me" and "Dun Dun." Atlanta would not be the same without Jeezy and Gucci Mane, *Thug Motivation 101* shares a similar importance to *Trap House*. Even if the concept of regional music has suffered due to the internet breaking down barriers — no longer keeping us isolated or tethered only to the noise of our hometowns — regional hip hop still matters a great deal. A great example is how Big Boi, Young Thug and 2 Chainz all recently dropped albums on the same day. Three different projects, three different sounds, but all hailing from the same city. This is a level of representation one artist can not incarnate.

Big Boi represents an era of the past, a time when OutKast was an outfit of unpredictable musical explorers. As a solo artist and living legend, Big Boi continued to follow the beat of his own funky drum instead of attempting a youthful transformation. 2 Chainz fits into the present tense, a trap rapper who contains essential elements of the *Trap Muzik* that T.I. made infamous. Adapting and adjusting allowed him to survive the last 20 years in this industry and just now reach the peak of commercial success and visible adoration. He beat all the odds, dodged many pitfalls, and came out a giant. These are two older, more seasoned artists who have found their respected lanes.

Young Thug, on the other hand, is an anomaly. To call him a trap rapper seems shortsighted. With each album he moves further from the traditions of his contemporaries. *Beautiful Thugger Girls* is a genre-blender that could be a glimpse into the future, but the future is uncertain with Young Thug, an artist who lives in the moment for only a moment. Tomorrow his eccentric rhyme style and melodic musing could be delivered over gospel organs and Kirk Franklin sermons. He took experimenting where Big Boi would never go, stretched trap aesthetics beyond 2 Chainz' imagination, and broke the limits of weirdness that has been attached to him. A true oddity. A true ATLien.

Chance The Rapper and Chief Keef are, musically speaking, incompatible. Chance chased after the color of gospel and jazz during Keef's rise as the face of cold and thunderous drill music. The differences are too apparent to list, but they are both connected to their shared homeland of Chicago. In the early 2010s, an interesting split occurred, though. As the Windy City saw a band of drill artists sign major label record deals, Chance and a company of artistic poets started to build followings online. If you watched the two at once, it was impossible to deny their duality. Chance and Keef, King L and Mick Jenkins, Lil Durk and Vic Spencer, Lil Bibby and NoName — the differing narratives showcase the many neighborhoods of Chicago.

From harrowing street tales to poetic musing on the city's state, a vast array of perspectives was being presented. Keef and L saw their commercial peaks in 2013, as guests on Kanye's Yeezus. Three years later, Chance and Vic Mensa were the new Chicago kids on *The Life of Pablo*. *Acid Rap* may be the acclaimed classic but *Bang, Back From The Dead* and *Finally Rich* also deserve to be written in history. Chicago's renaissance doesn't start with Chance, it's intertwined with Keef, drill, and all the good, bad and ugly sparked from a teenager on house arrest.

Like Chicago, Southern California has a similar duality with artists like Kendrick and YG, Vince Staples and ScHoolboy Q, Boogie and Jay Rock. Different areas in California raised them, heavily influencing their real-life experiences, but their approaches differ.

Both Kendrick and YG went the narrative route with their debut albums, creating a cinematic, day-in-the-life audiobook. We see the madness of their lifestyles — there's no prison in Kendrick's story, and YG's is absent of any good kids. G-funk and gangster rap are still heavily affiliated with Cali's sunshine but every artist mentioned has approached the medium with fresh ideas and a genre-pushing passion. *Summertime '06* and *Blank Face LP* both earned a heaping of acclaim, but the master craftsmanship of both artists wasn't enough to push them into the upper echelon of rap stardom. The lack of widespread attention doesn't negate that *90059* was Jay Rock at his finest, an artistic facelift. Boogie's *Thirst 48* also fell through the cracks despite being an applaud-worthy follow-up to *The Reach*. California is many things, but it is far from artistically motionless.

The homes of grandparents tend to carry a distinguished smell. A natural scent that the nose and brain will register moments after inhaling. Eyes aren't required to view a full head of gray hairs to know you are in a house of elders. The first whiff upon entering will let it be known. Music works in a similar fashion, the way we innately register sound to a person or a place. This big, growing genre may devour its young, but a unique voice can not be silenced. Finding that voice, crafting the sound of home, building a universe for listeners to be lost in and fearlessly giving that to the world can change a region, alter a genre, and immortalize your name amongst the great.

J. Cole Was Signed by Jay-Z, Then He Was Left Alone

He stands outside Roc-The-Mic studios with a freshly burnt beat CD and a bottle of E&J praying, hoping, and waiting, for Jay Z. The waiting, there's always more waiting. It's night, the rain begins to pour. Two hours go by, his stomach is full of cheap liquor and raging butterflies as an expensive car pulls up. Hova has arrived. For a young man that once made a "Produce for Jay-Z or Die Trying" shirt, this was it, the reason he moved to New York, attending college in the City Of Dreams instead of staying in his home state of North Carolina. When the opportunity comes, standing in front of the man who could hand him his ticket off cheap couches and overdue rent, words refuse to form. He stutters and stammers. Jay sees the CD in his hand, a wall goes up in his eyes. "I don't want that, give it to one of them," he says. If this had happened to me, I would've walked away cursing Jay's name, playing "Ether" all the way home, hoping that while he's recording American Gangster Beyoncé is in the arms of her true love, Memphis Bleek. Not J. Cole. He took his first encounter with Jay as a lesson learned, that getting on wouldn't be so easy.

A year later, it was Jay Z asking to meet the same kid he previously dismissed. Mark Pitts played one song which lead to a three-hour meeting which lead to multiple meetings (waiting, always more waiting) until eventually J. Cole was officially the first artist signed to Roc Nation. This is a story well known by fans, but I don't know if I truly appreciated how astounding the tale is until recently, especially from Jay's perspective.

"The real thing is that they weren't going to do rap, if that tells you like my position over there. They weren't

gonna do rap. I think Roc Nation was just gonna be a pop label" —J. Cole[11]

As Cole said in his Complex interview after the signing was announced, Roc Nation was created to be a label focused on pop music. Jay didn't want the resurrection of Roc-A-Fella but to recapture the success he had during his Def Jam presidency with Rihanna and Ne-Yo, but on an even larger scale. There wouldn't be any Diplomats or State Propertys, he wasn't seeking talent from the streets but voices that could reach the households he couldn't imagine while standing on Marcy Project blocks. Rita Ora, Willow Smith, Calvin Harris, these are the kind of artists that fit into that mold, the kind of artists that would be eaten alive standing in the Roc-A-Fella jungle with real lions from Philly and tigers from Harlem.   J. Cole was someone different. He wasn't a pop sensation or a hustler with imagination but a rapper passionate about rap, a hip hop artist through and through. So what made Hova make a detour in his plans, signing a rapper more focused on making hip hop history than dollar signs or fame? I have to believe Jay's intuition told him that this kid had that mythical "it."

"Lights Please" is the song that led to the first meeting, a song that showed a relationship between a young man full of angst toward the cold world and young women whose only passions are loud packs and casual sex. A record with zero crossover possibility, too slow for the clubs, too intellectual for radio, a businessman would've dismissed it. Listening to it now I think of Kanye West's "Jesus Walks," a song that challenges the accustomed and accepted. I imagine Jay listening to it and thinking it would sink in a world where Soulja Boy's "Kiss Me Through The Phone" and Jamie Foxx's "Blame It" were current Billboard hits. I imagine he saw attributes of his little brother, Kanye West. J. Cole didn't have his swagger or the enchanting ego of a mad scientist, but reading over his old interviews from this time frame it's clear he had a glow. Who stood before Jay was a passionate rapper that cared more about making good music than making good money. A producer that learned to make beats because he was tired of rapping over others' subpar productions. Southern roots with an east coast style, not from the streets but familiar with hardship. An anomaly.

After seeing the success of music's favorite college dropout, I don't think it was a coincidence that Jay's next big artist would be a college graduate. Another example of how J. Cole's selection further shows his separation from the artists Jay formally associated with on Roc-A-Fella. If he saw anything in Cole, it was that he lacked any obvious star power. There was no gimmick attached to his persona, no style that gleamed with magic, he was simply a dreamer that grew up on hip hop from the late '90s and early 2000s. This is the kid Jay prophesied about on the 2000 *Back Stage* Documentary; later and fittingly used on J. Cole's "Rise and Shine." He was looking into the future, a rapper born from his pre-retirement world that could reach a new demographic of fans witnessing the music at the end of gangster rap's era. If Jay saw any of this, along with the talent displayed on "The Warm Up," there's no way he could let J. Cole leave his office without signing a deal, even if a rapper wasn't in Jay's original blueprint for his new Roc Nation empire.

During the Roc-A-Fella era, Jay-Z used his co-sign to stamp the label up-and-comers and associates, similar to how Rick Ross functions now on MMG. Jay's growing likeness was meant to bring allure to other acts like Freeway, Beans and Bleek. It wasn't just a feature, Jay had entire songs on their albums. "Dear Summer" is a classic Jay Z song that appears on Memphis Bleek's 534. The last song on Beanie Sigel's The Truth is "Anything," another Jay Z solo record. Not to mention The Dynasty album, a Roc-A-Fella compilation marketed as a Jay solo LP that was meant to showcase the talent he was housing. Jay appeared in their videos, studio sessions, magazine covers, the Roc was a family and he sat at the table's head. Roc Nation didn't have a chair for Cole, to the outside world their relationship was like Vernon Dursley and Harry Potter. The internet has countless jokes about how the two have surprisingly few pictures together, I could only find one video where Jay is speaking to Cole. J. Cole has yet to produce for Jay and only received one feature from the boss since his signing in 2009. A feature that he had to wait for (waiting, always more waiting) so long that his albums mastering was stopped and had to be pushed back a week. It's easy to claim that Jay just doesn't care, that J. Cole was a side project for him, an investment he didn't invest much time in.

"It was a time when he was in all of the Roc-A-Fella artist videos. He's older now and has different priorities. Jay is a businessman. He signed me, that's enough. I respect that Jay lets me do what I want to do." —J. Cole[12]

You don't relate J. Cole to Jay-Z in the same way as the artists during the Roc-A-Fella era. No one ever says Cole is successful because Jay-Z made him. In fact, the further he goes from a Jay-Z guest verse, the more successful he's become. I think Jay's lack of public support tactic turned out to be a blessing in disguise, perhaps Jay's intent all along. He removed his name so that his artist could glow if the moment presented itself. Their relationship is based on trust and the belief that Cole didn't need a giant to lift him, that he had potential to grow into a giant himself. I remember hearing Big Sean rapping over "Say You Will," confessing his frustration with the lack of support from Kanye and the label: "But honestly I wish that I could take you off tour, Put you in the studio so you could focus more on my shit." I believe this is the attitude of most artists that sign under a bigger artist, they have certain expectations, and it turns into a waiting game. It's a sentiment that I never saw in J. Cole's music or character. He was driven, determined, with or without a deal he would make it. Jay-Z found a rapper that he wouldn't have to babysit. Introduce him to the world and let him sink or swim. J. Cole's destiny was always in his own hands.

"One thing I appreciate about Jay-Z is he let me do it my way and let me figure it out. ... He never compromised or interfered with my creative process. There was never a point when he was like, "I need to come in and play big brother and show you how to do this." He let me figure it out, and it feels better to win like that. It feels better winning knowing that I figured this thing out on my own and if it wouldn't have worked, I would have been OK with bumping my head and failing on my own terms, rather than winning on somebody else's" —J. Cole[13]

Later Jay would sign Jay Electronica, meaning that from 2009 to 2015 J. Cole was essentially the only active rapper on Roc Nation, a label founded by one of the greatest rappers of all-time. Cole's been surrounded by producers, songwriters and potential popstars, yet somehow became the label's biggest and brightest investment. He went from getting the coldest shoulder outside of a studio to a hip-hop leader in his own right, from "Mr. Nice Watch" to rapping about getting robbed for a nice watch.

Playlists and the Future
of Lyrical Rap

Childish Gambino's "Redbone" has achieved a level of commercial conquest that's completely uncharted territory for the Stone Mountain, Georgia-born multi-faceted creative. Daniel Glass, president of Glassnote Records, recently cited Spotify's RapCaviar playlist as the launching pad that sent the single soaring. This is the power of a curated playlist with over seven million subscribers.

When East Atlanta's 6LACK was at the genesis of his blossoming career, his hit single "PRBLMS" brought him millions of eyes and ears. He was new, fairly unknown, and still under the radar of radio—but he had Apple Music. The streaming service not only premiered the record but was able to spread "PRBLMS" across 10 different Apple Music playlists. Unlike Spotify, Apple Music doesn't reveal how many of their millions of subscribers utilize playlists but it's more than enough to jumpstart a promising music career. The blogs can't claim him, radio wasn't first; the old guard has become the tortoise in this ever-evolving era.

Curated playlists like Spotify's Rap Caviar and Apple Music's The A-List: Hip-Hop have also become a leading source of music discovery, able to break songs, accelerate hits, and present new faces to their immense listener base.

For artists, getting placed on a prominent playlist has become nearly as important as radio play. "Labels obsess over that," says Ben Swanson, co-owner of indie label Secretly Group, which represents rockers like the War on Drugs.[14]

In July, 2017 it was reported that hip hop is the most popular music genre for the first time in U.S. history, a feat accomplished thanks to on-demand services like Spotify and Apple Music where rap and R&B are dominating. What the statistics don't show, however, is that while mainstream rap and artists with a mainstream-esque approach to rap are being given all the tools to succeed, underground traditionalists aren't receiving the same convenience.

The next Drake has a promising path to an audience of millions if his melodies and singing appeals to ears accustomed to rapping and singing that coexist as a singular art form, but what about the next Jay Electronica? Unfortunately — or fortunately, depending on your music preference — trap rappers and hybrid rapper-singers have an advantage in rap's current climate. The sounds of Gucci Mane and 6LACK have a wider appeal than Earl Sweatshirt and Oddisee, a reality that is reflected in some of rap's biggest playlists.

The song "Sorcerer" by milo doesn't sonically complement Cardi B's "Bodak Yellow," but both deserve the same awareness. Skyzoo's "95 Bad Boy Logo" and J.I.D.'s "Hasta Luego" should be highlighted for their potent lyrical prowess but don't earn the same number of placements as Lil Pump's "Boss" or 21 Savage's "Bank Account." It's not a question of better or worse but rather a lack of balance.

Where does the lyrical lyricist — or simply a more traditional rapper — exist in the rise of algorithmic-developed streaming services and human-curated playlists? Do rhyme bars, in the most traditional sense, have a thriving home to spotlight those writing rhymes in the underground?

In order to get answers to these questions, I spoke with Carl Chery, the Head of Hip-Hop/R&B Programming at Apple Music. It was Chery who received an email from 6LACK's manager, Seam Famoso, which led to "PRBLMS" being championed by Apple Music.

Carl is a real industry OG. From working at XXL as a journalist to acquiring a post at Beats Music in 2012 (before the service became Apple Music), he knows music discovery and he knows hip-hop. It's a bit comforting knowing the man who is behind all the Apple hip-hop playlists is someone deeply engrossed in the culture. But even the biggest hip-hop head understands we aren't in the age of wizardry lyricism.

"Before everything went online there was a clear separation," Chery explained. "You never had the biggest artists in music, or in hip hop, on the same platform as emerging artists or artists no one ever heard about. That's what the blogs did. You had Drake on NahRight." Chery went on to reminisce about how blogs brought a balance between the emerging mainstream and underground darlings. It was a duality that didn't exist when radio was the industry's leading tyrant.

When asked about an artist who leans more toward traditional rhyming without the usage of melodic enhancement in their rap style, Chery mentioned Walterboro, South Carolina native Nick Grant with glowing praise. Earlier this year, he premiered Nick's "Luxury Vintage Rap" on Zane Lowe's popular Beats 1 radio show — the same show that premiered 6LACKs "PRBLMS" and helped place the song on multiple playlists. He calls the record, "Organized Noize production that sounds like Public Enemy and he's rapping the whole time with a bunch of punchlines."

Chery elaborated further on the path of a lyrical artist:

"There's no melody, maybe one song off the mixtape that uses melody, but I've played Nick Grant before on some of the biggest playlists on the service. I'm a little bit more careful when I play that kind of artist just because that's not exactly the current landscape. Mumble rap just takes off faster. It's just what happens. If you're a more lyrical artist, it's going to take you a little bit more time to get to a certain point. What's the last lyrical rapper that became a star? Chance. Probably Chance. He didn't get there overnight, it took him four projects to get there. When you look back on Kendrick, he did it step by step. Same with Cole. Any lyrical rapper that I can think of did it step by step."

Chery understands that he's seated in a powerful and influential chair. He understands the importance of championing lyricism and music with a message. "For me, it's important to still give them a shot on the platform and the right playlist," he said. For a lyricist, that "right playlist" could be Apple Music's BARS. Originally titled Lyrics To Go — an homage to the A Tribe Called Quest track on Midnight Marauders — the playlist was developed after Chery had an epiphany that the current generation of youngsters seeking out the latest playlists predates the golden era of Tribe and they likely wouldn't understand the reference. Once the name was changed, the numbers began to surge.

Buddy, J.I.D., Jalen Santoy, and Dreezy all have at least one record featured on the playlist alongside Kendrick, Lauryn Hill, Ghostface Killah, and De La Soul. BARS is closer to more classic hip hop records, but seeing the newcomers alongside legends and legendary records is a positive step in a right direction. It's still a rather new playlist, one that Chery admits he hasn't yet had time to dedicate to growing, but he has high hopes for what it could become.

When asked if he foresees a future where popular playlists can be driven by new lyricists, Chery seemed hopeful:

"I think it can grow into that. If you look at Kendrick and the year he's having. Kendrick is influential, but I think with him having such a commercially successful year, and him being around for so long now, you're going to start seeing the influence a little more now. Sometimes, you come in and people don't realize how influential you are. It takes time. Sure there's a lot of mumble rap, and to have a meteoric rise doesn't really happen with lyricists, but the guys at the top can always rap. I don't know if Drake is on BARS right now but he should be. You can say what you want about him, he can rap. J. Cole can rap. Chance can rap. We can go back to the beginning of hip-hop. The top guys in hip hop could always rap. You might've had someone who had a good year — no offense — but like a Nelly because he had some pop hits. But at the end of the day the top guy can always rap."

Even as an acclaimed rapper, Kendrick Lamar earning the highest-selling album (so far) of 2017 is a rather impressive accomplishment. Unlike the jazzy foundation of *To Pimp A Butterfly*, *DAMN.* leans closer toward the soundscape of modern rap. A song like "LOYALTY" shows Kendrick is able to adapt, create a record for radio, but he's still able to bless rap fans with album cuts like "DNA," "FEAR" and "DUCKWORTH."

During our conversation, I mentioned Mir Fontane to Chery, the New Jersey rapper signed to 300 Entertainment who has a popular single ("Frank Ocean") on Spotify. Mir isn't a "mumble rapper" but he's able to make music fitting of mainstream rap's current sound. On the flip side, Mir can also craft a record like "$horty $tory," which showcases a natural storytelling prowess that would be admired in hip hop's yesteryears.

In a recent meeting with Trippie Redd, a young rockstar rapper in the same musical lineage as Lil Uzi Vert, Chery was blown away by the bar-filled "Can You Rap Like Me?" but to date, it's the least popular song from his *A Love Letter to You* mixtape. "It's literally the most intelligent song I have on my tape, with the least amount of views," Redd told Pigeons & Planes in a recent interview.[15]

The new generation isn't as one-dimensional as some would perceive. As Chery explained, it's mostly a matter of strategy.

"Maybe it is a thing where some of these guys want to be lyrical, [but] they come in and try to figure out a different entry point. What I said earlier about the top guys being lyrical, always, I don't think everyone is having that conversation. I think the perception is that guy who I found out about in March by September has a million followers on Twitter and Instagram, a hit song, and he's on Instagram talking on the money phone, he's everywhere. It creates the perception that it's the way to go, maybe that's why people — I don't want to call it microwave music — still gravitate towards that. There's always going to be a window to that quick scheme. But Kendrick has been around for a couple years, he's not going anywhere. All the guys that we've mentioned earlier—Drake's been around nine years, I know people will be mad about me mentioning him with the other guys but the guy got bars."

It's disheartening to think that every artist may have to adapt in order to showcase their wide ranging, artistic palette, but this approach isn't new. Joe Budden had to drop a classic dance record ("Pump It Up") before he could release his deeply introspective *Joe Budden* debut on Def Jam. Visibility isn't acquired just by being the nicest with the bars. One of the most interesting takeaways from my conversation with Carl is that, when it comes to bars, he believes lyricism is a bit deeper than complex rhyme schemes and clever punchlines. Not everyone will agree, but there's something to his perspective and how the bar for bars can be up for discussion.

"The OGs will be mad at me for saying this but the meaning of bars has become different. A lyricist will always be a lyricist. All the guys that I named earlier in addition to J.I.D., those guys are lyrical. We talking about imagery, wordplay, and being clever, but the thing is, there's also a skill in making a song that's fun to rap along to. Cardi B has the hottest song out right now, "Bodak Yellow." She says, "Got a bag and fixed my teeth," that's a bar! It's not lyrical, but you have a reaction to it. You're like, 'Oh, shit, that's a dope line.' Or like Baka Not Nice, that guy from Drake's camp, I've been talking about that song for the last 48 hours and I keep quoting a different line. He said, 'Just remember, I'm a shooter first and rap is not my thing,' see, you laughed. He's not lyrical but that's a bar. There's an art to saying certain things that connect to people. Me and my friend were talking about perfect verses. Years ago, I would've named you Mos Def on 'Two Words' or something that's lyrical. But now, I feel like 21 Savage's first verse on 'X' is a perfect verse. He caught everything perfect, he has the references that make you say, 'WTF did he just say,' and it's fun to rap along to. Just like Offset on 'Bad and Boujee' is a perfect verse."

What Carl is referring to is something I've been intrigued by since Young Guru introduced the idea of a "trick." It's a skill long utilized by JAY-Z, who quickly realized that in order to sell albums he had to stop rapping like Common Sense. Drake, Kanye, and even Kendrick are all masters of the trick. Without question, "HUMBLE" is an entire song built on the concept of tricks. It won't be remembered as Kendrick's most lyrical record, but sold-out arenas rapping every word will cement "HUMBLE" as Kendrick's most impressive trick yet.

Amidst lyrical rap's uncertain future, there are more questions than answers, but Carl is optimistic, going so far as to cite J.I.D, Nick Grant, Buddy, Smino, and IDK (formally known as Jay IDK) as the next crop of lyrical artists to take off. "There can't be a certain type of artist where there's no room for them," said Chery when I asked him to give aspiring lyrics artists a piece of advice. "We'll probably get to a point where I'm not the only one curating a playlist that caters to lyricism."

There was a time where I put my trust into Shake and Meka, Eskay and Kevin Nottingham, DJBooth and OnSmash, and countless other blogs and bloggers. They were the gatekeepers who introduced me to everyone from The Cool Kids to Elzhi, and while I still look to them, the new era has new gatekeepers and they're curating playlists for millions. Carl hasn't forgotten about the wordplay wizards and Olympic lyricists, he's aware, and that awareness could lead BARS to become the next big playlist that introduces the world to the successor of "Exhibit C."

Even If It Destroys You:
Lil Wayne and the Muse Called
Drugs & Vice

Watching Lil Wayne from 2006–2009 was like witnessing someone that wasn't a human being. He seemed invincible, that his lungs could inhale pounds on pounds of kush smoke, his body could handle an endless waterfall of Lean, and he would still deliver the most potent of bars.

Lil Wayne was 27 years old in 2009. A year after selling a million copies of *Tha Carter 3*, and a year before trying to sell us the catastrophe that is *Rebirth*. His mixtapes were already deemed classics in the underground, "Lollipop" hitting number one broke him into the mainstream, and his protégés Drake and Nicki Minaj were starting their careers. He was arguably the best rapper alive, with the vices of a rock star, his untimely death would've been devastating but expected. There's only so much a man can test the waters of his mortality, but the same substances that would bring his destruction were aiding in his creative expression. In a way, his career is fascinating, as he descended deeper into the darkness his acclaim shined the brightest. The industry would be shaken to its core, the rest of the year would be dedicated to glorifying his contributions and endless amounts of tribute songs. To this day, Wayne is one of hip-hop's most notable stars, but in that moment of time, who was higher? Who else was riding on a course to destruction? Wayne could've crashed and exploded into fireworks.

I remember listening to Mac Miller's *Faces* and thinking this is an A&R's nightmare, TMZ's wet dream, middle finger to critics, damn impressive, and a cry for help. It was obvious that drugs were musing the music, unlocking his potential, and he spoke about it with gallows humor. Addiction and death are greeted like dinner guests, every lamented lyric ends in lol. Mac attacks issues like a Comedy Central roast comedian, poking plight with a pitchfork. I'll proclaim it his best project yet. Lines like, "I know my father probably wish I would just smoke pot, my grandma probably slap me for the drugs I got, I'm a crackhead but I bought her diamonds, we love rocks," is brilliant and equally cringing. Obviously he had found the same artistic stride that had Wayne running circles around his contemporaries, walking down a creative passageway that leads to rave reviews and tombstones. In that same black hole you'll find the Slim Shady that everyone wishes would stand up, but Marshall Mathers is in a better place because of it. When an artist finally emerges from the swirling madness, the music is never the same and the reactions always leave me baffled. It has to be conflicting wanting to better yourself while your fans would rather you be in hell creating heavenly art.

A$AP Yams recently passed away and it still feels surreal. You never think about the drugs winning, even after countless deaths. Young Thug gives me the same eerie feeling of Wayne when he was diving into a pool of destruction. Weezy is his idol, he's in Birdman's birdcage, he's inside the same wild and drunken cesspool that birthed his favorite rapper. Future is another rapper that is giving off this vibe of losing control. He has this line on Travi$ Scott's "High Fashion" that I've been stuck on, "This lean got me nauseous, but I keep on using."

With Wayne he always seemed immune to the substances. Looking at these artists with older eyes, I find myself worrying about their wellbeing, but the music is good. Once you gain fame rapping about a certain lifestyle, you have to keep living it, even if it destroys you. We witness what drugs did to Gucci Mane, how they almost got the best of Danny Brown, ScHoolboy's wanton consumption, but the fans couldn't be more enthralled. If you so happen to hit rock bottom, the cheers only get louder. It's such a twisted reality for artists. I recently stumbled upon Amy Winehouse final performance before passing, and it's unbearable to watch. To think someone recorded that and uploaded to the net, it's heart-wrenching. You want great music, but you want the artist to survive their trials and tribulations.

It's not just the drugs. Internal struggle also weighs on an artist's soul. We all deal with depression and sadness. Personally, I think artists are born hypersensitive. Their feelings are intense, extreme, enhanced, and that's where creativity is born. It's what allows them to see what we overlook, and to bring forth emotions in a way that it touches our souls. The passing of Capital Steez surprised me, such a promising young man. Kendrick recently confessed to struggling with inner-turmoil. Listening to "U" always leaves me feeling empty. The picture of him sitting on a pile of money, holding a giant bottle of wine, and wearing the expression of a man coping with a problem that can't be solved with direct deposit or booze. Aren't you suppose to enjoy the fruits of your labor? Aren't you suppose to rejoice once you reach the bosom of success? Like J. Cole so poetically stated, "The good news is nigga you came a long way, the bad news is nigga you went the wrong way." J. Cole always comes off cool, calm and collected. I can't imagine waking up and feeling like Nirvana fans on 4/5/1994.

Since I was a small boy, I never imagined a long life. Gray hairs, grandchildren, retirement homes, all thoughts that I couldn't fathom. It wasn't about living fast, or dying young, but simply no true yearning to deal with the aches and struggles of old age. I think hip-hop has a similar mentality. We live in moments, song to song, album to album, drug to drug, girl to girl, thinking somehow we will be forever young. We scream at the top of our lungs, bring us vices, bring us risk, and bring us life. In reality, time is weighing down on us at every second. That these young bodies will begin to feel the abuse, that our souls can only take so much debauchery. Moderation and cleansing, it's something that has to become a part of the discussion. Hopefully no rapper has to be inducted into the 27 Club. The culture has to age like wine, and not cellphones.

Notes & References

1 Obaro, Tomi, "Chicagoans of the Year 2015: Chance the Rapper," *Chicago Magazine*, http://www.chicagomag.com/Chicago-Magazine/December-2015/Chicagoans-of-the-Year-2015-Chance-the-Rapper/.

2 Siegel, Alan, "The Education of 'The Wire,'" *The Ringer* (June 1, 2017), https://www.theringer.com/2017/6/1/16045406/the-wire-15th-anniversary-hbo-season-4-79e80c01f167.

3 Nosnitsky, Andrew Kendrick, "Lamar Talks Rap, Religion And The Reagan Era," MTV (July 11, 2011) http://www.mtv.com/news/2694080/kendrick-lamar-talks-rap-religion-and-the-reagan-era/.

4 Marsh, Steve, "Kendrick Lamar: Rapper of the Year," *GG* (November 12, 2013) https://www.gq.com/story/kendrick-lamar-men-of-the-year-rapper.

5 "Exclusive: Kendrick Lamar Sings Taylor Swift's 'Shake It Off,'" *Fader* (November 11, 2014) http://www.thefader.com/2014/11/04/kendrick-lamar-interview-halloween-taylor-swift.

6 "King Kendrick Decodes Eight To Pimp A Butterfly Tracks," MTV (2015) https://mail.google.com/mail/u/0/?shva=1#search/Article+link/15f7201561f9cc33?projector=1.

7 Coscarelli, Joe "Kendrick Lamar on His New Album and the Weight of Clarity," New York Times (March 16, 2015) https://www.nytimes.com/2015/03/22/arts/music/kendrick-lamar-on-his-new-album-and-the-weight-of-clarity.html.

8 "17 Religious References on Kendrick Lamar's 'Untitled Unmastered' Project," Billboard (March 4, 2016) http://edit.billboard.com/articles/columns/hip-hop/6898223/kendrick-lamar-untitled-unmastered-religious-references.

9 Lewis, Miles Marshall, "Kendrick Lamar Talks Politics, Spirituality, Music + More (May 26, 2015) http://www.ebony.com/entertainment-culture/kendrick-talks-politics-spirituality-music-more-333#ixzz4yJI6imzP.

10 Halliday, Josh, "LimeWire shut down by federal court," The Guardian (October 27, 2010) https://www.theguardian.com/technology/2010/oct/27/limewire-shut-down.

11 "J. Cole Talks Roc Nation, Meeting Jay-Z & 'The Warm Up' Mixtape," *Complex* (May 2, 2009) http://www.complex.com/music/2009/05/j-cole-talks-roc-nation-meeting-jay-z-the-warm-up-mixtape.

12 Srhett, "J. Cole On 'Born Sinner,' Alleged Jay-Z Beef, More," *Jet Magazine* (June 4, 2013) https://www.jetmag.com/entertainment/j-cole-interview/.

13 Associated Press interview (2012).

14 Knopper, Steve "How Spotify Playlists Create Hits," Rolling Stone (August 5, 2017) http://www.rollingstone.com/music/news/inside-spotifys-playlists-curators-and-fake-artists-w497702.

15 "Trippie Redd Interview," *Pigeons & Planes* (August 4, 2017) https://www.youtube.com/watch?time_continue=3&v=UKDWVDGJbmo.

Part 2
MUSIC REVIEWS/ RETROSPECTIVES

Summertime '06:
A Vince Staples Retrospective

The same kid that once said, "Rap ain't never did shit for a nigga with no options, you want some positivity go listen to some Common," is dropping his Def Jam debut album next week. It's astounding how far Vince Staples has come. I first found him during the early days of Odd Future, when their music was a double dose of mischievous immaturity, full of presumptuous vulgarity and rebellious carelessness. The first time I heard his mixtape, *Shyne Coldchain Vol 1*, chills galloped down my spine. It was his voice that stood out, a colorless, soft tone completely vacant of emotion. He spoke of godless gangbangers that witness death too soon, too often, and was engaged in this cycle of endless, inescapable dread. To them it wasn't dread but the circle of life. To live and die in Long Beach. There was a terrifying honesty about his lyricism, he spoke a frank truth that wasn't sugarcoated by optimism, and his views on race, religion, and justice were stirred into his first and third person perspective of what was unfolding around him. There wasn't any remorse, regret, or hope. He said "hades was my birthplace" and I believed him.

Vince Staples was the kid you were warned about, the quiet, most dangerous elephant in the room. He seemed like a normal kid, looked like a normal kid, but he had been to hell and back without receiving a visible scar or blemish. He reveals the untold in his music, illustrating a lifestyle that unravels the glorification of gangster personas with the unseen reality. There's no low-riders and duffel bags full of cash, just PlayStation and dead friends, broken homes and skipped classes, lost love and dying morality. Did I mention he raps extremely well? His attention to detail is literary, poetic, lacking only the eloquence, a word that doesn't exist where he comes from. His first mixtape showcased his talent for creating cinematic narratives that felt like reminiscent tales and events yet to unfold. All the beats original, only one song included a hook, the project lacked a proper mix, it wasn't a demo for the labels, but a treasure for underground rap fans looking for something unfiltered, pure, with some edge. He had plenty of edge.

Vince beat the odds, rap actually did do something for someone with no options, and I believe he has turned that into his purpose. His double disc Def Jam debut would be an ode to the summer of '06. I've read interviews where he confessed his goal was to enlighten listeners on what was occurring in his neighborhood during one of his wildest years. We listen to ScHoolboy Q and YG, they can make being gangster sound enthralling, exciting, hitting licks, popping glocks, stealing girls, the fast life. That's not what Vince wants to represent. Most of his music throughout the years has centered around stolen youth. He had a childhood, one without innocence. In 2006 he was only 13, a teenager, wearing Polo like Young Dro, like most of us that spent our days and nights shoulder leaning, but in past songs he has hinted at the gruesome circumstances he was living in. Like on "Feelin' the Love" from *Hell Can Wait*, where he references the year in the second verse: "2006 I said I had to get my money right, shit I refuse to hear my stomach growl another night, might put a burner right up in your mouth and free your mind." His home wasn't Compton, but it was a mad city and he wasn't a good kid. Vince was here to be horrifyingly honest.

Summertime '06 starts with the serene sound of seagulls and the laughter of children while the ominous drum stutters in the background, the song ends with a gunshot. It goes into one of the most important songs I've heard this year. "Lift Me Up" is everything we could want from a rapper that's conscious of the subjects that America wants swept under graves while looking at himself in the mirror. He admits to struggling with skin color and his conscious, wanting a new Ferrari but knowing he needs to fight the power. Knowing that he stands in front of white crowds, rapping the n-word and aware they would never set foot anywhere near his home. He's internally conflicted, wrestling these demons over a lochness bassline that vibrates power and terror. This is a great representation of the kind of rapper that Vince is. This is the song you need to hear.

Summertime '06 is an album full of statements, this is the album that finally showcases Vince Staples as an artist. He's been growing gradually, each mixtape and EP showcasing a rapper growing artistically. From a mixtape with barely any hooks to conceptual records, this album is a testament to how far he has come. Vince's early appeal relied heavily on charisma, all his technical shortcomings masked by his captivating storytelling and wordplay. He doesn't carry this album with strictly powerful rhymes, it's curated to feel major, big, intricate production, bridges, harmonies, and Vince even sings an entire song without rapping a line. It's a leap forward, a true jump toward becoming the kind of rapper that can stand out in an over-clustered industry.

"Love will tear us apart. Nov 30th, 2005 was the beginning of the loss. The following summer multiplied it. Beaten paths, crowded with the hopeless. Same song every day, listening to the words of a dead man destroyed by his own mind and body. Why? Because at the end of the day we're all dead anyway. At least where I come from. Love tore us all apart. Love for self, love for separation, love for the little we all had, love for each other, where we came from. Jabari, Chris, Shard, Tom, Richy, Tyson, Tony, Shelly, Phil, Marcel, Brandon, Steve, Jaron, Tay. Too many to name, too much to forget. Some lost to prison, some lost to Forest Lawn, some turned snitch. Some still here but it will never

be the same. Bandanas, Stealing Levis and Nike Sb's. Derringers and Sidekicks. It's crazy how little you notice and how greatly those things impact. Summer of 2006, the beginning of the end of everything I thought I knew. Youth was stolen from my city that Summer and I'm left alone to tell the story. This might not make sense but that's because none of it does, we're stuck. Love tore us all apart. Summertime '06, June 30th.
—Vince Staples' Instagram

While staring at Vince Staples the fully polished artist, it leaves me yearning for the simplicity of his formative projects. He's still an excellent lyricist, cracking jaws with his truth, but it's the surrounding elements that can be too much. The production feels overwhelming, I want to zoom in on the words, but there are sounds blossoming from every direction. It works on records like "Jump Off The Roof," "Norf Norf" and "Street Punks," but on others like "3230" the trap elements are fighting with Vince's flow. Classic records like "Nate" and "Earth Science" are strong because they are records that are carried by his lyricism. He's the kind of rapper to start a song off with "Fuck your dead homies." As soon as I hear those words, stripped down and raw, I'm captivated, I'm pulled into the moment. The change in sound is likely to appeal to a larger, vaster audience. We've seen the results of "Senorita" live, that's the kind of sound that allows you to spit furiously without boring your audience into a coma, and I appreciate it. It also reminds me how much I appreciated what Vince was creating when the resources weren't accessible, a phenomenon newcomers to Staples' music simply won't experience.

Vince sounds more alive on this album, that cold-hearted monotone has found a bit of hope. There still isn't any sugarcoating, he isn't kidding, you'll hear him touch upon J. Cole's commentary from "Firing Squad" without naming names and Kendrick's

49

"Blacker The Berry" without the intense aggression. He's much younger, years behind, but he shares their concern for black music, black people, and the world in general. I once had a conversation with a colleague about whether or not rappers should feel compelled to speak on the issues that are engulfing the world. I only want artists that feel compelled to speak because they have a message that can hopefully influence more people to speak. Vince Staples is here to deliver. Songs like "Might Be Wrong" and "Like It Is" are definitely a testament to the times we are living in. Vince is rare, he straddles that line between being a gangster rapper and unapologetically socially aware. In many ways, it's the purest definition of gangster rap.

I Don't Like *Illmatic*:
My Battle Against
Hip Hop Elitism

My introduction to *Illmatic*, Nas's debut and widely considered classic album, was like being the last friend to lose their virginity - is this what everyone else was so worked up about? Others spoke about the album like a father watching his son score the winning goal in the last seconds of overtime. They would use words that most saved for their wives or girlfriends: perfect, flawless. I believed them before I ever pressed play. I wasn't fed hype, I was fed the rules, the Bible, the holy truth of hip hop. The countless hip-hop forums I visited always had the same views. I was hungry to discover the best music and they always recommended starting with the classics. I never questioned who bestowed these titles, every opinion was unified, this was real hip hop.

I was young, too young to believe strongly in my own tastes. Every friend I asked and every website I visited, the recommendations seemed to be similar, and the word "classic" was the only reason. I didn't know what to expect, but I knew I was supposed to like it. But I didn't like *Illmatic*, and I didn't like *Reasonable Doubt* either. I did, however, gravitate toward Pac's *All Eyez On Me* and Kanye's *Late Registration*. No one cared to tell me the importance of these albums, just that they were held in the highest acclaim. It's easy to learn the lingo. Know which albums to praise, which legends to love, and you'll be embraced like a brethren. You don't need to have a single thought, all the thinking is done for you, just follow the leaders and recite the scriptures. Having an opinion outside the general consensus isn't allowed, you'll be exiled to an alternative genre if you don't act in accordance with our united perspective. Who am I to disturb the foundation that was laid before my birth? Before I bought my first CD, the undeniable, unanimous classics already existed. Who am I to voice my distaste for the albums that built this culture? Who am I to be happy in the present, carelessly ignoring the past?

I once told a classmate that Nas's *Lost Tape* was my favorite album by him, he looked at me as if I said George Bush loves black people. He hit me with a barrage of, "*Illmatic* has this, *Stillmatic* has that" and "*It Was Written* is the greatest hip hop album of all time." He was reciting what I always heard, what was always said when Nas' name was mentioned, but what about the personal connection? "Doo Rags" and "Nothing Lasts Forever" are songs I got lost in for hours. On "Blaze A 50" the storytelling is too vivid, I get chills every time she sniffs that line of glass. "Drunk By Myself" makes me feel like I'm right in the passenger seat, and "Untitled" is sage-level lyricism. Not to mention, the beat selection is incredible. It's an odd feeling defending your subjective opinion; hip hop heads will convince you that your ears are broken. Being from the South is bad enough in their eyes, we impelled poisonous daggers into the heart of their culture.

So I stopped debating music, I stopped searching for recommendations. It's exhausting feeling like your every like and dislike has to be defended and dissected. As I got older, I was able to appreciate the music I sought to understand. A few months ago I sat and listened to "The Genesis" on repeat for an hour, because it sounds like the New York City I romanticize. From the slang to the sounds of the subway, it's a place that I can't reach when listening to French Montana or Troy Ave.

While talking to a colleague one day about feeling the pressures of hip hop elitism, I realized that I did the same thing to my little brother. He has this knack for recommending artists during their indie starvation period and those artists almost always become well-fed superstars. He told me about Rich Homie Quan in 2012, but I didn't care for any music he had to offer, citing the fact that my brother had never heard a Jay-Z or Kanye album as my reasoning. What does he know about rap music? For most of his high school years we were stuck in this cycle of claiming the other had bad taste. When he adamantly tried to convince me this Autotune crooning, dirty Sprite drinking, Free Bandz representing rapper would be the Future, I vehemently called him crazy. He told me about this rapper that was replicating Lil Wayne, had the hair, tattoos, was even vocally similar, and I brushed him aside. He was always ahead while I was looking behind, his ears are fixated on the present, listening for whatever resonates with his personal preference. I thought about him after watching Young Thug say he would never buy a Jay-Z album: "If you're 30, 40 years old, you're not getting listened to by minors. Like, Jay Z has some of the sickest lyrics ever, but I would never buy his CD, just because of my age and because of his age. By the time I turn that old, I ain't gonna be doing what he's doing."[16]

I didn't think Thug's statement was rude or disrespectful. It was a very honest, interesting look at how his younger audience perceives Jay. Witnessing how outraged it made people, I thought he pissed on *The Blueprint*, or dropped a deuce on *The Black Album*. He's a kid that grew up in a post-retirement Jay-Z world, Lil Wayne is his idol, what do we expect from him? What do we expect from the kids that don't know Missy's prestigious history? There are going to be kids who never heard of "Cop Killer" but have seen Ice T play a police officer. There are going to be kids that will see LL Cool J as the corny GRAMMY host and be completely oblivious to "I Need Love," "My Radio," "Momma Said Knock You Out," "I'm Bad," or "Around the Way Girl." It's not just Jay, hip hop is getting older, the audience is getting younger, and the internet is full of angry messages that aren't helping.

I don't know when I started judging someone based on the music they listen to, but it became more important than their political views. Last year, I was distracting a young lady while my friend tried to ask her friend out for a date, music is a common conversation, and somehow Nas got brought up. She's only 19, the same age as my little brother, but that doesn't excuse her from calling The God MC boring, and that she'd rather listen to her favorite rapper, K-Camp. At the age of 23, that was the day I gave up on younger women. Instead of recommending my personal favorite records, I labeled her a lost cause and unfollowed her in real life. When did I become this monster?! I joined the same circle of elitism that made me feel unwelcomed when my views didn't correlate with theirs. I'm no better because of what's in my iTunes. Music is personal, subjective, it shouldn't make you feel entitled.

We live in a time when we're able to express personal opinions on global platforms and we still get caught up with being "right" or "wrong." You can shove 101 reasons why I should love *My Beautiful Dark Twisted Fantasy* down my throat, but that doesn't mean I have to share your affection. It's a lesson my little brother taught me. I think Meek Mill is Classic Lay's potato chips, but my brother hails Meek as Flamin' Hot Cheetos. My brother would rather listen to *My Krazy Life* than *good kid m.A.A.D city*. He went through a phase of loving Sosa, but didn't care for Vic Mensa and Chance The Rapper. I can't force him to see hip hop through my ears, and I love him for it. He's one of the few people I know that purely enjoys the music he likes without being influenced by lists, album reviews, and popular opinion. The best we can do is try and reach them, teach them, but respect that they have their own likes and dislikes. Don't just spout that Nas is great, introduce Nas through YouTube links, Spotify playlists, any method is better than caps locks and swear words. Be the walking stick for the blind and oblivious, you can't expect everyone to share your musical awareness. So now I'm on a mission to mature and stop judging people based on music....except for women who claim Wale as their favorite poet, and grown men that wear Trukfit.

My friend and former colleague Nathan once said to me that he cried a little when I admitted I hadn't really listened to Ghostface, which made me laugh, because I also didn't admit that the only Ghost album I'd heard is *Ghostdini: Wizard Of Poetry In Emerald City*, which is almost worse than not hearing Ghostface at all.

Chasing a Classic:
A Jay-Z Retrospective

Jay-Z was greeted with applause after releasing *Reasonable Doubt* in 1996, a highly revered debut that offered Jaz O's former protégé a seat at the table amongst New York's elite. He wasn't embraced as a genius prodigy like Nas after he dropped *Illmatic*. He wasn't yet considered a talent large enough to escape the massive shadow of the Notorious B.I.G.'s *Ready To Die*. But Jay-Z was seen as a respected word wizard who brought a sense of cinema to his Mafioso perspective.

Reasonable Doubt received immediate admiration, acclaim and ovation, but it wasn't loud enough. JAY wanted the classic stamp, the highest approval, the loudest possible applause for any hip hop artist. At the time, "classic" was synonymous with perfection, a flawless album from front to back. You couldn't be regarded as the best breathing without achieving that designation — *Reasonable Doubt* was one mic short (*The Source Magazine's* coveted 5 mics) of reaching that greatness. The missing mic would come later, years later, but the chip on JAY's shoulder was already apparent.

Every new Jay-Z album to follow *Reasonable Doubt* would deliver classic singles and timeless verses. But he couldn't escape cringing duds and forgettable attempts at commercial viability. His name grew, his place at the table was made permanent, but the instant, critical classic continued to elude him. It was a rapper's purgatory, a few flaws short of perfection. By 2001, JAY was in his fifth summer as a rap star, the flagship artist of the Roc-A-Fella regime and a prominent figure expanding into pop culture's psyche. Despite all that was accomplished, his eyes never left the crown.

Remembering this moment of JAY-Z's career is fitting when we're on the cusp of *4:44*, his 12th solo studio album (or 13th if you count *The Dynasty: Roc La Familia*). The number four has a deep-rooted significance in the Brooklyn MC's life. Some would even say he has an obsession with fours. Born on the 4th of December, married on the 4th of April, named his sports bars after the rare feat of 40 home runs and 40 stolen bases in a single MLB season. Even Blue Ivy's name can be poetically linked to the roman numeral form of four. The list is long and the infatuation runs deep. What JAY has yet to do is release a fourth installment of any of his album series.

In My Lifetime stopped after volume 3. But with so little information surrounding 4:44, rumors have started to spread that it could potentially be Jay's fourth *Blueprint* album. Just like the number four, Jay holds *The Blueprint* trilogy close to his heart. There's only four albums that Jay has removed from all streaming services that are not Tidal — *Reasonable Doubt* and the three Blueprints. This isn't a coincidence. Keeping them from competitors could be seen as a move to entice subscribers, but that's a shortsighted observation. If Jay-Z intends to continue what he began in 2001, now is an excellent opportunity to revisit how each album has played a specific role in his artistry. The common thread linking these albums was a desire to be placed in hip hop's highest echelon, classic status.

"Anybody got beats?" A simple question. Just Blaze has stated that's how it began. Three simple words led to the genesis of what became JAY-Z's *The Blueprint*. No big discussion was had, no meeting of the Roc-A-Fella braintrust — JAY's desire to rap turned into a three-day recording session more mythical than the misplacing of 92 bricks. Magic tends to occur when an ordinary request is asked by an extraordinary man, not by an ordinary man looking for the extraordinary. Something special occurred as JAY entrapped himself in a bubble of soulful samples in order to shed any overthinking. A small, tight-knit group of producers who complemented one another was enlisted and chemistry took precedence over commercial prosperity. Kanye West, Just Blaze and Bink! applied the foundation, setting up the musical bed of water for Hov to walk upon. Jay had foes to finish and rumors to dismiss, tears he couldn't shed and a throne to seize.

Bruce Lee once said, "Empty your mind, be formless, shapeless — like water." It's a perfect analogy to describe the seamless grace of how *The Blueprint* flows. Jay is, without effort, his most fluid and precise, focused and charismatic. If you ever watched the way Muhammad Ali would dance in the ring during his prime boxing years, that's the Jay who dominates *The Blueprint*.

No one has ever stated that Jay's passion was to make the perfect album for hip hop heads and rap enthusiasts. It almost seems like *The Blueprint* was an earnest attempt at spilling his soul, rather than approval seeking, but even on the same day that America grieved over the deadliest terrorist attacks in this country's history, Jay-Z was applauded. It was the loudest ovation of his entire career. Critics and fans, stans and naysayers, even his enemies would have to tip their hats through their hate. The curse of failed classics lifted, the throne was finally his to take.

Once you reach the pinnacle of excellence, there comes all the beauty of victory and all the spoils of being the biggest target in the room. *The Blueprint* turned Jay-Z into a giant, one that didn't slow down after reaching the treasure he had been searching for. It's as if the thrill of conquering one mountain made him want to plant his flag on an even higher, more difficult peak. Writing and recording for his next project began immediately, even while on tour. If *The Blueprint* solidified that Jay was among the best alive, *The Blueprint 2: The Gift & Curse* was a blockbuster sequel meant to raise the bar into the heavens, an attempt to challenge the dead.

"Nah B, All the greats like 2Pac and Biggie did double discs. To put you in that league, you have to do one."

Young Guru, both engineer and musical confidant, admitted this was the conversation that eventually led to the decision to make 2002's *The Blueprint 2* a double disc. Guru may take the blame for planting the seeds, but Jay-Z saw this as his opportunity to reckon with two of the greatest all-time chair holders. So he doubled the music, doing months of recording instead of weeks. Sampling and conversing with Biggie on the intro wasn't a coincidence.

Taking a play from Pac for "03 Bonnie & Clyde" wasn't just a nod of respect. Even the name, *The Blueprint 2*, was a ploy for how he wanted the album to be received — through the same classic standards as its predecessor. He attacked commercially by collaborating with Beyoncé, Pharrell and Sean Paul; threw salt into the bloody wounds of his adversaries; and proved that fame hadn't deteriorated his talent with impressive records like "Hovi Baby," "Diamond is Forever," "Meet The Parents" and "A Ballad For the Fallen Soldier."

Most of the music was excellent, boasting a high level of lyricism and exquisite production, but while *The Blueprint* was nimble, *The Blueprint 2* was bloated. He was a few steps short on his stairway to heaven. It was a humbling reminder of being mortal and the scars of overreaching. Carving off the fat, much *like* The Blueprint 2.1 eventually did, would've made a far more compelling argument for a second coming.

As a competitor, JAY is very much driven by the spirit of an athlete. No matter the medium, if there isn't a challenge to overcome, he doesn't feel compelled to try. Hov was the first artist to release a double disc album on Def Jam, and with the mainstream music industry seeing the viability in soul samples again, *The Blueprint 2* was made as a fight against the gifts and curses of being the biggest figure in rap. Sadly, it became an excess of music that came out between two acclaimed classics. Wedged against *The Blueprint* and *The Black Album*, this is why *The Blueprint 2* will forever be seen as Jay-Z's Titanic, the luxury cruise ship that is remembered for sinking.

"If you look at [the number] 3, all they did was connect lines. The whole thing about this album, how I approached it, is that I wanted to make a new classic to start that all over again — to go back to making classic albums like the ones we grew up listening to." That was Jay-Z during an interview with MTV, discussing the album cover for *The Blueprint 3*. Much like *The Blueprint 2*, it was an album that flirted with the concept of classic recognition.

The Blueprint 3 is also the third album in Jay's post-retirement catalog. *Kingdom Come* was a reintroduction of sorts, *American Gangster* was a return to form, so on his third at bat, Jay wanted to go back to the idea of classic rap albums in a post-Soulja Boy ringtone era. A natural competitor, Hov had plenty to assess and strike down. "DOA" was meant to be "Takeover," but against Auto-Tune and a generational approach towards making music, not local lyrical rivals Nas and Mobb Deep. It was exciting for only a moment, the idea that Jay could end T-Pain's reign. But he couldn't extinguish the sound that still runs rampant in music's mainstream. His failed attempt to finish Auto-Tune is a great example of what is good and terrible about *The Blueprint 3* — the aging Jay-Z is resistant to the trends of the times, but fails to set any new precedents.

He was famous enough to take Oprah Winfrey to Marcy Projects, had the hottest woman in the world carrying his last name and his child, and was able to make an anthem for New York City that will live on in eternity, but he had lost the fire to truly burn down the opponents in his path. Kanye West's production didn't have the flair of the first *Blueprint*, and leaning on new artists instead of up-and-coming producers failed to evoke new life and spirited energy. The third *Blueprint* is burdened by age, but not in the literal sense, "Thank You" is proof that the wrinkles of time didn't spoil his gift for gab, but it did absorb all the rebelliousness in his pores. Despite having an anthem for eternal youth, *The Blueprint 3* sounded like it was recorded in the beach chair from

Kingdom Come. Highlights aside, Hov's hope to reignite the hip hop album is instead a collection too deep in the throes of an idea and not execution. But what The Blueprint 3 did do was mark JAY Z as an icon larger than life itself. Even in falling short, he leaps light years ahead. Being a living legend in rap was a position he held since his 2003 retirement, but The Blueprint 3 escalated him into being a pop culture juggernaut.

"Empire State Of Mind" was the massive hit he'd never had, his first and only No. 1 Billboard Hot 100 song as a solo artist. The Kanye and Rihanna collaboration "Run This Town" peaked at No.2. Some of the other highs include the unforgettable "So Ambitious" and the Kid Cudi-assisted "Already Home." But the entire project doesn't come together. Even the great moments won't leave most listeners eager to return.

What Jay accomplished with *The Blueprint 3* will live much longer than the album itself. Classic is synonymous with perfection, but it wasn't until The Blueprint 3 that Jay-Z was synonymous with hip hop.

A Blend of Modern Nostalgia: How Adult Swim and J Dilla Inspired the Music of Thelonious Martin

The allure of fruit that's forbidden has tempted men and women since the day Adam and Eve took a life-altering bite from an off-limit apple in God's garden. I've always loved how the biblical story illustrated the human weakness to temptation's whisper. Temptation is a voice that's enticing and seductive — filling the earlobe with bad ideas that focus on pleasure and never the consequence. Children are naturally drawn to the forbidden — a hunger for curiosity, a thirst for trouble, and a need to discover what exists behind the locked door that only adults have a key to. In some households, the television was both a best friend and a mysterious stranger. There was always a time at night where what was shown wasn't for young eyes, programming made specifically for adults.

Chicago producer Thelonious Martin remembers 1999, when he was only 6 years old, how his father made clear that the show "South Park" wasn't meant for him. It was his first introduction to an animated series where children were not the intended audience.

"For any kids, when your parent goes to sleep and you're still awake, anything past this point is unfiltered, unsupervised, and there's no guideline to it," Thelonious reminisces during our phone call. He recalls how the airing of an episode of "The Sopranos" was a signal that it was bedtime, how "Sex in The City" was a series his mother would watch while he ate dinner, and knowing that both shows weren't for him. There was a clear distinction between television after-school and television after-dark. As he got older, his interest in late night television rose. Like every young man lucky enough to have cable television between 2001-2006, his life changed after staying up one night and seeing B.E.T. Uncut; a rite-of-passage for babies born in the '90s. More important than B.E.T.'s artfully raunchy videos, there was another adult block of programming that had a huge impact on Thelonious: Cartoon Network's Adult Swim. Every child knew Adult Swim was meant for an older audience, but like all forbidden fruit, you couldn't help but venture into uncharted waters.

A middle school tech teacher introduced a young Thelonious to GarageBand, an Apple audio workstation that was the doorway into production for many hip hop producers. Making loops and chopping up samples was something that he played with, a hobby to dabble in but nothing that he considered to be his future. Coming home from school, he would turn on Cartoon Network and immerse himself in a world of audio and videos. Gundam Wing would be playing in the background as he taught himself the basics of making beats. It was a ritual that spilled over into Adult Swim, and he would hear "the bumps", the short television teasers that play in-between commercial breaks. No longer than 15 seconds, they would show text or various images with instrumentals playing in the background. While he would work on his own beats, Thelonious would look up and hear music from Flying Lotus, DOOM, and Madlib, brilliant beatsmiths who reached mainstream ears despite being underground darlings. One night, Adult Swim played a bump that would inspire him to become a producer:

"The Bump that made me want to start taking beats seriously was "Outro," the intro to *Donuts*. I was like, 'whoa.' I ran to the computer and immediately started researching Dilla. Sadly, by this time, he had already passed. I got more attuned with his discography and realized that some of his music wasn't new to me. My mom would play Badu (Erykah Badu) in the crib, she would play D'Angelo in the crib, all The Soulquarians shit, so to me I was already listening to Dilla, without knowing. I will say Adult Swim put me onto J. Dilla, and after that, I begged my mom to buy me a laptop so I could start making beats. Freshman year of high school is when it all started."

J. Dilla and Adult Swim changed his life. You take away the bumps, J. Dilla, and Adult Swim, and there's a good chance Thelonious Martin doesn't blossom into one of Chicago's most promising producers. Some of the most inspiring stories in music are the ones that allow the subject to come full-circle. It took eight years for Thelonious to hear one of his own beats on Adult Swim, a bump that played during the first time Toonami aired Akira (a very impactful and influential cult-classic anime movie from '88). It was a full-circle moment for Thelonious for many reasons: "I thought to myself, there's a kid right now who was in my shoes where I was at 14-15 seeing this, hearing the music, and thinking, 'Yo I want to do this or this is inspiring to the point I want to create.'"

More important than his music being on Adult Swim is the man who made it happen:

"Jason DeMarco is like the creator of Toonami and the SVP/Creative Director for Adult Swim. He's responsible for a lot of the music that got onto Adult Swim, especially the Stones Throw stuff. That's Dilla, Doom, and Madlib. When my music got onto Adult Swim, he was the guy. He put Dilla on Adult Swim, so he's the guy that's responsible for me even starting to make music. I have a great work relationship with them, it's incredible to work with people that inspired me. Hopefully, I'm inspiring the next batch of beatmakers."

Late Night Programming, Thelonious's sophomore album, is an ode to television, Adult Swim, and his musical influences. From the first track to the last, the runtime is 24 minutes long; the length of a half-hour television show not including commercials. If you let it run from last to first, it's a smooth transition, as if the listener allowed the next episode to continue even though it's a rerun. Every song is strategically placed. There are familiar skits and bumps from Adult Swim, a song that represents when it gets so late that you start to see infomercials, and the album ends with a hilarious Everest commercial, which is usually a sign you've been up too late. There's no rapper features, which is a change of pace from his 2014 *Wunderkid* debut album that featured heavy hitters like Mac Miller, Curren$y, Smoke DZA, and Ab-Soul. The album was successful, a strong combination of soulful instrumentals and stellar rap verses, but it was missing something, it was missing Thelonious' presence.

"It was more like a showcase," Thelonious says of *Late Night Programming*. A thought that didn't come until *Wunderkid*. *Late Night Programming* might be missing friends, but every bit of the album represents Theo. It even features his voice. He wanted *Late Night Programming* to be more cohesive, cinematic, and reflective of who he is. To hear this album is to get a slice of Thelonious. It's a strong body of work, one of the most captivating beat tapes that I've heard all year. Part of that comes from the production sounding lively, powerful, but full of flavor and flair.

He explained to me how he approached drums, "I want kicks to be low and real strong to hit you in the body, and snares to snap real hard and hit you in the neck so when I put on the album, 'Neck brace recommended' that's real." This ideology comes from The Neptunes' *The Eighth Planet* documentary when Chad says, "Kick drums hit you in the chest, snare should snap you in the neck so you get a full body head nod by the person listening to the music." When the drums drop on "Open Credits" and your body is shaken to its core, you'll need that neck brace.

"It's important not to be afraid to acknowledge your influences," says Thelonious. "I wouldn't be where I am today without my influences. It's important to showcase that. Your idols won't be your idols unless you give them the proper credit that they need and deserve."

We talked about Pete Rock, and how he would set the tone for songs by implementing an intro to the song that has absolutely nothing to do with the beat. Thelonious used the classic hip hop song "T.R.O.Y" as an example. Before the angelic horns blow there is a funky drum and bass that fades in and out within the first few seconds. It's a technique that Thelonious plays with, at both the beginning and ending of songs. It's a tiny detail but adds character to each song. Dave Chappelle is prominent throughout the tape, hilarious skits from "The Chappelle Show" are sprinkled about. If Dilla inspired his music, it was Dave that inspired his humor.

The influence from Dilla's *Donuts* is very apparent as well. You can hear the influence in the soulfulness, like the infamous Beastie Boy's "The New Style" making various cameos. The song "Adult Swim" is a three-minute ode to Dilla and Madlib, two of Thelonious's biggest influences. Kanye once said that J. Dilla's music sounds like good pussy. I think Thelonious Martin is the sound of reminiscing on that first good time you made love.

"The sound of it is a modern twist of the soul beats we fell in love with Dilla and Madlib and my modern twist to it, my 2016 touch to it," says Thelonius. "It's a voyage into nostalgia with a 2016 soundtrack. It plays into both words. My sound itself is more nostalgic, leaning on boom-bap and soul samples. It's a blend of modern nostalgia. The game truly pays back those who are grateful and those who have knowledge in their field. If you pay attention to those that came before you in your craft, the game will pay you back for it. That's how you know what waves are coming, that's how you know when to reinvent yourself, and to make progress."

Reminisce, that's what Thelonious wants from listeners as they swim through his sea of soul. Modern nostalgia is the perfect way to describe what you'll take in from *Late Night Programming*. It's rooted in both the past and present, taking from the forefathers and mixing it with what he's learned in this modern era of music making. He wants to bring back the feeling of sitting in front of the television — before Netflix and DVR — when shows demanded your attention. *Late Night Programming* is an album he wants you to experience.

"Growing up between television getting a little more wild, YouTube starting to grow into what it is, that 2008-2009, I used to go to the internet and on Imeem listen to Cool Kids and Wale mixtapes. The transition of T.V. where it was and becoming more crass and the internet coming into play my whole mind got molded in a different way than, say, if you were 15-16 in '95. It was so much more of a jump start, a boost, to what was going on. My mind had to develop much quicker, it was much more content to take in. There are good things to take from my parents, there are good things to take from television. I took the common sense from my parents and I took the comedy and entertainment element from television. I took the things I needed from the proper places." —Thelonious Martin

The above quote really captures what it means to be a baby born right before the internet took off, and having to live with its impact on the world. Lupe shouted out all the televisions that raised us on *Food & Liquor*, but in reality, television was more of a co-parent, the nanny that we all shared. Thelonious's parents weren't together, but they both shaped his world along with television. They were strict enough, but not overbearing. He was allowed to watch "The Chappelle Show" when he was 11 years old, but he was given *The Autobiography Of Malcolm X* at 10. His life has been mirrored by this strange but intriguing juxtaposition. Thelonious takes from his parents and co-parent, fruits gifted and the fruits forbidden, anime and movies, sports and comics, rock and rap, a true connoisseur of various arts and culture. I think that's why his music sounds like it isn't rooted in a time or a sound; his life and taste are diverse and so is his music.

808s & Heartache:
Kanye West's Personal Masterpiece

With each passing song, I wondered when the rapping would begin. Where was the Kanye that spoke of turning tragedy to triumph with a jaw wired shut? Where was the Kanye who touched the sky alongside Lupe? For three consecutive albums he had delivered, and yet, on his fourth offering, he failed to pierce my hip-hop soul like he once did.

My heart sunk into the sole of my shoe when he redirected and renamed *Good Ass Job*, but I wasn't prepared for him to completely revamp his artistry. This was a completely new Kanye, a singing Kanye, a tragic Kanye — the darkness of his 808s, the bleakness of his heartbreak didn't resonate with my 17-year-old desire for the old Kanye.

It was a little over a year after the release of *808s & Heartbreak*, the winter of my graduation year, when I tried the album once again. This was the coldest winter of my adolescence, an age of love and heartache, conflict and pain, guilt and longing — emotional scars that can be relieved by the ointment of music. A year can change a lot, especially when a woman enters and exits your life like some beautiful, dark, twisted fantasy. The very songs that I once wished to be filled with — buoyant boasts, slick brags, and inspirational lyricism — sounded perfect as Auto-Tune drenched life anecdotes from a man unafraid to wear the shattered heart on his microphone. He couldn't sing (he still can't, Kanye's shortcomings to some may be the Achilles' heel of *808s*), a flawed man with an imperfect technique is fitting of such a vulnerable album, but it adds a flavor that even a master singer isn't able to reproduce. I couldn't truly be welcomed into heartbreak before; it felt foreign, weird, but the once strange place had suddenly felt like home.

Over the years, Kanye's fourth album has continued to hold a special place in my music library. Its subject matter, heartbreak, has kept it from aging — an album that is relevant each time a former dream girl arrives in your nightmares, when dealing with a paranoid lover, or eclipsed in a game of cat and mouse by a heartless heroine. From front to back the music West was able to produce is enchanted by an execution of emotions you are likely to relive countless times throughout this lifetime. Not everyone will understand how it feels to drop out of college or graduate with a degree, but we all will be haunted by a former lover or the passing of a parent, and the despair of trying to keep it together while the world slowly crumbles all around.

Without a light at the end of his tunnel, Kanye envelops listeners in his therapeutic release disguised as a pop album. The album never wavers from its central themes — this dedicated focus to pouring out his soul is why the entire project flows like a descending elevator into the depths of his soul. It never stops being dark and heavy, the tone is black as midnight. I don't care about Complex's ranking of Kanye's album, but Brendan Klinkenberg nailed what lies underneath *808s*: "*808s* is a reflection on a Faustian bargain gone wrong, a message from a man who achieved everything he wanted — fame, fortune, critical adoration, and a place in canon — but realized too late that it was at too high a cost and, to his horror, there was no going back. *808s* is the sound of living with decisions you regret."

Abstract moments like "Street Lights," "Bad News" and "Coldest Winter" have always stood out for their songwriting. The beauty is in their simplicity — you feel as if you're in the cab underneath the streetlights, you feel as if you're in the room as bad news is harshly delivered, bringing death to a dream, and you can feel the unforgiving cold of lonely nights, uncertain if love will ever reenter your sleepless world. *808s* is the first time I remember artists covering Kanye records, and it's within those covers where you see the true magic of his writing. The Fray's version of "Heartless" removes the Auto-Tune and increases the poignant human ache of his words.

Daniel Caesar's "Streetcar" is a breathtaking rendition of "Street Lights" that breathes an even more chilling air to the masterful record. Daniel is the superior singer, but both songs are exquisite in the way they convey emotion.

The man who made a name for himself through soul samples removed all the soul from his beats. The man who was determined to be acknowledged as a rapper decided to sing of his pain. The man whose name is synonymous with confidence and egotism created a project where both traits are almost completely vacant. *808s & Heartbreak* is a selfie of Kanye at his most fragile, vulnerable, and creatively daring.

"Welcome To Heartbreak" and "Pinocchio Story" are my favorite portraits of Kanye West the man. He is an open vein bleeding in both cases. One encompasses a man juxtaposing his famous, lavish lifestyle against the conventional lives of acquaintances. This isn't the good life he once proclaimed, his life appears to be more of a fortress that he's trapped within. Sorrow fills the soul as he admits an inability to stop. He had come too far to go back, sacrificed too much to reset. "Pinocchio Story" gives a closer glimpse into his psyche, stripping him of the persona and revealing a man scarred by the loss of his mother, the loss of reality. Singing this song live, doing it in one take, trying to recreate the rawness of this rant would be impossible. This is Kanye at his most pure and lugubrious. This is a man who made it to paradise and realized that even the most beautiful utopia has a dark side.

When Chance The Rapper revealed his ranking of Kanye's albums, I wasn't shocked to find *808s* dead last. It's a subjective list like all lists, no different than Complex. I'm sure he could articulate his reasoning, but it's also rather common to see *808s* at the bottom when categorizing Ye's best music. It's rather unfair, out of all of Kanye's projects, that this is the one where rapping is almost nonexistent—the black sheep of his discography. I've slowly placed the album outside of Kanye's rap realm, choosing to instead categorize it as a unique body of work that he'll never recreate.

Every artist will likely have a moment when an inner voice is daring them to go beyond what's expected, pushing them to escape from the tangle of normalcy and make an album people could hate. It's been said countless times how *808s* was innovative, how it changed the scope of modern rap music, how it ushered in the age of Cudi and Drake, but that's not what makes the album special. Even if no one was impacted, even if the world wasn't altered, even if the album was a complete flop, it doesn't change the music.

During a time where Kanye didn't know what reality was, he made a project overflowing in realism. It's a quality that will always make the album relevant. Even after rap's infatuations with 808 drum sounds and Auto-Tune are dead, I believe this album will stand the test of time. It survives because of heartbreak, vulnerability, and honesty. It may be placed at the very bottom when discussing Kanye's rap albums, but it deserves to be ranked high as one of Kanye's most personal masterpieces.

Meet G Koop,
Your Favorite Producer's Secret
Sample Clearance Weapon

Underground hip hop enthusiasts rejoiced when Drake's *Nothing Was The Same* album featured production from the immensely talented Jake One. The producer laced the Toronto golden child with a beat that felt old and soulful, gentle and elegant, intricate and transfixing; by far one of the best on the album. He didn't do it alone, though. The track's creation was a group effort, as told to NPR in an in-depth interview[18] after the album was released.

The sample used to make "Furthest Thing" came from an unknown gospel record that Gene Brown sold to Jake. Gene is even more underground than Jake, an independent record collector who built a name in the shadows for outsourcing songs to producers. He sells the WAV files from his private collection. A problem arose during the sample clearance stage, however, and the owners who had rights to the song requested a ridiculous amount of money which put the record at risk. [Editor's note: For an in-depth examination of sampling and copyright law, read the book *The Art of Sampling* by Amir Said]

Luckily, Jake had an ace, someone who could save the record and save the label money: G Koop, an Oakland producer who specializes in replays of songs. G Koop works quickly and is able to send you a new version of the song that's almost identical to the original, but it's protected due to it being a studio-created interpolation.

Jake and G Koop's relationship began as student and piano teacher but would evolve into so much more over time. As a Berklee College of Music graduate, G Koop has a deep background in music theory and passed his knowledge down to Jake. His love for the past and his collection of old instruments like the Fender Rhodes, the Clavinet, and a number of old Fender Guitars brought the two closer as colleagues. Jake would teach him about making beats, and it completely revolutionized how he thought about production. What Jake saw in G Koop was someone who had the ear for sounds and the skills to replay them on the right instruments to keep the original feeling of the source material. He had stumbled upon a diamond when he was only looking for a piano teacher.

"Jake would send me samples and I would reinterpret them, learn them, listen to them, try to replace all the sounds, and he would chop them up and make beats," says G Koop. "He would send it back to me sounding nothing like the sample. He would change the hell out of them. As my name got around as someone who could do this type of thing, I would get artists and labels reaching out to me. If they can't clear the sound, [are] not sure what the sample is, or if the sample [costs] too much, they would ask me to reinterpret the music. I would listen with the goal of getting down to the essence of what it is, dissect it, and put it together backwards. If the notes go up, I would take the same notes and go down. If the chord progression goes this way, I would go that way. I pretty much reverse shit."

Understanding the instrumentation, figuring out each instrument used, is what makes what G Koop does amazing. Ear training was taught intensely at Berklee, and it's a skill that he uses to reinterpret samples. Hearing records, hearing melodies, and being forced to sing them back drilled in the prowess necessary in his line of work. It's more than just recreating, you have to understand the essence of the sample.

He told me during our conversation that finding the instrumental's vibe is all about the instruments used. Once you find out what creates the sound, you can recreate the feeling.

"When I finished school, all I did was sit around and listen to Miles Davis records and play the trumpet solos on my guitar to the point I couldn't tell the difference between me and Miles. I wanted to hear that as one voice. I learned to copy, and as a result you soak up the phrasing, you soak up the melodic movement. You soak up the rhythms and feels. The deeper you go into an instrument, the deeper you go into music theory and the mechanics of music in general, you're going to have a deeper understanding to how you create music. All tools that you add to your arsenal. The point of this story is I studied my ass off to master my craft."

The dream of a life in music tends to begin at an early age, a single moment of pure, magnetizing magic that sends you down the path of an artist. G Koop remembers being a child enamored of The Beatles' *Sgt. Pepper's Lonely Hearts Club Band* album, where the vast sea of musical details lassoed around his ears and pulled him in. Music was always around him (his father had a huge collection of records) constantly filling up his eardrums.

The legend that his parents love telling is the story of how his first word was "doobie," a request for them to play The Doobie Brothers' album he loved so much. When he got older, his first job was working at a record store. Naturally, being immersed in music created a desire to make his own. He grew up believing that he would be a guitar player, following in the footsteps of his heroes Eddie Van Halen and Jimi Hendrix. The future he foresaw was a life in a band, a life as a singer, a life as a songwriter; working in music was always the end goal.

There's a vastness to the music industry, an endless number of roads that can lead you to an unexpected destination. "I didn't know what beatmaking was, I never thought about this as a way of making a living," he told me. Adapting has allowed him to stay afloat in this ever-changing industry. Originally, he moved to California in 2002 to start a jazz band, the first one was called The People's Quintet. If you're familiar with Blue Note Records and jazz from the '50s and '60s then you'd be familiar with G Koop's drummer, Donald "Duck" Bailey. Sadly, having a jazz legend who played alongside Jimmy Smith and John Coltrane didn't change the fact that it was a dry period for the jazz era. No one was hiring bands, so once the group disbanded, G Koop bought his first computer and dove into Pro Tools and Reason production software. Being exposed to various kinds of music and learning to play an array of instruments all prepared him for the next stage of his career.

G Koop's name shouldn't be new to fans of Atmosphere, Jake One or Brother Ali, he's been working with some of the underground's most acclaimed darlings for years. But with the boom of "Bad and Boujee," you might notice his name in the production credits alongside Metro Boomin. He also appears on Future and Jay Z's "I Got The Keys" with Southside of 808 Mafia. When that song first hit the web, he wondered if it would be his commercial peak. Of course, months later Migos and Metro helped him secure his first No. 1, the biggest song of his career.

What I found interesting is how G Koop was able to get co-production credits. It's a fascinating process:

"A few years ago, I started to do stuff in this lane where I'm in the studio just creating ideas and melodies. I had this super strong network of heavyweight producers that are making all the heavyweight songs and getting all the big placements in the game that fuck with me. I would send them stuff, they'd sample it, and it would be in the record. We would share the credits, share the production, all that. The sample pack for 'Bad and Boujee' was one that I did in January of this past year. I sent it to Metro Boomin and from that sample pack we did 'Bad & Boujee,' and also 21 Savage's 'Ocean Drive' from the *Savage Mode* album. My elements to those songs were made in the same week."

Both "Ocean Drive" and "Bad and Boujee" were created using the same sample pack. I wonder what else was created through this form of collaboration? Since G Koop is creating original compositions, labels and producers don't have to worry about sample clearance. The musical beds he creates for producers to make into masterpieces could very well become a new way into the game.

Koop lays down the foundation for others to build a house upon, but he does this with specific producers in mind. Having a large Rolodex of producers, he's able to reach S1, Southside, Metro Boomin and countless others. With the explosion of "Bad and Boujee," I'm sure fists are pounding on his door. After ten years in the game, this is his time. The best thing you can be in this business is an asset. If they need you, your phone will never stop ringing. Labels need him to save them from sample woes, and producers will soon see him as a hit-making partner.

"We find the right people to use the tracks. I'm able to be me, and be free in my own space and my own time. The game kind of comes to me on a certain level. It's such a blessing. I'm so grateful. I've helped a lot of people save a lot of money on these clearances. I'm like the Wolf from *Pulp Fiction*. I help situations move along in the way that they should. Ultimately, I like to make great music. There's really no rules. Try shit. I've been blessed to try things and a lot of it sticks."

The heart of G Koop's story is about one man's love for music and how he was able to turn that love into a promising career. It all starts with wanting to be a guitar hero and going through the highs and lows of life without losing the passion for music. From being a record store employee to graduating from Berklee, every step moved him closer to being the creator he is today. Samples have been a huge part of hip hop, but they've also been a huge roadblock in other cases.

In 2012, G Koop produced a bulk of the music that appears on the third solo album by Gift Of Gab, entitled *The Next Logical Progression*. I see what G Koop is doing now as the next logical step

77

for producers who are gifted with strong ears and a comprehensive understanding of music theory. He didn't become the next Van Halen or Hendrix, but G Koop is slowly reaching a position where he has an influence on today's sound. He wants to make guitars a more prominent sound in hip hop, to make that the sound of the mainstream. The fact he's even considering this as a possibility shows the power you can have despite playing from behind the scenes. If he can pull it off, his heroes will be proud.

Killing Jay-Z:
4:44 Is Jay-Z's
Most Vulnerable Voice

"The Ruler's Back" wasn't just a song title paying homage to Slick Rick, but a classic album opener bringing to the throne an invincible conqueror. Jay-Z carries himself like Luke Cage meets Alexander The Great, an unstoppable force in every way. He's always had that mysterious air about him as if there was no way to penetrate his armor. It's the reason why I'm so stunned by the intro to his album *4:44*, a self-evaluation so critical that it's like Achilles contemplating stabbing his own heel to cleanse the sins. We truly get to witness his thoughts in a way unlike any other. There are no grandiose horns or benevolent drums; this isn't a ruler returning but an emperor shedding all of his old clothes.

Killing Jay-Z was the only way Shawn Carter could speak openly and honestly. It took casting away the very ego he once wore as a crown to unlock the seal keeping all these thoughts and emotions buried. He took it back to stabbing Un; just the mere mention cut me deeper than the knife he used that night. That's one confession I never thought would be said in this lifetime. Even his statement about egging on Solange, acknowledging how he further influenced the friction that unfolded in the elevator. "You can't heal what you never reveal" is a piercing lyric, and the moment he begins to vomit his truth as if the recording booth was a drunk therapy session.

Revealing to heal seems to be the mission statement for *4:44*. Not only healing his own heart but, by examining where he has fallen short in the past, the very men and women who look up to him can learn and cherish these lessons. Hov said he sold crack so we wouldn't have to, and now he's giving game that will hopefully allow us to see the power in vulnerability and crushing the ego in the name of growth.

4:44 wants to highlight how blessings can be born from pain, that hard knock lessons will make you better if you accept them as lessons and not just trials that must be overcome. It took a bit of pain for him to see his wrongs. Mistakes made him a better man. Jay has been working toward this maturity since *Kingdom Come*, even though he had the mindset that there was no emotional connection to his wealthy rapper half. Jay-Z has never been richer, he's boasting about being a billionaire, but the entire album is still relatable to even the most quarter-searching couch potato. This isn't the rap album belittling you for what you don't have, but saying you can have this too.

Acceptance is a theme of *4:44* that's handled in an introspective way. Jay is constantly looking back at all his wrongdoings and admitting why they were wrong. There's a lyric on "The Story of O.J." that grabbed me — of course, the deeper context of the song should shine brightest, but I couldn't help but be in awe of "I bought every V12 engine, wish I could take it back to the beginning." He finishes the verse explaining how investing in Dumbo, an up-and-coming neighborhood in Brooklyn, NY, would've been a more lucrative decision. This is the same man who made "Imaginary Player," one of the greatest examples of arrogant bravado in American history:

And now you got these young cats acting like they slung caps / All in they dumb rap, talking about how they funds stack / When I see them in the street, I don't see none of that / Damn playboy, where the fuck is the Hummer at? / Where is all the ice with all the platinum under that?

He goes through each verse on "Imaginary Player" looking down upon other rappers who aren't drinking better, who aren't riding bigger, and whose diamonds twinkle while his shine —

materialism galore. That's who Jay-Z was, proud of everything that money brought him. The Jay-Z on *4:44* once again reinvents bragging, so happy to be making investments that don't depreciate but double in value as time spins. Just listen to his tone on "Legacy," a fatherly warmth of a man holding an angel in his lap and telling her the world is hers. He now brags about how all this money will be passed down, allowing a financial freedom to his family and children that he never had growing up. This is a dad who was allowed a second chance not only to be a family man but to pass down mature decisions to others. We all know that good credit is better than making it rain in Magic City, but has a rapper ever said it?

On his sophomore album, T.I. confronts himself on "T.I. vs. T.I.P." Hearing him have an internal conflict allows listeners to comprehend the struggle of separating the man he was and the man he was becoming. The drastic change in his lifestyle created a split in personalities, a gentleman trying to best the music industry versus the former drug dealer who can't let go of keeping it real.

Jay-Z's story is a similar one, but he made a transition in ways T.I. couldn't fathom. Jay kept it silent, maneuvering in the industry as if the rap game was no different than the crack game — hence the stabbing of Un. But he adjusted, traded throwbacks for tailored suits and became more of a CEO than just another rapper. He continued down the road of an emotionless hustler even as his life got better, giving only glimmers of who he was outside the boasting and bragging.

Unlike T.I., "Kill Jay-Z" finds Shawn killing off his other self rather than continuing to coexist. Maturity is a form of letting go of childish ways and for Jay, maturity is becoming more open, honest, and reflective.

Jay-Z doesn't stay dead, though, he makes a grand return on "Bam" as vicious as we've ever heard him. He came back to remind Shawn why Jay-Z was necessary for their survival. Jay is the one who hustled on those blocks, how they survived the coldest winters. "Sometimes you need your ego to remind these fools." Being vulnerable means taking off your armor and remaining invincible. "Bam" is the return of the ruler, if just for a moment. There's very little duality between Jay and Shawn on *4:44*, but there's no need for Jay to have a voice, this is Shawn's album.

I'm predicting a thousand articles will be written contrasting "Song Cry" and "4:44," two of Hov's most touching records. What I love most about maturity can be found in the last verse of "Song Cry":

That's your fault, how many times you forgiven me? / How was I to know that you was plain sick of me? / I know the way a nigga livin' was whack / But you don't get a nigga back like that! / Shit, I'm a man with pride, you don't do shit like that / You don't just pick up and leave and leave me sick like that / You don't throw away what we had, just like that / I was just fuckin' them girls, I was gon' get right back / They say you can't turn a bad girl good / But once a good girl's gone bad, she's gone forever / I'll mourn forever / Shit, I've got to live with the fact I did you wrong forever

He's blaming this woman for forgiving all of his wrongdoings. She was supposed to wait — the cheating didn't warrant her to move on — he was coming right back. He closes the verse promising to mourn her forever as if the guilt would plague him until the earth ends. He didn't believe it because he didn't fight for her. He just moved on to do wrong elsewhere.

Married Shawn Carter, however, the husband with three kids, you can feel his hurt. You can feel that his wrongdoings weren't a blemish but a haunting scar that burned. It's as if he suddenly was aware of consequences, that his world was about to crumble. "I would probably die with all this shame" and "My heart breaks for the day I had to explain my mistakes" are so much more heart-wrenching than "I've got to live with the fact I did you wrong forever." Because one just lacks the painful sincerity of having to own up and face your mistakes rather than moving on. Shawn is emotionless no more.

Jay-Z reminded us that he is still a mortal man. He is flawed, but he admits these flaws with a sense of clarity that you only obtain once facing the consequences of your actions. This is the dad-rap, grown-man album that evolution allowed him to make. Not as an artist but as a man. We never stop growing old, but we can cease to grow up. Fortunately for hip hop, Jay-Z is still here to share his maturation.

I Was Wrong About *Illmatic*

The final golden glow of a setting sun is beauty that speaks directly to the eyes. No context is needed, no explanation necessary, when the sky goes from its standard baby blue to hues of orange, red, and pink, the radiance can remove air from lungs. Sunsets represent a universal idea of instinctive appreciation, to be seen is to be loved.

Albums acclaimed as classics became of interest during my teenage submersion into hip hop. Various rap forums described the classics as perfect, albums without a single flaw or song worth skipping. I prematurely concluded that classics — when heard — were instinctively loved, audio sunsets.

A Tribe Called Quest's *Low End Theory,* Tupac's *All Eyez On Me, Notorious B.I.G.'s Life After Death,* Big L's *Lifestylez ov da Poor & Dangerous,* and Nas' *Illmatic* were recurring recommendations in my search for the gold standard. Especially Nas. His name was the most frequent across internet forums, chat rooms, magazines and blog sites. In their own way they all decreed his 1994 debut to hip hop what Francis Coppola's The Godfather is to cinema.

Before hearing *Illmatic,* the idea of "the greatest hip hop album ever" was drilled into my mindset. It was like opening a book, but before reading the first chapter being told the writing would make Shakespeare feel inferior. Masterpiece is what I thought when pressing play, but masterpiece wasn't the thought when the album ended.

I assumed listening was enough, that the reasons for massive acclamation would reveal themselves. It was a naive belief that anyone with functioning ears could acknowledge a spectacular album capable of causing cultural shifts. While each song played, innately, there wasn't a sense of instinctive enthusiasm. It was good, enjoyable, but I was left waiting on some unspoken surge that would send me to join the other wolves and howl to the moon of its excellence. The surge never came.

14 years after the initial release, I struggled with recognizing why it stood out like a giant drinking tea in a dwarf house. Wasn't a classic supposed to transcend the wear and tear of time? Questions of classics and its status swimmed around my thoughts while trying to pinpoint exactly what made *Illmatic* more special than Lupe's *The Cool* or Kanye's *College Dropout*, modern classics upheld by my generation.

At the time I was 15 going on 16. Lil Wayne was my favorite rapper, *Dedication 2* my favorite mixtape, and Kanye West's *Late Registration* my favorite album. T.I.'s *King*, Young Jeezy's *Thug Motivation 101*, Lil Wayne's *Carter II*, Lupe Fiasco's *Food & Liquor*, and Ludacris's *Release Therapy* were rotating honorable mentions. They were albums of the moment, representing my entry point into hip-hop as a culture of interest. My ears were modernized, mostly southern, and largely influenced by whatever was encouraged by mass media. Radio and B.E.T. were still the providers for what was new and hip.

Atlanta raised me, the city had more impact on my musical taste than either of my parents. I saw the rise of crunk and the death of snap. I saw dope boys turn superstars and Outkast years after the declaration that the south had something to say. My entry point into rap wasn't through a museum where what came before was rightfully highlighted, dissected, and elaborated. Age, not just ageism, plays a role in how music is embraced and digested. Not everyone naturally gravitates to the sounds and styles of old masters, especially when encapsulated by the present.

It was the internet, not a knowledgeable OG who encouraged digging into hip hop's past. There were no guides, just a bunch of posts saying what should be listened to. Discovering the pillars of excellence to all who came before and after was easy, but the why took deeper inquiring. Albums aren't sunsets, the radiance can be appreciated, but without proper context there's a wall of misunderstanding. I was born too late to experience the second golden era of hip hop, and still too young to fully appreciate the music when it graced adolescent ears. Maturity isn't puberty, it doesn't occur overnight. Life and its humbling experiences are instrumental in leading to wiser, more sophisticated perspectives. The same goes for musical taste — it grows with open mindedness, research, phases, and expanding beyond spaces of comfort.

A few years ago, I attempted to write about hip hop elitism and classic albums from an outsider's perspective. The piece pointed blame at hip hop elitist for enforcing a pressuring groupthink on anyone who enters the sacred sanctuary of hip hop. So much of it was based on my perceived notion of subjective individuality and how it didn't appear to be accepted. Everyone recited the same top 5s, loved the same classics, and championed what had always been glorified. The initial idea was born from my first impression of *Illmatic*, the strange feeling of alienation after not receiving the album like so many. The article, I admit, poorly executes a perspective that is shortsighted. Growing up in hip hop helped me understand that subjectively liking an album doesn't change its impact on history. Cultural significance goes much deeper than any subjective thought. Classics aren't meant to be beloved because of some sense of eternal awesomeness, but because of how they define, represent, impact and/or change where hip hop was.

Being younger, engrossed in your generation's offerings allows an easy neglect to the past. If you grew up in wonderment by mixtape Wayne's punchlines and tenacity, Slick Rick's storytelling won't have the same attraction. Sound, approach, and style are vastly different. For me, *Illmatic* was a new, completely unexplored world. I found it enticing much later in life, once reaching my early 20s. A bit more aware of '90s hip hop and how the era of Rakim transitioned into the dawn of Nas. A newfound allure was found when I returned to the dusty boom bap and poetic realism.

Playing *Illmatic* is like flipping through a black and white photo book of Queensbridge, New York in the early '90s. Unfamiliar faces, but a comfortable nostalgia exist in these stories of youthful coming-of-age. The breakbeats that once sounded ancient and old became enchanting, the lyricism that seem to lack dynamism was smooth yet sharp, elegant and captivating, and full of detailed imagery like the writing of F. Scott Fitzgerald — but if Gatsby was black, young, and raised in America's largest public housing. Realizing the flaws of rap albums heavy with commercial corniness and banal shortcomings only made *Illmatic's* flawlessness stand like a majestic unicorn in a field of aging stallions. It took me knowing more, hearing more, and comprehending music differently to see what was always there.

To a blind man the sunset isn't a spectacle, but just another moment occurring in his colorless world. It took a few years before the color of an album like *Illmatic* could truly beam in all its vibrancy. Not all albums released before my time were received with the same gradual acceptance. I loved Tribe's jazziness, Tupac's bravado, and Biggie's voice. The smallest detail can make an artist appeasing, a tiny quality that draws you in. I will say *Illmatic* sparked my revisit of other classics, listening to them with unbiased ears, all expectations wiped away. Some were better than others. I prefer Raekwon's *Only Built 4 Cuban Linx* over Dr. Dre's *The Chronic*, Jay-Z's *Reasonable Doubt* over Snoop Dogg's *Doggystyle*. But it's a favoritism of the East Coast over the West. Preference will always take precedence.

The going back phase happens naturally. I'm watching as my little brother is coming around to Jay-Z. For years he would only listen to rappers from home, if you weren't Atlanta, he wasn't listening. He was a teenager who wanted to hear those young men living where he lived, walking the same streets he walked. They were his artists, voices for his generation. He's older now, intrigued by the old legends and promising new legends. As his taste expands, he'll find the old masters where I found them, and hopefully he listens while digging into their cultural significance. That's part of being timeless, being so relative to a period that anyone looking back has to acknowledge your presence, impact, and influence.

I think of Jazz often, how a John Coltrane solo can have different effects on each eardrum that hears it. The same A Love Supreme that can bring a man to tears, will cause another to sheepishly request a change in song. Music isn't rocket science, it doesn't take a classroom to conclude subjectively what's good and bad. But there are times, on a much deeper level, where an explanation can change how someone perceives what they heard. Reading about hip hop has helped me understand the beauty of little details that would've gone unnoticed. Children of tomorrow might hear Kendrick Lamar's *good kid, m.A.A.d city* and not experience the same headphone-over-heels love that greets me with each listen. The music is good, but what *good kid, m.A.A.d city* means to hip hop is far more important. You can always mature into artistic appreciation, but knowing the history is vital for comprehending the magnitude one album can have.

Music and music history has to be treated like sacred torches — cherished like treasure and passed down like expensive inheritance. Whether it's cultural classics or personal favorites, the significance of what we love matters as long as we share them with those we love. Hip hop is better than a sunset, it is a musical universe so deep a lifetime can be spent exploring, dissecting, and defining for the torchbearers who will lead the culture into its future. Pray they don't forget the past, and if they don't, *Illmatic* will be there, patiently waiting for the next generation. Another group of kids to grow old with a true classic hip hop album.

Notes & References

16 Sullivan, Eric, "Story: Young Thug," GQ (February 3, 2015) https://www.gq.com/story/young-thug.

17 Reid, Shaheem "Jay-Z Elaborates On Blueprint 3 Album Cover" MTV (August 4, 2009) http://www.mtv.com/news/1617577/jay-z-elaborates-on-blueprint-3-album-cover/.

18 Matson, Andrew, "This Beat's For You: The Making Of Drake's 'Furthest Thing,'" NPR (October 2, 2013). https://www.npr.org/sections/therecord/2013/10/01/228235377/the-making-of-drakes furthest-thing.

Part 3
ART, CRAFT
& THE INDUSTRY

The Creative Vision
of The Little Homies

"Don't all dogs go to heaven? Don't Gangsta's boogie? Do owl shit stank? Lions, Tigers, & Bears. But *To Pimp A Butterfly*. It's the American dream nigga," That was the caption on Kendrick's Instagram the night he released the album art for To Pimp A Butterfly. Lil Homie is cited as the wordsmith, but there's no tag to his personal Instagram, his identity remained a mystery. Matthew Trammell wrote a story for FADER the day after acknowledging the renowned French photographer Denis Rouvre as the artist who captured the iconic image and also confirmed through TDE that Dave Free and Kendrick Lamar were the ones who came up with the brilliant cover's concept. At the very end of the piece, Matthew references the quote, calling Lil Homie, "A nameless genius that just might be staring us in the face." He was referring to the cover and all the joyous, black faces that stared back at us gleefully, one possibly being the undercover poet who announced the title of Kendrick's long-awaited sophomore album. He wasn't wrong, the Lil Homie is on the cover and he is also mentioned by name in the article, except he didn't know it. No one did.

Dave Free and Kendrick Lamar decided to become The Little Homies during Kendrick's transitional period away from K-Dot. He was starting to truly find himself as an artist and they needed to represent that change visually. Dave Free detailed the story back in August of last year when The Little Homies started getting attention for being credited as co-directors in all of Kendrick's music videos, everyone except "King Kunta" (although Director X told Complex[19] that Kendrick was involved for two whole days with the video's editing process). In his interview with Andres Tardio for MTV,[20] he recalled the "Ignorance Is Bliss" video, which was written by Kendrick and directed by Dave with assistance from O.G. Michael Mihail. The video had no budget, no major label backing or even an expensive camera, "Ignorance Is Bliss" was far from being MTV-ready but that's where it started, the blueprint for The Little Homies. Dave and Kendrick as the creative visionaries who just needed the right people to help bring their ideas to life. The way they brought Mihail in to help with choreography is no different than selecting Denis Rouvre to shoot the cover for *To Pimp A Butterfly*.

"The Little Homies actually came about one day when me and Kendrick were sitting down at the studio and one of our other videos came on. Everything is always a collaborative effort, so it would have so many names on there. And Kendrick was like, 'Yo, we're from Top Dawg Entertainment — so let's change the concept of what we do together and let's make it a brand, something under the TDE umbrella. Why not be The Little Homies?'" —Dave Free[21]

Despite the relatively little attention surrounding The Little Homies, the creative duo has quietly become a big deal in hip hop's realm of visual arts. If you look back on their last year of work, you'll discover they have released nothing but creative and stunning videos. The Little Homies adapted the same collaborative mentality and meticulous precision that Kendrick uses to create his music and applied it to his visual artistry. Alexandre Moors, the director of "i," gave a bit of insight into working with The Little Homies in his interview with Vibe after the video's release, saying that Dave and Kendrick aren't on the sidelines following his orders, both were heavily involved in the video's process. The duo had so many ideas they could have been stretched into five or six visuals — Alex's biggest worry was not being able to fit them all into one video. For example, it was Kendrick who visualized him getting his hair braided in the club and the iconic scene where he's hanging his head out of the lowrider. Alexandre confirmed that it's inspired by Heath Ledger's Joker from *The Dark Knight*.

Throughout "i" dance is used to showcase joy, a reccurring theme in The Little Homies visuals for *To Pimp A Butterfly*. Colin Tilley, the co-director for "Alright" (a much darker video than "i"), told MTV[22] that the dancers used were to represent positivity. Dancing, especially in black culture, is a form of expression that can be passionate, fun, and celebratory, the dancers in "Alright" embody this. They are meant to bring a sense of positivity to balance out all the negatives that plague the mad city. "i" uses dance in the same way — they dance through the street passing the homeless, passing a black man being arrested by two white police officers, passing the window of a man ready to commit suicide, you see both the joy and pain next to one another. You'll notice that theme in most of Kendrick's *To Pimp A Butterfly* videos — the portrayal of a world that's never just good or just bad but balanced. Despite all the internal and external evils, Kendrick is the beam of light, an infectious positivity waking up the people around him.

"As the concept continued to develop, I had a lot of great conversations with Kendrick and Dave. We just kept hammering the concept home to really keep digging deeper and deeper. I've never actually worked with an artist like Kendrick that wants to keep pushing the creative to a whole 'nother world. Every little detail matters to him," says Tilley.[23]

In Colin's interview with MTV, he mentioned that Dave Free called him about shooting the video and that their idea was to have Kendrick floating. The three of them put their heads together and formulated a treatment built on that foundation, a flying Kendrick. The soaring K-Dot symbolizes a hero-like character, someone that the people can look to, chase after, a superman. "Alright" gives you the contrast of good and bad, especially with the powerful beginning scenes that portray a city engulfed in madness. The clip of "Cartoon & Cereal" is gold and should've been nominated for a MTV Video Music Award despite only being a few seconds. Cutting through the madness is a flying Kendrick, hope personified, catching the eyes of people down the street, being held up by the mob, being chased by the kids, the same way he was chased and followed while dancing in "i." The idea of hope and positivity only begets more hope and positivity. It's powerful that they decided to have an officer shoot him down. Once again the case of the man who is supposed to protect and serve is stealing a man's life and hope from the community. Colin says Kendrick's smile at the end is meant to mean, "Everything is still gonna be alright," which alludes to the bigger idea of killing the man but not killing the dream, not killing hope.

The officer shoots the flying Kendrick with his finger and not his gun, realism was thrown out the moment Kendrick and company were being carried in a car by four police officers. All these touches of imagination help me realize that one of The Little Homies trademarks is teetering between realism and fantasy. Take "These Walls" for example. Kendrick bursts through the wall while the girl is dancing on him. Humorous but also extremely far-fetched. The Joe Wei-directed "For Free" moves at a dizzying pace, cramming a plethora of imagery into the two-minute music video. From the opening with the saxophone player blaring from the window to the end when a dozen Kendricks are seen in the front yard, it's a theatrical, bizarre but engrossing watch. There's plenty of split-second symbolism that will take multiple views to absorb, but watching Kendrick chase the scantily clad woman around reminding her that the dick isn't free balances the serious with the fun.

"We work with certain people for certain projects. It's very strategic. When it comes to executing and creating the ideas, we're not guys who say, "Do whatever." We're very much involved. There have been times where people have seen me pick up a camera and I'll start shooting sh-t myself because I want things done a certain way. We convey that message to anyone we work with, so they know that's what we expect. And to be honest, we've had nothing but positive outcomes."
—Dave Free

Glowing, fluorescent lighting is commonly used in The Little Homies videos, giving almost all their visuals a dream-like feeling. "i" is gorgeously shot, especially the opening scene in a dimly lit club that comes off as a wonderland for those seeking to groove until the rising sun passes the setting moon. The motel scene in "These Walls" are drenched in lush reds, blues, oranges and greens. The visuals for "For Sale" also make use of luminous orange yellows with a touch of heavy grain.

In the second half of the short film, "God Is Gangsta," co-directed by PANAMAERA, Kendrick walks and hangs upside down through colorful Paris at Le Silencio, full of women who embody the temptation of Lucy. He seems dazed, uninterested, almost as if he's sleepwalking through the wave of clothed and naked seductive vixens. There are clips of a baptism that are cut in-between the women and the cryptic messages that flash every few seconds. Another example of how, through his artistry, Kendrick sought God to escape the industry's Lucies.

The location being Paris at Le Silencio can't be coincidental. The strange nightclub is owned by filmmaker David Lynch, renowned for his movies and television series that, full of surrealism, toe the line between fascinating and disturbing. The first half of "God Is Gangster" is directed by Psycho Films (can't be a coincidence) and the visual rendition of "U" feels like something from the mind of Lynch. Kendrick's acting is convincing, he appears to be truly losing his mind in this tiny room, trying to submerge his struggles in whiskey. The screaming and frantic moving is unlike anything Kendrick has done on camera, which is fitting of "U" since his soul-crushing confession of guilt and even suicidal thoughts seemed completely out of character. In the second verse is where things take a turn for the strange — the bottle that is spinning on the table doesn't stop, the mirror in the corner begins to reflect a Kendrick that isn't moving like the man rapping in the camera, it's like Kendrick's Twin Peaks nightmare sequence. (Looks like Childish Gambino isn't the only rap artist inspired by Lynch.)

The Lil Homies have mostly been credited for their work with Kendrick but Dave admitted in his interview that they have goals of branching out and doing more with outside artists. Starting within the squad is a start, both Jay Rock and ScHoolboy Q have visuals co-directed by the duo. Jay Rock's "90059" (also directed by PANAMAERA) is rather intricate, the first half of the visual is SZA driving Jay around in a straightjacket-wearing a Hannibal Lecter mask. Things get strange after he's let loose, the latter half is Jay running from the police like CJ from San Andreas. It's rather epic and very fitting of the song's rather deranged lyrics. Q's "Groovy Tony" (also directed by Jack Begert) is rough and raw, the video captures the murderous persona that is more menacing than Larenz Tate in 1993. He's crushing bodies at a junkyard in the mouth of a crane, shooting his chopper, crashing his whip and stealing faces. A gangster so terrorizing that he lights his blunt using the fire that's burning his arm. There are some excellent angles used that help make this video one of Q's most creative. Both videos are strong and carry a touch of the abnormal and imaginativeness that can be found in Kendrick's visuals.

Along with music videos, The Little Homies are also the

masterminds behind Kendrick's stage content. Dave revealed that the B.E.T Awards and SNL performances were all them. It's not surprising, the same concepts that encompass the videos are extended on stage. Especially dance. He had a black couple waltzing on Ellen while he performed "These Walls." The crew of dancers that help change "Alright" into an impressive experience on B.E.T. Just look at how the camera angles and lighting are done masterfully on Jimmy Fallon, and of course the breathtaking GRAMMY's performance.[24] From the transition from prisoners to proud African dancers, it was unlike anything I've ever seen. That's something The Little Homies have mastered, taking songs you've heard before and making them feel new and fresh again. No Kendrick performance is the same, he will change up the song order, take verses and place them at the beginning or end of other records. Or like in the "Alright" music video, create a new song just for the moment, to give the fans a reason to come back. There's always a reason to hear and see him again.

What was Kendrick's involvement in the creative process?

In her intervie with Billboard, stylist Dianne Garcia said of styling Kendrick's GRAMMY performance: "He was involved in the sense that he knew exactly what he wanted. He showed me a photo of the prisoners and was like 'This is my inspiration.' There were these guys walking in a chain gang and he said, 'I want them to look like this.' And I knew that he wanted the African guys to glow in the dark because they were going to go into a sequence where everything was going to be dark and they were going be lit with UV lights."

The Little Homies have one of the most creative visions in all of music. If Dave Free and Kendrick Lamar continue their exceptional run of highly creative and deeply engaging music videos, they will be looked at with the same admiration as the leading music video directors of our time. A sign that the Little Homies may soon be heading for the big screen.

This Is the Remix:
The Evolution of the Hip Hop Remix
from Diddy to Drake

During the early '90s while A&Ring at Uptown Records, Diddy was the mastermind behind the early development of legendary R&B group Jodeci. Puff had a vision to expand their single "Come and Talk To Me" beyond the reigns of R&B and reach an audience engrossed in hip hop. He took their vocals and reconstructed the soulful ballad around a sample of EPMD's "You're A Customer," also including the drum loop from The Honey Dippers' "Impeach The President." The dance floor wasn't new to the future mogul; throwing parties was a big part of his executive beginnings, and he knew a familiar rhythm would cause the hip hop kids to dance. Diddy discovered his blueprint to commercial prosperity by foreseeing mass appeal in nostalgia and novelty.

What Diddy did in '92 was unlike Coldcut's remix of Eric B & Rakim's "Paid In Full" or Pete Rock's retouch of Public Enemy's "Shut 'Em Down." Producer remixes weren't uncommon—the concept of the remix originated from Jamaican dance music in the '60s, found new meaning in the '70s with disco, and continued to find a place in modern music. Puffy's newfound ambition to adapt a form of remixing that utilized samples with a twist worked for Jodeci. The success inspired him to use Mary J. Blige's highly favored debut album as a vessel to further explore how far he could push his reinvention. There was no full-length R&B remix project predating *What's the 411?*, it was Puffy who brought it to life and the commercial triumph proved the power of pairing old and new; hip hop and R&B.

97

Diddy's vision was on the crossover potential that remixing allowed: two chances to break records through two different mediums. One of the biggest, more unforgettable moments of the mid-'90s in hip hop was Mariah Carey fighting her label for a hip hop remix to her hit single, "Fantasy." This was 1995, Mariah was a pop princess and hip hop's commercial appeal wasn't yet solidified. The two worlds were separate, and the executives didn't understand why she was so adamant about bringing this rare and raw element to her clean and pristine image. Not only did Mariah go hip hop, she brought the otherworldly Ol' Dirty Bastard along as her Prince Charming. Imagine the look of confusion in the Columbia office the day ODB's vocals reached the suits.

Neither artist was signed to Bad Boy, but Diddy was one of the producers on the track. He made sure his name was involved with the first huge remix joining the worlds of pop and hip hop, which eventually opened up doors for contemporaries like Jermaine Dupri and Irv Gotti to follow in his footsteps with So So Def and Murder Inc.

The entire industry would actually follow, but everyone knew Puffy was the pioneer. He wouldn't let anyone forget about it, either. Countless classic, Diddy-engineered remixes throughout the '90s and 2000s became engraved in history while the originals aren't as immortal; Craig Mack's "Flava In Ya Ear," Biggie's "One More Chance/Stay With Me," Jagged Edge's "Let's Get Married," Mobb Deep's "Quiet Storm," to name only a few. Revitalizing singles with new production or features became the wave of repurposing music. There was an art to topping the previous version, but it wouldn't last. Nothing in the music industry ever does.

A change occurred during the mid-2000s, though, when the remix ceased to be an art form that produced new instrumentation. In a 2010 interview with SoulCulture, Just Blaze provided insight into what inspired such a small but noticeable change.[25] Simply, radio's Nielsen BDS spin generator, which tracks how often a song is played on the radio, only attributed remix spins to the original record's total provided the beat is unchanged. By keeping the production untouched, both the single and the remix would account for the same amount of spins. Preferring the remix over the original no longer mattered, as Nielsen would judge them as a single entity. Then again, if the production is changed for the remix, or the beat is slowed down or sped up, the radio's computer system would recognize the new version as a completely different record. A new beat suddenly meant lower spin totals, not ideal for measuring a song's success. Puff was a banger guy, he prided himself on having the hottest hit, but the remix format he helped to popularize was killed because it made tracing hits more difficult.

Dupri's "Welcome To Atlanta" couldn't have a Coast 2 Coast remix with each new location getting production to match its heralded city, Puff and Snoop would have to represent for the East and West over one of Jermaine's Southern slappers. When the remix format changed, the focus was no longer on crafting production that could push a single into new spaces but finding the right feature to push the music further. Destiny's Child was a group of young, innocent darlings who wanted a "Soldier," so it fit the song's theme to get thuggish ruggish rappers like T.I. and Lil Wayne for the remix. This predates the two being commercial phenoms, and Wayne especially benefited from crossing over into space where he didn't have much footing post-Hot Boys.

Unlike Lil Wayne, who used the remix as a way of rising up from the underground, André 3000 utilized the medium to keep from vanishing from the mainstream. Around the time of *Idlewild*, the last OutKast album, Three Stacks began to make guest appearances on scorching remixes of others' hot singles, laying down extravagant verses on DJ Unk's "Walk It Out," Lloyd's "You," Jay Z's "30 Something" and more. He became a fine example of how the remix spectacle could be turned into a sensation due to an unlikely visitor; there was no way to predict what song he would arrive on and that only added to what made each appearance monumental.

Around the time of André's appearance on "Walk It Out," the industry began to also see a rise in the mega posse cut remix. It became imperative for every ringtone seller to follow up their verse with a verse from every hot rapper in the game. The labels began to move with an Avenger mentality, seeing power and popularity in adding big names for bigger numbers. Songs like Rich Boy's "Throw Some D's," Chris Brown's "Deuces" and Ke$ha's "Sleazy" all benefitted from, among others, André's participation. And due to the South's rising dominance a majority of these massive remixes featured Southern rap stars like Lil Wayne, T-Pain, Rick Ross and Ace Hood, who seemed to pop up on almost every rap tune that broke Billboard's Hot 100. The Game's "One Blood" remix is still one of the most grandiose, star-studded remixes of the massive remix era. 25 artists contributed verses, stretching the song out to be 12 minutes long — a legendary feat that even brought Ja Rule back from hip hop obscurity.

The biggest winner of the massive remix era was DJ Khaled. His singles were already filled with legions of rappers, so it was a seamless transition to turn his phonebook into a massive remix assembly line. The "I'm So Hood" remix in 2007 started the trend he would continue to lean upon, each one getting bigger and calling upon more artists to add bars to the fray. He went big with the "All I Do Is Win" remix, followed by the enormous "Welcome To My Hood" remix. Just like Diddy did before him, Khaled found room to take over through the remix.

While Khaled may have been known for orchestrating some of the biggest remixes during the posse-cut era, the most memorable single-turned-remix remains "Touch It." Busta Rhymes brought out DMX, Mary J. Blige, Missy Elliott, Rah Digga, Lloyd Banks and newcomer Papoose to boost his single to legendary status. Pap's appearance alone took him from an underground emcee to a top prospect. During this time, radio was still prevalent, television still had networks where rap videos were playing, and it was common for remixes to receive massive spins and even visual representation. Big records received big remixes, it was the era of seeing rappers move in herds.

Like everything else in the industry, the internet marked the next big wave of change for the remix. Ringtones died, radio began to lose its dominant grip and singles began playing an entirely different role as a way of promotion.

With the days of bringing in 17 disparate emcees for a remix slowly dying, the power of a remix shifted to a single co-sign. Now, all you needed was one verse from a huge star to take your name beyond the stars.

Drake is the poster child for this kind of contribution to a lesser-known artist's track, always keeping an eye out for how he can become a part of bubbling movements. From Future's "Tony Montana" to Migos' "Versace" to iLoveMakonnen's "Tuesday," the Drake remix became a coveted commodity, turning underground acts into the "next big thing." Look at how South London's Dave recently saw a huge boost in awareness once Drake remixed his 2016 single, "Wanna Know." In the age of streaming and social media, remixes have allowed for an easy, immediate introduction to a much wider fanbase; whether it's Fetty Wap or Wizkid, aligning with one sole artist in this age is worth more than a thousand features.

Of course, there's also the remix as an internet event. Anytime Black Hippy decides to come together and destroy an instrumental, hearts skip beats. Kanye West on "Timmy Turner" was expected to be much bigger but his touch isn't what it once was. Jay Z appearing on Kendrick's "Don't Kill My Vibe" and Remy and Fat Joe's "All The Way Up" was worth 100 artists. There's a novelty to certain remixes now, only a select few blow up. But the awareness of collaboration is massive for followings.

In addition to impacting the remix game, the internet also shifted the focus away from Nielsen BDS spins and toward streaming numbers. DJ Luke Nasty can now chart by making a song over Anderson Paak's "Might Be" and T-Nasty's "Nasty Freestyle" was much bigger than Bandit Gang Marco's "Nasty." Can you imagine if this form of charting was possible during the mixtape Weezy era? "Sky's The Limit" would have soared while Mike Jones' "Mr. Jones" would have languished in ZShare obscurity. Instead of doing official remixes, rappers can now just grab beats, make their own rendition and pray (read: pay) the song is cleared.

This current era of the internet remix is where producers stand to reemerge. Skilled beatmakers now have multiple platforms to release their remixes, edits, and flips to an audience of fans who are always intrigued by new takes on their favorite singles. It's taking the Diddy approach of pairing vocals with new production but without needing the rapper to participate. I've spent countless hours listening to Knxwledge's *Wrap Taypes*, a collection of rap songs that he has tweaked and warped over his preferred production. Kaytranada got his big break by posting an immaculate remix of Janet Jackson's "If," and now he is one of the biggest producers maneuvering through the House genre. I've played GreenSLLME's version of "Bad and Boujee" more than the original. Sango made me realize how much we need Bryson Tiller and GoldLink to get their hands on Dilla beats. What Stwo did to 21's "X" should completely erase the original from existence. And Ducko's edit of Kanye's "Heartless" and 21 Savage's "No Heart" will make you rethink logic. Everything returns full circle, and producers have to take advantage of the climate and realize how vitality could be a remix away.

Live From Chattanooga
With Isaiah Rashad

Blue and beautiful, not a single cloud could be found in the sky as a sign indicated our entrance into Chattanooga, TN; scenery fitting of a Thomas Cole landscape painting or a Ryan McGinley photograph. The sun glowed from above, a radiant yellow that beamed uninterrupted, unchallenged, unrivaled. This very sun would go unnoticed on an ordinary day, any other Thursday the ball of fire right below the heavens would simply be a symbol of one of life's most consistent patterns. The sun did as the sun has always done, but while driving through downtown Chattanooga, I couldn't help but think of Isaiah Rashad's lyric, "I think the sunshine should feel how I feel, how I feel."

It was the day Rashad was coming home to perform. What better way to be welcomed than by a gorgeous afternoon? Tonight he would be the highest star, the apple of all eyes, a sun too bright to be eclipsed by clouds, and the weather was a symbolic representation of Chattanooga's son returning home.

Isaiah's homecoming was my first time back in his Tennessee hometown since a fifth-grade field trip. Memories of my adolescent aquarium adventure had been long forgotten, but after my first bite of Champy's fried chicken and a satisfying sip of Miller High Life, I knew this would be a far more memorable trip.

I loved the calm, patient Southern spirit that soaks into your skin the minute you slow down and take a deep breath. No one seemed to be in a rush, no one moved with a sense of urgency — even during rush hour, the roads were without rage. It wasn't until arriving at the venue did I begin to feel that tonight wasn't just another ordinary stop on the Lil Sunny Tour.

"Y'all ready to turn up for Zaywop!?" an enthusiastic voice

questioned, as Isaiah strolled through the crowd toward the venue's entrance. His face wore a grin, the kind of drunken expression displayed when excitement and intoxication are in perfect harmony. As he opened the door into the Revelry Room, another car drove by playing *The Sun's Tirade* at an unruly, peace-disturbing volume. It was the third, or possibly the fourth vehicle to speed through playing Rashad's long-awaited sequel to *Cilvia Demo*. Everyone from the jolly drivers to the drunk walkers were in high spirits, happily entering the venue. I watched them with the eyes of an outsider, witnessing firsthand the elation of a hometown celebrating an offspring's return.

Four days earlier, I was at Zay's Atlanta show, where the line resembled a large leviathan that coiled around the building. Rain fell hard, causing the crowd to become anxious and impatient. I couldn't blame them for wanting to rush inside. Chattanooga was different, the natives lingered outside. Music was played loudly, weed was passed, beer was shared — all that happened outside foretold a crowd who was ready to celebrate.

When opening act Tut took his first steps onto the stage, he was welcomed to warm applause and loving cheers. Tut is another homegrown artist making a return visit, and there are high hopes that he'll be the next emcee to prosper in a major way. On stage, he reminds me of Curren$y — easy-going and nonchalant but precise, his carefree spirit never creeping into carelessness. Seeing Tut live was a good reminder to revisit his *Preacher's Son* mixtape that was released in 2015; the kind of Southern rap that feels like old Cadillacs, smoky jazz clubs, and AriZona Iced Tea on your grandmother's porch during the hottest summer months.

There's an interesting contrast between Tut and Maryland's Jay IDK, the only other opener who took the stage. Jay has a commanding presence, from the way he comes out with a mask on to how he demands the crowd to chant his name. Jay has the charisma of an Army general; the crowd stayed mostly transfixed throughout his entire performance. He has found comfort onstage, he has made music that translates well in a performative setting, and will only get better from here. Each time our paths cross, his star quality shines a bit brighter.

As Jay closed out his set, I maneuvered into the center of the room, where you find the fans who aren't too cool and aren't too rambunctious. Chattanooga was still calm, but the whispers broke out into yells as Isaiah's DJ Chris Calor walked out onstage. There was very little build up — Kendrick's "m.A.A.d city" to get the energy to roof-scorching levels. Before we knew it, Isaiah was on stage reciting the lyrics to "Smile." An interesting intro since the loosie didn't find a home on either one of his albums.

The beauty of the internet is that songs that simply linger on SoundCloud can still make it to the stage and every word is known. Frenzy. An intoxicating passion filled the room as song after song reminded us why we were here. Onstage, the way Isaiah's lyrics are delivered are passionate, he understands how to project and really engage the crowd. There's no theatrics, just a man with a microphone telling the stories from his life.

Seeing Isaiah live made me realize how his hiatus between *Cilvia Demo* and *The Sun's Tirade* meant his music was heard mostly in intimate settings — thunderous bangers are meant for plenty of company, but personal records like "Heavenly Father" really work best when you're alone. I never expected to hear a crowd of people sing in unison, "And I been losing more than just my mind, gathering what's left of self-respect." It's hard enough to recite your demons into a microphone, but to perform them for hordes of people, night in and night out must also lay heavy on the soul.

There were joyous moments, like rapping "Damn, that Vince Vaughn is a funny cat" together during "Soliloquy," but it was hard not to just fall silent and watch the man pour out his truth while confessing how he saw his son but missed his daughter during "Dressed Like Rappers." To see Isaiah live is like witnessing a man speak his gospel, reading straight from the book of Zaywop.

My trip to Chattanooga was inspired by the feeling that an artist returning to their hometown must inspire a single moment of magic; something that wouldn't happen anywhere else on a tour. I didn't know when it would happen or what it would be, but I believed it would occur. In Atlanta — and I imagine on all the other tour stops — Zay performed an a cappella version of "Rope." It's another rather personal song, but also a crowd pleaser. The music stops, he begins singing "Then my daddy call me yesterday," and all the air is sucked from the room.

As the hoarse words were sung into the mic, the passion in his voice shook all who spectated.

It was the same song, but the way the words were delivered cut deeper.

He sang while staring directly at his father who was in the crowd as if they were the only two people in the entire building. "I love you, I love you, I love you."

Every time "I love you" was belted out, a new wave of chills was sent down my spine. It was like being baptized in an ocean of his emotions, and each one was heavier than the last.

Onstage, Isaiah testified, and we all watched without uttering a single sound. I looked to the left, I looked to the right, and the same men I was previously jumping around with were frozen as if we were locked into a staring contest with Medusa.

The show, of course, continued — the fun was brought back in full force once all The House members came out to perform "Park." The mob of men would stay on stage and turn up until the last song. The show ended how it began, with a song from Kendrick. The sounds of "Alright" echoed through the venue right before Isaiah left the stage. Even after the crowd begged for one more song, the rapper never returned.

I believe that even if the show abruptly ended after that final "I love you," my soul would've been content. In an age where everything feels fake and curated, that raw moment between father and son was pure. Real is what people love about Isaiah — he is no different than the rest of us in our mid-twenties trying to figure it all out. Fighting with our vices, wrestling with our demons, confronting our past, celebrating the present, and hoping for the brightest future.

I would later see Isaiah's father backstage — a tiny, older man who reminded me of all the jazz musicians who dedicated their lives to a life on the road; life with their instrument. During our brief exchange, he admitted to being proud of his son, as I imagine any father would be. He seemed to be a nice man, very gracious, but I couldn't help but hear the lyrics to "Hereditary" as he spoke.

In addition to Isaiah's father, there were other close and extended family members backstage, including Isaiah's mother, stepfather, cousins, friends, peers — and at the very center was the rising rap star, their lil' sun. To be at home, what could be better than performing for a sold-out crowd and seeing people you've known all your life stare at you with pride in their eyes? The look they gave Zay is one that you only see at college graduations, family reunions and NBA drafts.

Memories were made that night in Revelry Room, the kind that will be talked about until his next return. The best thing an artist can do is leave you wanting more, and more is what Chattanooga asked for.

"I love you," Isaiah said to his father, and "I love you," is what Chattanooga said back. Not in the heat of the moment, but in the way that they arrived and in the way that they left.

Kid Cudi, Kevin Abstract, and the Art of Leaving Home

New York City. I saw it as an artist paradise through the eyes of a young writer. I craved to walk the streets that hip hop was birthed on, to gaze at the graffiti on the subway walls like paintings by Picasso, to be devoured by the city that has crushed dreams and raised legends. From afar, the city called me like it has so many, a voice luring me from the hospitable south, from my home, to enter the merciless lair of hustlers and go-getters.

I read stories of how Arthur Rimbaud took a one-way ticket to Paris and how that set the course for him to change poetry. Stories of how Jean-Michel Basquiat started rebelling at an early age by running away from home, and how that spirit of defiance never left as he turned the art world upside down. I looked up to the artist that didn't play it safe, that dared to run away, taking the midnight train into the unknown with no money, no ticket home, pushed by their beliefs that they will make it. I never bought my ticket - my balls weren't made of brass, my heart didn't pump the blood of a radical. I played it safe, but I never stopped admiring those that didn't.

Kevin Abstract tweeted, "Buy a helmet, steal a bike, run away from home," attached with a picture of him wearing a motorcycle helmet with California behind him stretching into the distance. The headline for his USA Today profile reads, "The best thing Kevin Abstract ever did for himself was run away from home." He's a teenager, 19, the same age as I was when daydreams of running away flirted with my reality. He escaped his home life, moving around a bit before taking a risk in Los Angeles. Kevin is an artist that is following his creative vision and not accepting the circumstances of his surroundings. There's a line from his single "Echo":

"He was a bad son, He was a bad son, So he left home, so he left home."

I'm not fit to write Genius annotations, but I relate the lyric to his actual life — a son that doesn't fit his family's conventional way of living so he ran away. The bad son, the artist. "Echo" is a beautiful ballad, cut from the same side of the moon as *Man On The Moon* Cudi and *808's* Kanye, a song that you lose yourself in, by an artist who is prepared to lose it all for his art. He will go far.

One of Kevin's biggest influences is the ever elusive Frank Ocean. One thing they have in common is both artists left from their hometowns for the city of angels. Frank was born in California but moved to New Orleans at age five and was raised there until after Katrina. As told in a 2012 GQ story, he drove cross country with his then-girlfriend, only $1,100 in his pocket and demos to record in professional L.A. studios.[26] A stay that was supposed to last only six weeks turned into six years. If he would've returned to New Orleans, his story would be vastly different. So much of his growth as an artist happened in L.A., there's no guarantee he would sign with Def Jam or more importantly, join Odd Future, the turning point. Imagine Frank signing to Cash Money — trying to fit their aesthetic, singing all the hooks Drake was too busy for. There was very little hope for him at home. To fly, Frank had to cross the country, he had to run away.

Kid Cudi has a similar story of moving away from Cleveland, Ohio — the place that raised him since birth — to New York in hopes of making it. Luckily, he had an uncle that lived in the South Bronx that gave him a roof when he decided to make the voyage. With only $500 in his pocket and a demo, he made the move in 2004, to live with someone he never met in a city he didn't know. In his 2009 cover story with Complex, Cudi said if it wasn't for his uncle letting him stay for those first few months, there would be no Kid Cudi.[27] Unlike Ohio, New York is an unpredictable land of opportunity, you don't know who is around every corner, be it a mugger or megastar. New York brought Cudi everything he needed to enter the next phase of his career, no matter how popular "Day N Nite" was on MySpace, the doors wouldn't have opened for him at home. There's plenty of cities with talented artists that get overlooked strictly because they don't live where the eyes are watching.

What's a hit record if it's never heard? What's a superstar if he or she is never seen? Your location can be the difference between an uphill battle or a downhill slope to prosperity.

Houston, Texas isn't some uncharted, deserted island in hip hop. There's plenty of hip hop history and cultural impact in the H-Town, but it still doesn't rank up in ideal geographical territory in comparison to Atlanta, New York and L.A. The biggest Houston rapper in recent years, Travi$ Scott didn't break out in his home city. Travi$ really embodies the Kevin Abstract lyric, a bad son whose parents didn't see his vision as an artist, they wanted him to finish school and get a realistic job in a realistic field. He dropped out of school, lied to his mom about needing money for books, and bought a flight to New York burning with ambition to prove everyone wrong and make his dreams come true. It didn't happen in New York, so after four months of trying and not seeing results, he tried his luck in L.A. Things were happening but not fast enough.

Finally, he returned home to Houston, but it wasn't a warm welcome. He was a liar that had nothing to show for his deceit, his parents kicked him out. With no place to go he returned to L.A. with no money, just a promise he could crash on a friend's couch. There were 14 text messages from T.I. waiting for him when the plane landed. Finally from the soil of all his labor, the seeds planted were starting to grow.

Iggy Azalea has one of rap's biggest run-away stories. She was 16 when she decided to leave Australia, drop out of high school and pursue a rap career in the United States. It's a pretty ballsy move for a young girl to enter a foreign country with the hopes of becoming a rap artist, insane when you start to really think about it. But she did it, leaving behind everything and everyone, moving from Miami to Houston and then Atlanta. The move eventually led to rewards, she met the right people, connects in the industry she would've never came across back home.

"HipHopDX: To switch subjects a bit, you have an interesting story. You do not see a lot of female rappers from Australia in the United States. You ran away from home when you were 16. While you were flying here, what was going through your head? At 16, kids aren't usually thinking about doing something like that...

Iggy Azalea: There are lots of things that kids do that make them feel invincible. Driving drunk, going to parties and doing stupid shit. I just think that coming to America was such a dream and fantasy and I wanted to make it happen. It didn't dawn on me on how big of a deal it was until when I was about to leave for the airport and I was lying in bed the entire night before. I couldn't sleep thinking maybe I shouldn't go or what if I die, what would happen to my family. I didn't want to go. I woke up in the morning and my mom was crying and I wanted to cry too. She said, "Please don't let anything happen to you or people will think I am a bad mom." I said, "Okay, I promise I won't." As I was on the plane I kind of shat myself the whole way there until I finally got to Miami. Customs had to escort me as a child because I didn't know how to do anything. It was overwhelming and exciting at the same time. Once I got to Miami it was nothing like I thought it would be. I thought it would be like CSI Miami with all bright colors and fancy drinks. It was not like that at all."[28]

Kari Faux is another young, artsy woman on the rise. She's been making noise online since her Laugh Now, Die Later EP. When Childish Gambino jumped on her "No Small Talk" record even more eyes were looking in her direction, and with good reason, she's the first artist to get the Gambino stamp since Chance. The two now share the same manager and one of the reasons Kari left Little Rock for Los Angeles. Her debut album, *Lost En Los Angeles* is coming soon but she also started a separate project *LELA*. Instead of being overwhelmed by the loneliness she felt while being away from home, she started to interview others that came to L.A with similar pursuits and who were also facing a similar loneliness. It's one aspect of escaping that isn't acknowledged enough, all the parties and celebrities can't fill the void of home sweet home.

Art has the ability to expand your horizons, open up possibilities to explore places on maps and globes that you only see on T.V. and Tumblr. No matter the medium, going above and beyond for your art can mean leaving home. It seems like a teenage fantasy to fly from the nest and return with the world in your palms, that can be the reality for anyone who doesn't hesitate to uproot and be guided by their passion. When Kanye was waiting on his spaceship, he didn't stay at the GAP. He packed the U-Haul and went from Chicago to New York because waiting doesn't bring anything but anxiousness and regret. Those five beats a day for three summers would've meant nothing if he hadn't been where the right people could hear them.

To take over the world, it means being unafraid. I was afraid, in many ways I still am, this home is the only one I've ever known. The internet allowed me to make my dream come true without leaving, but I know there's more to the world than my little south Atlanta. I still flirt with the idea of leaving, I still watch New York from afar, the teenage desire is still there. The day might come when the opportunity to leave will present itself, and I can't let fear keep me from going.

Inside the Conspiracy Theory World of Childish Gambino's Music Videos

The first time I saw Childish Gambino was the "Freaks and Geeks" music video. It was a minimalistic one-shot in an abandoned garage and he was a young, jubilant fireball that had a bad cause of rapper hands. The rap reminded me of a tattoo-free, suburban Lil Wayne, but I liked it. I was in. I was watching, and I kept watching. And what I've been watching over the three years since "Freaks and Geeks" came out is the development of an artist now consistently making the best, most compelling, most interesting videos in music.

Case in point, while the world was intoxicated over Bino's "Sober" music video last week, I was trying to connect the dots. To most people, Gambino's last album, *Because the Internet*, was just an album. But to fans and those who cared enough to really look, it was also the soundtrack to a screenplay that Childish wrote and released. The screenplay's story, and the "Boy" character, actually started at the end of his debut album, *Camp*. The final song of *Camp*, "That Power," ends with a coming-of-age narrative that details a nameless, 13-year-old boy facing rejection, heartbreak, and ultimately enlightenment on the bus ride home. That's where the *Because the Internet* screenplay picks up, with The Boy getting off the bus, picked up by a chauffeur and his father, who just so happens to be Rick Ross.

Knowing that background, let's revisit Gambino's enigmatic short film, *Clapping for the Wrong Reasons*. When the film was first released, the general consensus was that it was a cryptic, plotless gathering of famous faces. Abella Anderson (who was also in his "3005" lyric video) floats around like a ghost, Trinidad Jame$ bests Chance the Rapper in a game of Connect 4, Danielle Fishel

113

reminds the world why jungle fever exists and Flying Lotus kicks a much sought-after freestyle. It was like watching a full-length episode of MTV Cribs. And when Clapping For The Wrong Reasons was released in August, there was no announcement of an album, no screenplay, there was little announced at all. It was confusing and intriguing.

But now, re-reading the screenplay, all the dots are (almost) connected. *Clapping for the Wrong Reasons* is both a look at the creative process of making *Because the Internet* the album and a bridge between *Camp* and *Because the Internet*. It's 15 years later and The Boy being picked up from camp is now a grown man, or maybe more accurately a man stuck in a sort of perpetual adolescence. While the story in *Clapping for the Wrong Reasons* doesn't appear in the screenplay, all the same details are there: the Buddha statue, the infinity pool, the spiral staircase—the person that calls at the beginning of the movie is likely asking for Rick Ross, the owner of the mansion.

And that's where the screenplay picks up. (Seriously, if you haven't already, go read the screenplay.[29] This will all make more sense, I promise.) The premise behind the screenplay was that the album's music would match the script perfectly: play Worldstar during the club shooting scene, Urn during the scene when his father dies, etc. In that sense, Because the Internet was actually less like an album and more the soundtrack for a movie that hadn't been made yet, although Gambino has been making that movie, video by video, over the last five months.

Things haven't been going according to script though. The album and script were supposed to form an interactive experience, going back and forth like a modern day flipbook, and so it only seemed natural that the videos from the album would fall in line too. Shouldn't the video treatments be an extension of what's been written? But instead, the music videos have been purposefully different.

Take "3005." The script has the song playing during a wedding scene; fittingly it does sound like wedding vows if you remove the morbid and worrisome verses. Instead of capturing that wedding imagery though, we get a Ferris Wheel with only Childish and a teddy bear in focus. The bear is silent, blinking, and his head moves as if he was Gambino's thunder buddy. Gambino raps without acknowledging his companion and when the hook comes in, the camera zooms into his blank expression, capturing their surroundings before refocusing back on the original subjects. You notice that the bear has been attacked at the beginning of his second verse, and by the end of the second chorus, he's been brutally beaten. There have been many speculations about what this means, but my favorite is that the bear is a representation of Gambino's childishness and the death of his innocence, but that has nothing to do with the script. There's also a very suspicious fire in the background. So many questions and possibilities.

"The Worst Guys" is another instance where the music video concept diverges from the script. In the script, there's a huge party going on at The Boy's house. Marcus, who is played by Chance The Rapper in the story, just fucked in a steam shower and compares the climax to busting one in a Prince music video. (Not really sure I understand the reference, but that's something that should've been committed to video.) The Boy, meanwhile, is put in a predicament where he's in his father's room, with two girls who only want…well, the song says it all. The video, on the other hand, is essentially just a beach date with friends that more closely matches the "Crawl" scene from the script instead of "The Worst Guys." Weed, friends, at first glimpse it seems like the most friendly and straight-forward video Gambino's released; maybe he got tired of the complex world of the album, script, and videos and just wanted to make a cool video. But look more closely. At the 1:45 and 1:48 marks there's something noticeably wrong with his leg—why? Things are never as simple as they seem

115

in Gambino's world.

I thought about the possibilities that The Boy and Childish Gambino are unrelated, completely different people, despite having the unkempt afro and signature white tee, but to an extent, "Sweatpants" killed that theory. In the script The Boy orders 12 bottles in the club, I'm going to assume a combination of Rozay and Ciroc, before heading to a dinner with his boys. And here the music video echoes the script; there's a diner, a group of friends, but of course there's a twist. Gambino walks through multiple times in a weird loop-like state. Putting a quarter into a jukebox, checking his cell phone outside, and rejoining his friends. After each loop, his surroundings slowly begin to resemble him. By the video end, he's literally standing in a room where everyone is wearing his face. It's a freaky sight, completely unorthodox, but oddly humorous.

The final video released from *Because the Internet*, "Telegraph Ave" is where everything goes from zero to over 9,000. Jhene Aiko is his co-star, but in the script, her character Naomi doesn't come into the story until toward the end; "Telegraph Ave" is the soundtrack for his trip to an old flame. There's no romantic utopia, no gorgeous setting, and definitely no alien. The music videos, by contrast, were utterly unpredictable, from romantic comedy to sci-fi horror at the drop of a hat. Was this a glimpse into The Boy and Naomi's future? Some completely different story?

Gambino has yet to comment on the revised edition of his script, so we're left to guess and hypothesize, which I can only assume is the way he likes it. In a way, it's like a movie that diverts from the book. The music videos have been maintaining an overlapping but also separate storyline, where The Boy is everything but a boy. There are some common themes running throughout all of Gambino's work that provide some clues—for example, water.

The first video related to the story, post-*Clapping for the Wrong Reasons*, was the trailer for "Yaphet Kotto." Even though it wasn't a song on the album, the trailer has a "submerged Gambino" and at the end of the script, The Boy visualizes his death by drowning:

"The Boy looks to the pool in the backyard and sees his own body floating lifeless. Eyes wide, bubbles clinging to his face. Orange, yellow, and brown leaves float above him. His left shoe floating far ahead, probably from struggling at some point. Next to the pool, Naomi and Steve stand over him. Neither is crying or really seem too upset. They just look on as if the movie they were watching took an abrupt turn and they're mildly interested rather than satisfied. It looks peaceful. Fitting. He'd like to go out like that."[30]

Similarly, the script comes to a close with an open ending. What if the boy drowned, and while in the water an alien took over his vessel. What if "The Boy" is nameless because he was never born, and Rick Ross is the leader that aliens spoke to when they finally decided to show themselves? He is the biggest boss thus far. That would make "The Boy" a foreign exchange student from Mars. What the "gold tooth" from *Clapping for the Wrong Reasons* has to do with eating Trinidad Jame$!? Alternative realities, parallel universe, the possibilities are pretty endless, and once you scratch the surface of Gambino's art it's not hard to quickly find yourself wearing a tin foil hat, tumbling down the rabbit hole.

But even if Gambino has averted completely from the script and his followers have found themselves in quasi-conspiracy theory territory, his videos do have a stable common ground, an internal common theme. In every one there's a false sense of normality, the ordinary is temporal before the paranormal unveils itself. This concept reminds me of his infamous Instagram post[31] when he unveiled some personal thoughts that sat on the rim of his mind. Before that, we saw Donald Glover as this hipster actor, decent rapper, funny comedian, and quickly that changed to questions about his sanity and possible suicidal thoughts.

He also conveys this false sense of knowing in his videos and quickly flips the script. Sometimes it's subtle like the suspicious fire in the background of "3005," or like his latest video, "Sober." The setting is a fast-food, diner-esque establishment. It's late night, and Gambino seems to be completely intoxicated. He attempts to charm his way into the arms of a young woman awaiting her food, he totters between being creepy and charming. The video could've simply ridden this course until the end. But then a random pigeon flies out of his shirt, cracking an egg with a message on the inside, Gambino hits an impossible Matrix-esque dance move on the table, the lights flicker, it's like something ominous and supernatural is omitting from the eccentric gentlemen.

"Sober" is from the *Kauai EP*, the musical sequel to *Because the Internet*, and it hints that the *Kauai* videos seem to be writing the next chapter in the story. Or maybe, in retrospect, the "Telegraph Ave" video more closely related to the themes of *Kauai* than *Because the Internet* — could there be another screenplay coming that will make sense of this all? One that will connect the dots the way Clapping turned out to connect *Camp* and *Because the Internet*?

Right now I have far more questions than answers, which in many ways is exciting. Along with Hiro Murai, who has been in the director's chair since *Clapping for the Wrong Reasons* and is known for his ominous themes and supernatural occurrences in his past work with Flying Lotus and Earl are proof enough, Donald is exploring the idea of what a music video can be in 2015. They're two very creative minds that are drawing from the darkness, exchanging flashy for depth, without losing the fun. Even though he isn't necessarily widely acclaimed and credited, Childish Gambino continues to prove why he's becoming one of hip hop's most electric acts with every video release.

He's evolved from the jubilant fireball in the garage. I don't think any other artist has made the leaps and bounds that Gambino has, the progress from his beginning to now is outstanding. He's found his voice, his imagination, his definition of "bigger" and is fearlessly delivering some of the best content in the game. How many other artists are putting this much thought and work into their releases? Who else is offering up the kind of material with enough depth to make fans develop intricately complex, completely-insane-but-maybe-not-insane-at-all-but-maybe-insane theories?

A Movie Script for J. Cole's
2014 Forest Hills Drive

ACT I: INNOCENCE

EXT. J. COLE'S HOME (2014 FOREST HILLS DRIVE, FAYETTEVILLE NORTH CAROLINA) — NIGHT

A two story home is illuminated underneath the moonlight. It's rather simple, the lawn is tended to, instead of a car there's a bicycle in the driveway, the kind of modest home you expect to find in a small town. On this night there's a peculiar man perched on top of the roof like a gargoyle. He sits still, appearing to be lost in thought. He snaps from his trance when a car drives by, honking and yelling about loving him. He smirks, waving, carefully maneuvering to re-enter the home through a window as the camera moves toward the door, entering inside.

CUT TO:
INT. INSIDE HOME — CONTINUOUS

A light piano plays as the camera zooms around the empty living room. A "for sale" sign leans against the all-white wall. There's nothing indicating that anyone has lived here in some time, but it's clean, well kept. Up the steps, onto the second floor, there's light seeping from a cracked door. Upon entering you see a man laying on the bed jotting thoughts into a notebook. His face is hidden.

PLAY "THE INTRO"

It's the only room in the home that's furnished, it's rather messy. A cereal bowl sits by the bed, shirts are sprawled on the floor, there are posters of '90s rap albums and basketball players covering an entire wall. A handful of shirts are hung on a rack. There's a tiny TV, a cassette player, and an analog beat machine giving off a nostalgic feel, it's a room that is strongly reminiscent of simpler times. The man leans forward, finally showing his young but mature face, flashing a cheesy grin confidently presenting his million dollar crooked smile. He flashes the composition notebook to the camera revealing the lyrics that have been sung in the background. While it's written in ink, there's a specific line highlighted: "You take the time to look behind and say, "Look where I came, look how far I done came." They say that dreams come true, when they do it's a beautiful thing. Do you wanna be happy?". Slowly the scene fades out as his cellphone rings and a woman's voice can be heard screaming, "Happy Birthday."

CUT TO:
INT. J. COLE'S BIRTHDAY PARTY (2014 FOREST HILLS DRIVE, FAYETTEVILLE NORTH CAROLINA) — NIGHT

The empty living room is now full of people, balloons and decoration covers the once white plain walls, it's a party. This isn't the birthday party you expect from a big-time rapper, it's rather small, intimate, only his close family and friends are with him. A giant cake is rolled out with 30 candles. Cole closes his eyes as they sing happy birthday and he starts to get lost in thought.

PLAY "JANUARY 28TH"

He starts mentally shuffling through his life, looking back on the years. Thinking of all the highlights and lows. There's a realization that this is the first birthday in his childhood home

121

since he graduated high school in 2003. "What did I use to wish for?" he thinks to himself. He chuckles. "Every birthday I would wish to make a million dollars from a rap tune." His eyes open and he blows out the candles, the screen goes black.

CUT TO:
INT. U.S. ARMY BASE IN FRANKFURT, GERMANY — DAY

The cries of a baby are heard as a doctor's voice exclaims, "It's a boy!" The doctor turns around to ask if the man wants to hold his son but the man who was just behind him is nowhere to be found. He would never be found again. The doctor hands the baby to the mother. She holds him tenderly as if he's the most precious jewel on Earth. When asked about his name, she pauses before saying, "Jermaine Lamarr Cole. My little king."

CUT TO:
INT. MATH CLASSROOM, CIRCA 2003 — DAY

A loud smack awakes a young Jermaine from his daydream. The baby is now a boy, not yet a man. He's staring into the eyes of his math teacher, who leans forward and requests that Mr. Cole come up front to work out the problem on the board. The class chuckles, Jermaine declines, sinking into his seat, knowing that standing was the last thing he wanted to do. He looks over to his right and catches the eye of the girl from his dream. Ever since Megan moved to the desk next to his he's had difficulty focusing. Long hair, brown skin, big booty, gorgeous. She's the one, the one he had to have. Months of note passing and wet dreaming pass by, until the question of sex finally appeared between exchanging of homework and jokes from The Simpsons. He keeps his nervousness below the surface, replying with boastful brags to give off the illusion that he's an experienced lover. Keeping secret that he's a virgin and hasn't been in pussy since the day he came out of one. Before he knows it there's a date set. Oh shit.

CUT TO:
INT. J. COLE'S HOME — DAY

A Monday through Friday montage of clips showing the callow Jermaine preparing for his first sexual experience. The clips capture the awkwardness of buying his first pack of condoms, sneaking to watch porn with the volume down, stressing about busting too quick. A combination of Carlton meets Will, more awkward than smooth, but still charming.

CUT TO:
INT. MEGAN'S HOUSE — NIGHT

The day arrives and he's sitting on her plump, pink queen size bed. Much like his room, she has a cassette player, tapes, posters, your average '90s girl bedroom. She sits down beside him and he silently prays she doesn't notice his sweaty palms and trembling knees.

PLAY "WET DREAMZ"

A fairly intense scene where they look into each other's eyes as she confesses to being a virgin. The screen fades out before revealing if they went all the way.

CUT TO:
INT. J. COLE'S HOME — DAY
Jermaine sits on the roof, writing into a composition notebook. Similar to the one that is seen in the movie's beginning. It's poetic

123

but stylized as a rap verse revealing a bit of depth to his character. His withered shoes and tattered clothes help illustrate his hardship and why he's so hungry for wealth. He wants the finer things that life has to offer. The scene ends with him slamming the notebook closed.

CUT TO:
EXT. TERRY SANFORD HIGH SCHOOL — DAY

It's the end of the day, the bell rings letting the students out, Jermaine starts to head home but before leaving he witnesses his friend, Vince, selling drugs in the hallway. This isn't new, they grew up together but on two totally different sides of the Ville. Vince was the hustler. Jermaine notices the stack of hundreds bulging from within his pocket. It's a giant wad, he's getting money, the opposite of Jermaine's empty pockets.

CUT TO:
INT. J. COLE'S HOME — DAY

Jermaine grabs his mom's keys after rushing home and heads out immediately, going to visit Vince. He pulls up to Vince's house, a home quietly falling apart, the grass needs to be cut. Vince comes out of the front door and sits with Cole in the car, which remains parked in the driveway.

PLAY "03' ADOLESCENCE"

CUT TO:
INT. J. COLE'S HOME — NIGHT

After getting back from Vince house, Jermaine walks in and notices the paper and skims through it. Stopping when he sees a familiar face, his friend Eddie. He knew Eddie for years, he was a good kid, innocent, would rather hit the books then hit a person but here he is in the newspaper for murder. He's shocked but also coming to terms that anybody can be a killer if pushed. Just hours before he was ready to deal drugs for riches. He heads to bed with a heavy heart.

INT. J. COLE'S DREAM — NIGHT

PLAY "TALE OF TWO CITIEZ"

Dream sequence: There's a couple walking home, the street is mostly empty and there's only one street light keeping the area from being pitch black. An all black Escalade speeds up on them, the window lets down, and a man holding a shotgun is demanding their wallet and purse. You notice that it's Jermaine who is holding the gun. When the man hesitates to give up his nice watch, a gunshot is heard.

Jermaine wakes up from the nightmare, realizing that if he didn't leave the Ville, the temptation of fast money would eventually entice him. He gets down on his knees and prays to God. "Your wish is my command" is repeated as the scene fades out.

FADE IN:
INT. BOARDING AIRPLANE TO HOLLYWOOD — DAY

After graduating, Jermaine decides not to pursue his education despite being accepted to St. John's University in New York. He takes the little money he received for finishing high school and buys a one-way ticket to Hollywood. He's going to make his dreams of rap and riches come true. He's excited but conflicted, the second verse represents a girl that could either be an actual woman or a personification of the Ville but there's a brief moment

of remorse. The plane takes off, he takes a deep breath, trying to prepare for whatever will happen next.
PLAY "ST. TROPEZ"

FADE OUT

ACT II: HOLLYWOOD COLE

TITLES ON BLACK READ: "10 Years later"
FADE IN:
INT. HOLLYWOOD CONDO — DAY TIME

The scene opens in a luxurious condo, the kind of place fit for a king. The walls are covered with plaques and magazine covers, indicating that he is no longer Jermaine but J. Cole and he's successful in Hollywood. Now an established rapper, he has a bit of fame and some riches.

PLAY "G.O.M.D"

He takes a call from home. He gets into a heated argument with whoever is on the line, being called Hollywood sends him over the edge. He spazzes about putting the city on the map and how he'll come back with the burner for anyone suggesting he can't come back and visit his hometown. This turns into a tangent about all the girls he has, all the homies that will ride, and that jealousy is the reason why there are haters back at home. He appears more arrogant than he was before, it's easy to assume that he's been corrupted by his new life. "Get off my dick" he yells before hanging up.

After hanging up, he inhales, closes his eyes, you see how deeply hurt Cole is by the allegations. He's conflicted, even asking God if he's changed but promises not to tell anyone. The introspective reflection puts him in an emotional space, he starts to reminisce about a woman that he is in a relationship with. Again, the confliction of wanting this woman, wanting her to have his kids, but still enthralled by the allure of groupies and women throwing themselves at him. It's the internal struggle for wanting love and lust.

CUT TO:
INT. FAMOUS HOLLYWOOD CLUB — NIGHT

J. Cole is in the club, living the life of a B-class celebrity. He seeps back into his arrogance, in these settings it's easy for an ego to be inflated. Showcasing the imbalance that he is struggling with. Bottle popping, champagne waterfalls, fully immersed in the nightlife when he really wants to hear songs about love and send messages to the girl he was thinking about earlier in the day.

CUT TO:
INT. HOLLYWOOD CONDO — DAY TIME

Cole's phone rings as a re-run of The Fresh Prince Of Bel-Air plays on his plasma screen. It's the fifth missed call. The woman, his girlfriend, is reacting to the break-up text that he sent a few hours ago. He's occupied with a bombshell so breathtaking he makes a man call his girlfriend and break-up without a second thought.

PLAY "NO ROLE MODELZ"

His relationship with women has obviously become twisted. He sees women as phony, opportunists that will sleep with anyone to reach the next plateau. You're in a city where everyone is an actress, model, singer, you need a defense mechanism or else you'll be taken advantage of. That's why he looks back on the past, on the women from the '90s as symbols of goddesses instead of the reality show women that he continues to meet. Saving them is loving them and they don't want love, they don't want to be saved.

FADE OUT

ACT III: CLARITY

FADE IN
INT. HOLLYWOOD CONDO — NIGHTTIME

PLAY "HELLO"

Alone in his condo, a drunk J. Cole calls an old flame and begins spilling his soul before she can even respond. While talking to this woman from his past, he's realizing things about himself. This is drunk clarity. Slowly coming to the realization that he has all these things but doesn't truly have a home, all these women but he's been neglecting love and the woman that he believed would end up as his wife has moved on. Even though she isn't responding, he continues to think back about how he became this man. "Reflection brings regrets, don't it?" The woman never responds; it's possible that he was too drunk to properly dial her number. Before blacking out he realizes what he has to do.

CUT TO:
INT. BOARDING AIRPLANE TO FAYETTEVILLE NORTH CAROLINA — DAY

PLAY "APPARENTLY"

While on a plane back home, he pulls out his notebook and starts writing like a man possessed. Word after word fills his notebook. He looks as relaxed as we've seen him in a long time, even with his long frame folded into a coach seat. He closes his eyes, the smallest smile on his face. Every mile away from Hollywood is a mile closer to the person he wants to be, surrounded by the people who love him.

CUT TO:
INT. J. COLE'S HOME (2014 FOREST HILLS DRIVE, FAYETTEVILLE NORTH CAROLINA) — DAY

PLAY "LOVE YOURZ"

J. Cole signs the papers to buy back his old home on the kitchen counter, his mother fighting back tears. All those years of struggling, the foreclosure, it's over. Not because the home's been returned but because Cole has. He now knows what no one ever told him. That it's not about what you don't have, but discovering that all you really need is love and happiness. It took leaving to realize that. It took returning to make things right.

PLAY "NOTES TO SELF"

ROLL CREDITS

It wasn't until Cole said that this album was made to be a soundtrack to a movie in his HBO documentary that I truly noticed how much it's structured like a linear narrative. If you connect the dots, it's a rather fluid story about a child that wanted riches through rap, went to Hollywood to acquire them, but after obtaining that dollar and accomplishing the dream, he still wasn't happy. Happiness, freedom, love, lust, riches, poverty, these are all recurring themes but they really fit together when viewed as one long story. But if there's a hitch in the album, something preventing the movie from fully coming to life in your mind, it's that Cole makes it a bit difficult to follow the timeline, and the differences between J. Cole the artist and J. Cole the character in this "movie" can become convoluted.

For example, a lot of the album has to do with looking back while moving forward. "January 28th" should be the birth of the character but it's not, the verses are all based in the present. It's not until the very end of the song that we hear the laughter of a baby. And what's particularly important about "Wet Dreamz" is that the story about his first time shows that there is a separation from the actual J. Cole (he previously told the "real," and far different, story in "Too Deep For the Intro"). This Jermaine in math class is a character. The same goes for "Apparently," when Cole says he was chasing panties in New York City (like the real Cole) instead of L.A., like the Cole character we'd been listening to. While both Cole's have similar backgrounds, right down to the same birthday and home address, they're not one and the same.

Still, the narrative flow largely still works...except when he follows "A Tale Of 2 Citiez" with "Firing Squad." "Firing Squad" references Iggy and Macklemore, which puts the song in the present tense. He jumps from being a child with rap dreams to being the rapper who is GRAMMY nominated, just to jump back to "St. Tropez" as a reference to moving toward Hollywood. If you take out "Firing Squad," "St. Tropez" is a good transition from being an aspiring artist in the Ville to making it to Hollywood. If Cole was truly attempting to create a movie, "Firing Squad" should have come somewhere around "Hello" and "Apparently," when he's an accomplished rapper realizing just how fake and empty the music industry is.

In a way, I see this as his *8 Mile* (or even Childish Gambino's *Because the Internet* film). Eminem isn't B. Rabbit, but you can draw some parallels between the actor and character. The same can be said for Cole, this album might feel autobiographical, but it's based off true events with a touch of fiction. Even with the flaws, though, the development of his character between the three acts is really impressive, and as often as I've played this album since it dropped, the story of Hollywood Cole has left me with a new-found appreciation of the album.

Cole could easily take *2014 Forest Hills Drive* to the big screen. He's already been on HBO once this year, now all he needs is a talented screenwriter who leaves his home in Atlanta and his job rap blogging to chase the bright movie lights of Hollywood.

Notes & References

19 Tharpe, Frazier, "Director X Breaks Down Kendrick Lamar's "King Kunta" Video," Complex (April 4, 2015) http://www.complex.com/music/2015/04/director-x-king-kunta-interview.

20 Tardio, Andress, "Here's How Kendrick Lamar And Dave Free Became Super Duo 'The Little Homies'" MTV (August 21, 2015) http://www.mtv.com/news/2246258/kendrick-lamar-dave-free-little-homies/.

21 Ibid.

22 Tardio, Andres, "We Got All The Answers About Kendrick Lamar's 'Alright' Video," MTV (June 30, 2015) http://www.mtv.com/news/2201127/kendrick-lamar-alright-video-colin-tilley/.

23 Ibid.

24 Singleton, Micah, "Grammys 2016: Watch Kendrick Lamar's stunning performance," The Verge (February 15, 2016) https://www.theverge.com/2016/2/15/11004624/grammys-2016-watch-kendrick-lamar-perform-alright-the-blacker-the-berry.

25 "What Happened To The Remix?" SoulCulture interview (May 18, 2010) https://www.youtube.com/watch?v=2H22JvHF5OM.

26 Wallace, Amy, "Frank Ocean: On Channel Orange, Meeting Odd Future, and His Tumblr Letter" GQ (November 20, 2012) https://www.gq.com/story/frank-ocean-interview-gq-december-2012.

27 "Kid Kudi," Complex (August 3, 2009) http://www.complex.com/music/2009/08/kid-cudi.

28 Tobias, Jonathan, "Iggy Azalea Speaks About Not Being Your Typical Rapper, Hip Hop Influences, And Modeling," HipHopDX (August 2, 2012) https://hiphopdx.com/interviews/id.1936/title.iggy-azalea-speaks-about-not-being-your-typical-rapper-hip-hop-influences-and-modeling.

29 Childish Gambino, Because the internet Screenplay - Part 1, Genius (2013) https://genius.com/Childish-gambino-because-the-internet-screenplay-part-1-annotated.

30 Ibid.

31 Childish Gambino, "Open Letter on Instagram," Genius https://genius.com/Childish-gambino-open-letter-on-instagram-lyrics

Part 4
PERSONAL ESSAYS

Vices and Duty:
Growing Old and the Music
You Take With You

My father's tools lay across the living room carpet of the apartment, to see them without him is viewing the stars without the moon. The same tools he once used to remove training wheels are now in the hands of my brother and his girlfriend. The two are building a dresser for their room — together they are an image of a mature relationship, in that moment their union seemed holier, more future-focused. It starts with building a dresser, then building a crib, and before you know it, you've built a life together; a life that ends in good memories, gray hairs, grandchildren, and rocking chairs. As the drill spun, as the hammer swung, as the screwdriver turned, I saw in the present a future that was once so far away — adulthood.

Our first weekend in the apartment, a gun accidentally went off and shot through the hallway carpet. Our neighbors underneath were unharmed but we were still threatened with eviction for early signs of unruliness. We were let off with a warning, and the party we planned for our eviction became a housewarming. Each following weekend was spent carelessly drunk — more bottles than bodies, more bodies than drugs — while balancing responsibilities and chasing dreams. We were like clowns juggling vices and duty. We worked, paid bills, did taxes. You could consider this adult living, but I saw us as kids pretending to be grown-ups, Peter Pan with facial hair minus the fairy dust.

We weren't in a rush to be our parents, but pursuing debauchery over virtue, hangovers over holy water, lust over love, today's thrills over tomorrow's promises, an endless cycle of turning up for the sake of being alive. The times were good, the times were fun, but what seemed to be a never-ending present slowly receded into yesterday's memories. Two years later, the kids who were dressing up are no longer pretending. I watched as apartments became houses, boys became gentlemen, girls became debutantes. Settling into the next phase of their lives began to transform people that I've known since the sandbox. Soon, new kids will be terrorizing the playground and this time, I'll know their parents.

Music tends to be a reflection of every point in my life, the embodiment of my soul. I first noticed a change in taste with the release of *Birds In The Trap Sing McKnight*. Travis Scott has never been my favorite, and the album was good, but it failed to compel my interest. Shallow, too shallow. The same feeling came as The Weeknd's *Starboy* filled my ears, sounding good, sounding pop, but ultimately too bland for recurring visits.

More girls, more plugs, more drinks, more Percocets — the formula for trap music had lost all zeal, and recently it has felt like being in some strange purgatory of living the same song over and over again. I can judge and enjoy it all objectively, able to perfectly articulate why Playboi Carti with Awful is preferred over A$AP, the thrill of *Savage Mode* and 21 Savage, the poetic prowess of Future, and why Migos are incredible together and apart. Yet, most of the music hasn't moved the spirit, stirred the soul, or inspired lasting plays. Yachty, Uzi, SahBabii, and NAV may have the teens, but their growing dominance over the mainstream has only solidified that I've grown out of that demographic. Knocking on the door to 26, I am not their target, I am not their audience, and so comes the early ache of age.

Khalid's *American Teen* has been in heavy rotation, a well-put-together debut by a promising young star, but there's an unavoidable realization that his music isn't targeted to those going through the quarter-life crisis that is the mid-twenties. It's in the title, there should be no surprise who the album is intended for.

"Young Dumb & Broke," the album's second song, is an anthem for the young, dumb, and broke high school kids across the nation. Despite being fairly young, in an endless search for wisdom, and struggling with money management, it's been almost 10 years since my days were spent in high school hallways. I'm grueling over thoughts of a reunion while he's celebrating an escape from the woes of public school education.

The teen stars of my day have grown older while trying to maintain a place of relevance. The ones who use to play on ringtones can't buy their way onto modern charts. With each passing year, the phrase "back in my day" grows closer to leaving my lips. Khalid's way of singing about love and loss with a mature sensibility has made him an enjoyable musical companion, but he has songs like "8TEEN" that would appeal much more to a younger me.

For every Khalid who is a voice for a generation of adults on the rise, there's an Anderson .Paak who sings for us who remember Blockbuster and Limewire, dial-up and Internet Explorer, phones before artificial intelligence and Jordans before the resells. He isn't the artist making songs for the girl you fall for in the hallway after homeroom, but ballads about dodging temptation on the way to your happy home, or songs for married couples who are trying to get their groove back — music about life that's been lived and not the excitement of life to come. Anderson isn't hiding that he's older, but wearing age like a vibrant bow tie that's impossible to overlook.

R&B is at the forefront of my personal music palette. From Steve Lacy to Sonder, Nao to Thundercat, JMSN to 6LACK, the resurgence of impeccable rhythm and blues has captured my heart and ears much more than modern hip hop these days. I hear less formula in the singers; there are no rules to follow, but rules to be made. SZA's "Drew Barrymore" is the sort of heartbreaking honesty that feels like claws wrapped around your soul; raw with passion and pain, the result is magic to the ears. I find it almost impossible to hear Solange's *A Seat at the Table* and not feel empowered; a surge to conquer the world with grace and fortitude by thirty. Spellbinding lyrics over minimal production, *A Seat at the Table* is an album only a woman who has seen life in the raw could make.

Because the Internet is an album loosely about being lost in a world of strong Wi-Fi and infinite connectability — the theme of my life, but it resonated strongest in my early twenties. I was in search of something deeper while balancing an existential crisis, much like The Boy. *"Awaken, My Love!"*, Childish Gambino's latest, speaks with a mature tone that is absent from *Because the Internet*. Gambino left all the childishness behind him to become an adult singing to his son, and with each listen I appreciate his evolution more. He grew up and needed a language for this new voice. I don't have a son, so I don't have a child to be taken from me, but I still get chills from the passion in his voice on "Baby Boy." *"Awaken, My Love!"* isn't the album of my present, but sometime in the years to come, it could be.

Divorce is a tragedy I've yet to experience, but Marvin Gaye's *Here, My Dear* — a heartfelt, soulful album written and recorded while going through his separation with Anna Gordy — has filled my recent nights. The number of emotions he's able to convey, explore and bleed during this turbulent time speaks for the amazing artist he was.

A true sign of age is the backstroke through the sea of oldies, diving deeper into the artists who have lived and died, digging up their art despite bodies that have been long buried.

Hip hop isn't dead. It may not dominate the mainstream, but there's an immense amount of good music coming out that doesn't require intoxication to find enjoyment. I may be in the minority but I'm prepared to argue *4 Your Eyez Only* is Cole's most refined album. It's a bit boring, but it's some of his most piercing and mature music. There's fear of death, love of life, cherishing wife and child, alongside bigger themes of racial profiling, systemic racism and the weight of fatherhood. Despite my disdain for the song, I couldn't help but hear "Foldin Clothes" as my brother slid another drawer into the dresser. Cole is no longer making music for college students, but for college graduates. Sallie Mae has been replaced by admitting Santa Claus is the personification of greed to his newborn.

Hip hop is youthful, the kids will always be the ones who will push culture forward. But kids aren't the ones who make you look forward to getting older. It is inevitable, time is always moving us forward. Age is of the mind they say, but youth has an expiration date. Anyone who is younger, or someone in my position staring at the crossroads, will eventually have to face the fact that your lifestyle won't always match the music that's popular. Enjoying music and connecting with it aren't always in harmony, and age influences how music touches each individual.

I'm far from an adequate, ideal adult. There's nothing "grown-up" about spending an entire day writing about hip hop and only eating Jell-O shots, knowing more about rap beef than political battles. I can't live off American Deli and Jack Daniels forever, I need nutrients and water. Music is no different, the older I age, the more nutrients will take precedence over junk food.

The movie *The Lion King* taught a generation that "Hakuna Matata" doesn't last forever. The notion of having no worries for the rest of your days is enticing, the kind of pipe dream you hope to accomplish. But even if you see that heaven for a day it will eventually come to an end. Everyone isn't destined to be king, but Simba's destiny is proof that the wheels of time never stop.

There's a future for us all, a day in the distance where we are older and our plates fuller, but it doesn't mean it won't be fun. I have to stop seeing suits as casket uniforms, marriage as a contract of eternal compromise, and 30 as the pen pal of death. I'm fighting the cancer that is time, but I'm slowly embracing that life will be long and that I'd rather enjoy my time here than resist what will not stop. It's becoming important to discover artists who take me to the past, who mirror my present, and who will make my eyes look forward to the future.

I Quit My Job
to Become a Writer

Midnight was sixty minutes away, but the sky was already filled with primary colors and gunshots were already welcoming the birth of a new year. If my life was a movie, this would be the final scene. Budding writer removes blue collar noose on the final day of 2014. On his final day of work, greeted by celebratory fireworks, he exits the loathsome building that was the bane of his 9-to-5 hours. The credits would roll as I tweet, " F R E E D O M", with Mozart's "The Marriage of Figaro" playing lightly in the background — an homage to *Shawshank Redemption*. It took Andy Dufresne 19 years to escape prison; I escaped mine in two.

On the outside, the building looked like an Olive Garden, on the inside they sold soup, salad, and wine. But if you ask me, my bosses were superintendents, my customers were wardens, my uniform a jumpsuit, my co-workers inmates, and the paycheck the bars that kept us confined.

As I drove away, I thought about Kanye West making three beats a day while working at the Gap. I thought about Charles Bukowski writing immortal poetry while slaving at the post office. Kurt Cobain dreaming of record deals while loathing being a janitor. Faces of great artists and their past jobs shuffled through my mind. I wondered how they handled the euphoria of freedom mixed with the anxiety of failure. Is there anything more fulfilling and equally terrifying than trusting your art to be a bridge to greener pastures? A starving artist isn't just a cute term to use when trying to sell music, this path has left many men homeless, penniless, and forgotten. There are graveyards full of brilliance that never got notarized, and graveyards full of talent who were too afraid to take the risk.

2015 is the beginning of my era as a writer. I'm committed to these words, and the journey that will unfold with this decision. Never will I fill out another job application, never will I succumb to doing a job that doesn't leave me fulfilled, and never again will I allow the concept of comfort to hinder my creative expression. Last year, my left lung collapsed, a moon man belittled my existence, my job refused to recognize my good work, hospital visits to friends and family were frequent. I felt like my face was stained by lemons thrown by the universe, and yet all I wanted to do was get the word down. Ever since the day I decided to be a writer, I never knew if I was going to be self-supporting, if I was going to be the greatest of all time, but I knew what I wanted on my tombstone. It wasn't Olive Garden host, McDonald's manager, lawyer, doctor, or president, I want to leave this world as a writer, for better or worse. That's my resolution, for this year and everyone that follows, to live my life as a writer. It's the only thing I've ever done well, the only thing that makes me feel alive.

The last few days have felt surreal like I'm in this dream state and I'm awaiting the vicious pinch to piss on my parade. If I'm able to use the creative writing born from the imagination of an adult embracing his second childhood and love for hip hop to keep Hot Pockets in the microwave, Eggos in the toaster, and WiFi in a two-bedroom apartment, then there's very little else I desire. For now, I hope this dream doesn't end. I have a long way to go, but I'm growing. Overcoming my little mistakes and killing my darlings is a huge goal of mine this year. Traveling is another. I can't be a reader of Jack Kerouac and never hit the road. My parents have yet to read any of my writing, time is becoming apparent in the physical form. Gray hair is blooming, movements are slowing down, watching them age is beautiful and frightening. I've always said their first piece of mine would be read inside of a magazine, the goal is a distant one, but not far from my mind. Or maybe the first time they read my writing, it will be in a book.

Brilliance and Vanity:
The Kanye West Method
for Managing Self-Worth

It was me and the most ungodly of hours, with only the moon, stars, and whatever song or album held my obsession; that is how I began writing about music. Money was a mere fantasy. The lottery seemed like a better gamble than being paid for writing. Years would go by before receiving the first slice of fruit for my labor and it brought an elation I relate to hitting the jackpot on a penny slot machine after tireless days and restless nights of pulling the lever. The victory was a sweet one. Luckily, I was in a position to relive the feeling, and the fantasy became a recurring blessing. Somewhere between quitting my old job and starting life anew as a writer, a wise mentor gave me some excellent advice: Always know your worth.

The worth of words is an abstract concept that I'm still struggling to understand. I went from feeling underpaid and underappreciated at Olive Garden to happily making money as a writer. Worth wasn't a question on my mind but when it did pop up, I found myself wondering if I was worth diamonds and gold or nickels and dimes? What is too much? What is not enough? Where was the metric system to gauge talent, passion, and place in this gigantic world of music and journalism? From freelancing to staff positions, how does one realize what they deserve to make?

Thinking about self-worth, what constantly came to mind was Kanye rapping "Give me fifty million or I'mma quit" on the eternal summer single "Mercy." It was easy to picture him storming into the Def Jam office, kicking over the coffee maker, breaking his Louis Vuitton briefcase against the office table, and demanding L.A. Reid showed him the money in an unwavering bark. Something about the line didn't seem far-fetched despite the outrageous amount; he's the same man rumored to have made the entire Def Jam office adjust their wardrobe from Friday casual to Easter Sunday just to preview *My Beautiful Dark Twisted Fantasy*. The line always represented that he knew his worth, the worth of his art, and wouldn't take anything less.

Kanye's confidence is what I've always admired. From my very first impression of him, he seemed as if he had more than most humans, an abundance of overflowing self-assurance. What made him the brash egotist of hip hop also seemed to be a sturdy shield protecting his innocence in an industry that crushes the weak and exploits the enchanted. From making those five beats a day for three summers to fighting for his chance to be heard as a rapper, his confidence never faltered. There isn't an instance I can remember where Kanye West didn't think he would be upheld as a great, if not the greatest.

As he grew more renowned so did his prolific ego. I can recall hearing chatter about Kanye needing to be humbled, that his narcissism overshadowed his genius; but often brilliance does not come without the vanity. Ye knew if he was going to talk big he had to deliver big. His inflated self-belief may have been criticized but Kanye never made excuses. He always stood behind his art and actions. From George Bush to Taylor Swift, he continued to stand before us as the outspoken poet with the aura of a spoiled prince and a voice loud enough to shake the heavens. I didn't always agree with his actions or antics, but he did everything with an admirable conviction — it's hard not to believe in the Kanye that believes in Kanye. A belief and conviction that I always hope would burn within me when the time called for it.

I started to view Kanye's confidence in a new light after recently revisiting "New Day," one of the deep cuts from *Watch the Throne*. Despite the theme of celebrating prestigious black excellence, the album doesn't have much return value for me. Returning to the record six years after its release, however, I have gained a new perspective for an old favorite.

"New Day" is special. RZA's mood-inducing sample of Nina Simone's "Feeling Good" that feels like a ghostly grandmother whispering from the other side is far more chilling than light-hearted. You can hear it in Kanye's tone as he shouts out RZA, there's a hoarseness as if he hasn't seen his bed in five sunrises. I remember the song as a letter to Ye and Jay's unborn sons, but hearing Kanye's verse in 2017 sounded much more like a man speaking in the mirror than one jotting thoughts in a notebook.

He begins with:

"And I'll never let my son have an ego."

This line comes from a man who has always worn his ego as a crown with more jewels than the Yeezus mask. I don't remember being stunned by it years ago, but it's shocking when isolated and questioned. Why would he not want his son to carry a similar sense of self-esteem or self-importance? You would think Kanye would raise his son like his mother raised him, but in this introspective look into the future, he would rather the junior of his dreams not inherit the prolific ego. From the opening line, he begins to unravel himself.

In reflecting on what it would be like to raise a child, Kanye saw something in the way he lived. Qualities about himself he wouldn't wish upon his offspring. I won't say he regrets the life he's led, but if he could change things, I don't know if he would do it all again. For example, how he might refuse to allow his son to attend a telethon, even if the world was ending? If the world was over a telethon wouldn't save it, but it makes you question how Kanye feels about his Katrina outburst. I remember how the black community applauded, but what was the backlash like? He publicly disparaged George W. Bush, taking a direct shot at America's 43rd president.

He goes as far as to say that he's raising his son as a Republican so that white people wouldn't assume he hates them. *Watch the Throne* happened post-Taylor. I didn't think he still carried whatever wounds he received from that backlash but it's apparent that being hated bothered him deeply. It's a bit sickening to see someone so strong wear an apologist cape, but it's hard to gauge strength when you truly don't know a man.

See, I just want him to have an easy life / Not like Yeezy life, just want him to be someone people like / Don't want him to be hated all the time, judged / Don't be like your daddy that would never budge
—Kanye West

An easy life. Someone who people will like. For someone so outgoing and brash, Kanye wished for the seed that would carry his name to know acceptance and spread kindness. To find love in high school and never venture into strip clubs. You can admire a man for his actions, but never experience any of the consequences. I don't know what it's like to be hated, but Kanye does. At the least, he feels like he does, and when you're famous, in the public eye, I wonder what it does to the psyche having to deal with being praised and facing disgust for your actions. What kind of worry does that bring? Well, the kind Kanye wouldn't want to pass down.

What is most intriguing about Ye is how much he doesn't want his son to be like him, especially when you contrast how many creatives admire him for all the things he's done. Before the birth of North West, there were countless kids who saw Kanye's art, style and personality as their blueprint. He was the father that birthed creative kids, but he didn't have to raise them, and they didn't have to carry his sins.

"New Day" shows a side of Ye that isn't the superhero but a man exhausted by never pulling his punches. A fighter who spent

145

his career fighting, and while we'll praise him for all the battles, we don't know the extent of the damages. After *Watch the Throne*, we started to see the slow transformation that would later cause many to ask for the old Kanye back.

The same acceptance he wished for his son would later be expressed through his attempts at entering fashion and slowly transitioning into a world where he felt change was necessary. Somewhere the confidence began to falter, the ego was crushed, and the shield was finally broken. The loud aura he once had seemed to grow silent. Even when Ye would rant, there was a disconnect; a piece of that old fire was missing.

In his interview with *DAZED*, Tyler, the Creator was asked about Kanye's passionate attempt to be accepted in Paris through fashion's gatekeepers. Tyler response is reminiscent of Kanye of old: "I could do a show in Paris without any of them. They're not stopping me. That's the thing. People think, 'I gotta be cool with these people to do this or I gotta get respect from the people to do this.'"[32]

Tyler had the answer that Sway also had, but Ye didn't want to listen. He no longer had that eye of the tiger to overcome without permission. That's why I see Kanye as an example of the bold, fearless bravery necessary to enter a creative field and truly be respected if you are gifted. You can't always be quiet. You can't always ask politely. But in the later stages of his career, he represents conforming and vying for acceptance. It's the big difference between how he entered hip hop and how he entered fashion: kicking down the door or knocking politely.

"New Day" represents the split between these two sides, Kanye the egotist and Kanye the conformist. In both cases he still innovates, he's still creative, and he's still a genius, but somewhere he begins to lose a piece of himself that was so imperative when he started. It's almost like everything he wished his son wouldn't inherit he begun removing from himself.

146

I'm still coming to terms with what it means to have self-worth as a writer. At the beginning of this year, I had an opportunity to write my first cover story for a magazine, but no compensation was offered. To know me is to know a magazine cover would be a dream come true. I wavered between the great experience and also knowing that the job was too big to end with only exposure. Deep down I knew I would've done it, but the superstar rapper I was meant to interview was unresponsive after agreeing to the story, and the cover story moved on to another artist and another writer.

Even though I wanted to be the Kanye of old, I felt like the conformist more than the egotist. I didn't like it. The magazine wasn't Ebony, but I look at their current fiasco and wonder why writers continue taking their offers after learning of their history of stiffing writers. After being so close to doing free work myself, I know the answer. The game is teaching me that to write means you'll have to fight for what you deserve, and sometimes fight for what you were promised.

I think we all wish to request $50 million for our art and know the only answer will be yes, but that's not happening. What I'm learning is that it is imperative to find that Kanye voice within yourself that's going to fight passionately for your worth once it's discovered. Be like Kanye and never budge unless you absolutely believe it's worth budging. No one hears the whisper, but everyone hears the yell. A little ego doesn't harm anyone, and a little pride might be the devil's advocate that will get you the pay that you deserve and not what they decide to give.

What watching the many phases of Kanye has taught me most is the importance of never losing a sense of self. It's okay to have confidence broken and the ego bruised, but you can't lose yourself. Not in love and not in hate, not when they cheer and not when they boo. All the money in the world isn't worth losing what can't be bought.

My Road to the White House
In the Hour Before Trump

Before Barack Obama was inaugurated as president, he was someone I believed was synonymous with joy and hope. It happened on the very day of his election. I was 17 years old, unable to vote, but I watched the polls, I saw the announcement, and I saw in my parents' eyes something unforgettable: joy and hope. Pure innocence is rare to see in adults, it's a gift given to children when they are born that is taken away as they grow older and more aware of the world surrounding them. To see them believe in such a man, to trust the change he promised to bring, it filled me with a naive sense of optimism. Before Kendrick Lamar uttered the words, it was President Obama who made me feel as if this country would be alright.

The last eight years weren't the easiest, or always the most joyous in America, but it was a counterbalance of beauty, beams of light that would shoot through the darkness. In all his years as president, Obama continued to be a symbol that change did occur, and despite all the resistance that more change could come. I believe this is the reason my parents were so adamant about visiting the White House before the new tenants arrived. If they couldn't meet the man, they could at least tour his then-home, and have a memory connected to his legacy. After an extensive background check and months of waiting, we were accepted to tour the White House. Our date was set for November 8th, the day a new president would be elected. It was a strange twist of fate that would bring us to DC on election day. There was a sense of hope that we would see the White House right before Barack left, and on the day that Hillary would be crowned as his successor.

Day 1: The Drive

We set out for DC as the sun was breaking through the clouds on the morning of November 6th. My company included two aunts, one uncle, one mother, one father, one grandmother and one great aunt — three generations of black Americans who lived through two terms of a black president. We took two SUVs, plenty of room for the nine-hour voyage. The drive would allow time for reading, music, and the ability to enjoy being in motion toward the epicenter of America. One of the first albums I played was Mos Def's *Black On Both Sides* while reading Mos Def's first-ever cover story from the year 2000. The interview is insightful, reading his views on hip-hop then and seeing how far we've come made for an interesting juxtaposition. At the very end, while talking about his role in Spike Lee's *Bamboozled*, he speaks on race, and how everything is designed to keep black people from appearing as human beings. He mentioned a name that I had never heard before, Amadou Diallo, an unarmed black man who, in 1999, was murdered — shot 41 times — by four NYPD officers. Each of the officers involved were eventually acquitted of all charges.

White folks been dealing with black folks in America... Everything is designed to keep you from being a human being. 'Cause if they have to look at you and deal with you as a human being, then they gotta start sharing the pie. They gotta start divvying up the pot equally. There's a parable, it says, "You want for your brother what you want for yourself." And that's the measure of brotherhood. If somebody's really down with you, and they sitting at the table and there's a pie, they gonna give you an equal piece. They may want the last piece and waiting to see if you want it. It's not like that with black people. We not viewed as human. Some people contest that, but it's like, they shoot Amadou Diallo 41 times. He was unarmed, and now the argument is, "Well, they didn't mean it." Which is just like, that's sorta besides the point

— whether they were defensive or not is not the argument. The argument is that they did it, and it was completely unjustified.[33]

Amadou Diallo's name stuck with me as I began reading James Baldwin's "A Report From Occupied Territory" — an essay written in 1966 about an incident that occurred in 1964. The essay begins with the story of Frank Stafford, a salesman who was brutally beaten by police officers after he simply asked, "Why are you beating him like that?" to an officer who was attacking a child. A question that would get him beaten, handcuffed, and taken down to the station where he felt the brute force of their assault. It was a beating that would lead to him losing his eye and one that forced him to wear a patch, a visible symbol for other police to know who he was. The fear of a second attack was so severe his lawyer asked him to keep someone with him at all times. The essay digs deeper into The Harlem Six and police brutality and gives a glimpse of what it meant to be black in America back in 1966. An image that sadly has too many similarities to 2016. You can't escape it through music, magazines or literature, at almost every turn there's a reminder of what it means to be black in this country.

Three of the policemen beat up the salesman in the streets. Then they took the young salesman, whose hands had been handcuffed behind his back, along with four others, much younger than the salesman, who were handcuffed in the same way, to the police station. There: "About thirty-five I'd say came into the room, and started beating, punching us in the jaw, in the stomach, in the chest, beating us with a padded club — spit on us, call us niggers, dogs, animals — they call us dogs and animals when I don't see why we are the dogs and animals the way they are beating us. Like they beat me they beat the other kids and the elderly fellow. They throw him almost through one of the radiators. I thought

he was dead over there.
—James Baldwin, "A Report from Occupied Territory"

We were in the eighth hour of our journey when we were forced to pull over due to issues with the car. There were some problems that became apparent back in North Carolina, but a quick trip to AutoZone left us with the belief that any issues with the battery were resolved. But soon, flashing lights indicated that a police officer had arrived behind us. The sight of his car sent a slight chill down my spine. It wasn't an overwhelming feeling, more of a tickle of fear. Maybe it was seeing my uncle standing outside of our broken-down vehicle that inspired the emotion — a big, black man who in that moment seemed to resemble an older Luke Cage, except he isn't bulletproof. As the white cop stepped from his patrol car, Terance Crutcher came to mind — innocent, unarmed, needing help to get home, and the Tusla police decided that he would return home in a casket. The duality of still having to face this kind of anxiety while in route to visit the home of our black president left me with a deep feeling of grief.

He did his job, and went about his business. It's all we want from officers, to do their job — protect and serve all Americans, not just the ones whom they deem fit to serve. It would be an hour-long wait for the tow truck to arrive. The furthest a truck could tow you is 100 miles, and we were 99 miles from our hotel — God or some higher power was on our side. It was cold in DC, much colder than the weather in Atlanta. We arrived safely in the night, roaming through the downtown area underneath the glowing streetlights. It felt strangely quiet, a place of such importance should feel like New York and not Alaska. We arrived at the hotel to fill our starving bellies and rest our weary souls. I played Daniel Caesar until sleep arrived.

Day 2: The Girl On The Bus

The next day began as a slight failure. We overslept and missed our chance to acquire tickets for The National Museum of African American History and Culture. They're very strict about the time you must be in line for a ticket, and since you can't buy your way in, there was no way to enter. We jumped on one of the buses that traveled to Martin Luther King's Memorial instead. Along the sides of the big statue read, "Out of the mountain of despair, a stone of hope." I wondered if you could build a mountain of hope from those stones, a thought that I would carry well past the election.

Our next stop was the Lincoln Memorial, a place swarming with people. When I stood at the very top, taking in the gorgeous view, there was a feeling of empowerment knowing that this is where Martin Luther King Jr. professed his dream. He looked out at those people and believed he could say all the right words to keep their spirits high, to keep them believing we were headed in the direction of better times. Then it was a sickening feeling, a moment of realization; of why he gave that speech, why he was fighting, and why he was killed. This feeling reminded me of what brought us to DC before: to march for Jena Six. That seemed so long ago, almost ten years. It was November then, cold, but thousands of people came out and marched. Walking through the nation's capital, feeling like you're at the center of America, there's a feeling of both pride and confliction. It eats at you how you could be born in America's bosom, raised on her soil, but treated as some lesser stepchild because of your race and skin color. You never get a chance to forget you aren't equal. Such heavy thoughts while in front of such a beautiful view.

On the bus ride back to our hotel a young woman sat beside me. She carried in her arms a little black girl — a tiny toddler that knew nothing of this world. She knew nothing of Lincoln or Martin, Trump or Hillary, hate or racism, she was pure innocence.

When she lifted her head to look at me, I saw the most beautiful brown eyes. In those eyes I realized that she had a chance to grow up to see a woman president, would go to school and learn of a black president, and it gave me hope that our small changes could be big for her future. Those innocent eyes knew nothing of this country's evils, of man's darkness, and of all the obstacles that were built against her before she was even born. She deserved to see a better tomorrow. Deep down, beyond all my conflictions, I still believed in the America that I call home. Home didn't always love me, but it doesn't always hate me either. Hopefully, it would never hate her, and a step in that direction would be electing our first female president over her opponent.

Day 3: Inside The White House

The next day I woke up and put on a sweatshirt that said, "Kanye West For President." There's a very slim chance that I will ever have the opportunity to endorse Mr. West at the White House again. It was early morning when we left the hotel, we saw a guard moments after exiting the taxi. He was strong, serious and holding a gun that most will only see during war. There's a sign that tells people not to pet the dogs, they aren't friendly. You have to go through two I.D. checks, one metal detector, and one thorough pat-down before entering the East Wing. As you walk through the security check there are pictures of Barack and his family along the walls, it's almost like a scrapbook of moments from the last eight years. People stared happily, but we all knew that in a few months these photos would be removed, and another family would take over this space. It wouldn't be the same.

There's something magical about walking through the White House with your grandmother knowing she never imagined that she would be here during a black man's presidency. She's a strong old sport that remembers darker days in America. I thought about how my mother is from a small town in Alabama, and how she can remember being one of the first black girls to attend an all-white school after the end of segregation. I remembered how she faced boycotts from adults who didn't want her there, how she faced their children who mistreated her, how she had to fight for no other reason than being born black and in Alabama. She's a strong woman who had to fight from an early age, and yet, has not an ounce of malice in her blood. She deserved to go into the White House and joke with a black Secret Service agent who was from a small town in Alabama that shared her surname. Watching my mother and her mother try and bribe him to meet the president with red velvet cake was priceless.

Gorgeous is an understatement when trying to describe the beauty of the White House structure. It truly feels like a palace fit for a king. What I loved the most are the giant portraits that hung from the walls. All the presidents and their wives are painted and placed somewhere in the enormous home after their term is completed. They all look like nobles or aristocrats — painted to appear big, bold, and powerful. These are the men of America's past, who held the most honorable position in the country, and Obama's portrait will be hung along with them after he leaves. Ronald Reagan didn't look like an evil man, more like a man that would host late-night television. The portrait of Bill Clinton got a lot of attention; people still love him like they love Michael Jackson. There was a portrait of Hillary hanging in a restricted area, but people still got as close as possible to take a picture.

At the very end of the tour, I saw an image that was unlike all the others. It wasn't vibrant, nor strong, but grim and melancholy. It was a painting of John F. Kennedy, and I stared at him for a very long time. Out of all the presidents, he appeared as the only one who was shouldering the burdens of an entire country's past sins and future promises. If a leader is supposed to represent his people, the portrait of Kennedy was the only one that resembled a mirror.

In the last eight years, Obama's appearance has aged like all men have aged, but there's a grayness to him, a weariness that wasn't there before. I see that grayness in Kennedy's portrait, maybe it's the inheritance of anyone that is fighting for the betterment of this country. The grayness that comes before the color of change. Or it could be the gray of knowing this country will kill you before ever changing.

The Day Trump Won

We were leaving DC when the votes were being tallied. Our vehicle was in Baltimore, in the hands of family who was getting it prepared for our trip back home. During the drive, I got a chance to reflect on the energy that I felt while in the downtown area. All day, everywhere I turned, Hillary's name was on the tip of every tongue. In the gift shop, in the elevator, in the taxi — even the children seemed to celebrate her victory early. The people of DC believed they knew who the next president would be. It felt as if Trump wasn't running, that he was just the opponent who had already lost. To say they were hopeful would be an understatement; they were certain. I guess we all were if I'm being honest. Trump reminded me of Heath Ledger's Joker — he has a quote that goes, "As you know, madness is like gravity...all it takes is a little push," and Trump was pushing with all his might. He was a man of malice, a disgusting balance of racism and sexism, who made it this far by feeding hatred. The racists and bigots ate up his message, devoured his views, and knighted him the leader of their revolution. I saw the rallies, I saw how that hatred was building up to something, but I never imagined it would erupt into a victory for him.

When it was announced that Trump had won, I was with my mother, and there was no joy or hope in her eyes. All I could see is deep disdain, as if she put all her trust into someone, and was hit with the realization that they had lied. The lie was that America had progressed beyond the country that it once was. Not only did he win, but we had to face the fact that more than 62 million fellow Americans voted to elect him. It's sickening that there are real people who don't believe in the dangers of climate change; people that want to ruin the lives of immigrants; people that couldn't give a damn about woman's rights; people so full of hatred they would rather elect an unqualified madman than put this country's future in the hands of a woman. I didn't agree with Hillary on all of her views, but I hated the idea of a Trump presidency more than anything else. I hate that this is our reality.

Our president-elect is being backed by the KKK and the American Nazi Party. They celebrated when he appointed Steve Bannon as his chief strategist. His vice president is Mike Pence — the Lex Luthor to Donald's Joker. Their combined evil is overwhelming. They are backed by a league of people who are violent, hateful and racist, who want nothing more than darkness. It feels as if we are living within two Americas, and the one that was victorious is the America that would rather our blood spill into the soil of this country than help build it up to be great.

I hate to live in a world where I have to question if my uncle will be murdered by a police officer just because he's big and black. I hate to live in a world where my children might come home and repeat to their grandmother and great grandmother the very things that were said to her 50 or 60 years ago. I hate to live in a world where I'm texting my Muslim friends trying to show my support knowing that they are frightened. I hate to live in a world where my colleagues and peers are trying to find the right words to explain to their sons and daughters why this man is our president and what that means about this country. This is a nightmare, our nightmare that we can't awake from. Yet, in a way, these are problems that would be here regardless if Trump won or lost. Going to Washington, D.C. felt like recognizing all the progress America has made, and by the time I left I was facing that we still have so much more progress to make.

America is the only home that I know. It's where I was born and where I was raised. It has taught me both love and hate. It has taught me both security and fear. I've seen possibilities to exceed all limitations, and I've seen the cage that traps all your potential. I've seen America elect a black man who promised change, and I've seen America elect a white man who promoted hate. To be black in America, to be a minority in America, is a constant state of confliction. This is the land of opportunity, the land of freedom, but you have to fight for it. Trump is just another challenger to fight against. I pray that this is a fight that will bring us closer, and from the darkness, an ultralight beam of change that will take us into the future. It's a bit naive, but to have any hope for the future is to be naive enough to believe that we can overcome.

I don't have the answers, but I'm searching for them — searching for the right steps so that I don't have to live in a world that is more of a nightmare than a dream. I just know that if you're angry, you must organize that anger. If you're frightened, we have to organize that fear. I still believe that more Americans want what's better for this country. This isn't hell, and if it was, what matters most is how we walk through it.

One Year Living Life With Frank Ocean's *Blonde*

The radiance of unwavering joy is personified in Pharrell's "Pink + White" piano melody. It is the sound of two butterflies mating upon a rainbow, elegant and beautiful. Seeking comfort within such vibrant colors, I played the song on repeat. In a room where love had begun to fade, Frank's "It's all downhill from here" felt like a pessimistic prophecy from an oracle who foresaw the forthcoming wildfire that would engulf paradise. The phrase vocalized a truth I wanted to elude: the inevitable end of a cherished love.

It's been one full year of these transfixing moments with Frank Ocean's *Blonde*. One year of my life in harmony with the lyrics, a painful unison.

There's a difference between listening and living with an album. The high volume of music saturating eyes and ears has something new always replacing the old. It's hard these days to find a body of work to be submerged in. Too many options and not enough ears or time.

What makes *Blonde* special is how the music is able to bare certain truths that couldn't be found elsewhere. When Frank exhales, "I'm not brave!" on "Seigfried" there's an arresting power in the stark statement. I recall memories where bravery wasn't anywhere to be found, and to express that emotion with words seemed taboo. Frank wasn't like me. He could admit fear, brawl with decisions, and confess his inner-most truths with unfiltered transparency. Sincerity didn't make him weak, it made him human. Just when he began to feel more mystic than man, Frank returned with his heart on a silver platter.

Blonde has been an easy album to live within, like discovering a voice who could narrate all the pieces of life that felt unarticulated. What is whispered, what is kept internal, what is written in journals with the words "If you read, you'll judge" scribbled across the front. There's something so incredibly impactful about his simplistic language and the feelings he conveys. The life painted is authentic; the highs of life, but more importantly the lows that follow.

Happiness in its most cliché incarnation makes brief appearances throughout the album's 17 songs. The only time Frank sounds genuinely overjoyed is during the first half of the criminally overlooked "Futura Free." It is the victory lap, a freestyle filled with humorous lines and carefree reflection. Blonde isn't a happy album, and yet it isn't bleak.

"Ivy," for example, doesn't allow the death of a failed union to eclipse the elation of their love. Last week's heartbreak will be healed by the weekend, no differently than the unrequited love described on "Nikes" is understood with mature comprehension. "I'm not him but I'll mean something to you" is affection that is bound to be a disaster, but the bliss was never meant to last. On the interlude "Good Guy," the blind date isn't a pleasant memory, but the clarity in the final line, "I know you don't need me right now and to you it's just a late night out," immortalizes the search for companionship and the reality of how it isn't easily obtained. Even the good guys aren't good enough.

There's a lack of naïve hope when Frank sings; there's no jadedness to protect his innocence. "Confusion is a luxury which only the very, very young can possibly afford and you are not that young anymore," James Baldwin wrote in his 1956 novel, *Giovanni's Room*. There's very little confusion in Frank's maturation. His growth as a man and songwriter can be heard in his perspective.

So much of what makes *Blonde* an immersive listen is how it doesn't sell the basic concepts of good or bad — it's more like finding a corner of heaven in hell, or a rising fire within the pearly gates. You can feel the ache in his world as he confesses eternal love on "White Ferrari" in contrast to the promise of relinquishing ownership on "Godspeed." Letting go is a theme that's explored across the album, and letting go tends to be the hardest part.

I've grown to appreciate the stripped-bare instrumentation. It's a necessary serenity — emotions aren't always loud and voracious. Sometimes the feelings that shake us to our core are the silent ones, hushed tornados that envelop our entire being rather than thunderstorms roaring across the skies.

It doesn't feel as if a year has passed since *Blonde* was presented to the world. The four years of waiting felt much longer in retrospect. But I guess it's the same reason Christmas Eve is so much longer than Christmas Day — anticipation slows the flow of time. When your days and nights move to the rhythms of the music, it's easy to become lost in them. The best music is there to be leaned upon during those unbearable days and those overwhelming nights in rooms with secrets only talking walls would reveal.

Growing up teaches you that love isn't just beautiful romance and overpowering heartache. Love, like life itself, is an expansive experience. It is the private dance between two hearts, and everyone moves to a different groove. The feelings of heavenly ecstasy and hellish regret aren't exclusive to any man or woman, we are all likely to feel both the halos and the heat. In life and in love, no matter the dire circumstances, pleasure can be found, if only for a moment.

Frank isn't sugar coating love as eternal bliss, but as waxed wings in a world with a merciless sun. It is the cold, harrowing honesty of his clear-eyed candor that made *Blonde* a constant companion throughout my 2016 and 2017. Moments of merriment were rarely christened by his sultry singing; the joys of life were scored by others. He was for after the parties, when the physical bodies had left and the ghosts of memories began to haunt. He was for after the bottles were empty, and self-control is forsaken in exchange for momentary satisfaction. He was for after the sex, when two bodies lay in darkness awaiting the dawn, unsure of where to go from there. He was for solitary car rides underneath dim lights, completely lost in thoughts that can only be mused upon in solitude.

Blonde is enriched by an intimacy of confessed emotions, an album that isn't just heard but felt. One year later, I'm still in my feelings.

Every Rapper Is Going to Die and So Will I

It was Valentine's Day. I stood in the V.I.P. area, surrounded by joyous faces and ambitious strippers, my pockets filled with Washingtons. Celebrating the birthday of a woman I didn't know, the cousin of a friend's friend, but I was too sober to carelessly indulge in their festivities. The music was bad, the strippers were average, and I started to zone out.

Death.

Somehow I found myself thinking about how we would die. I looked at a stripper covered in fluorescent lights. She was rocking lime green stilettos with the body of a basketball mistress and doing the same acrobatics that killed Dick Grayson's parents. She was beautiful, but the worms would feast on her one day. They will devour the man across from me buying the manufactured lust of a young woman with his old money. They will chew on the cigar-smoking, suit-wearing, drunk buffoon who keeps screaming "Turn up!" in my ear. While everyone threw their money, I sat in the rainstorm with death, wondering when, wondering how, and wondering why.

Hours after the club, five miles away from my home, my friend fell asleep behind the wheel. It was 4:30 A.M., we both were fatigued from a long night, and I was hoping my playlist of bouncy hits would keep us awake. We were on a bridge, the right side of the car ran up the concrete sidewalk. I freaked out, yelling his name, he awoke and swerved back onto the road, but not before a loud bang confirmed a tire was flat. The car could've flipped over. If another car was coming, it could have been a fatal collision. I could hear the laughter of hidden Gods.

When *If You're Reading This It's Too Late* dropped, I stayed stuck on Drake's "Legend." It wasn't riddled with bars, the singing wasn't anything glorious, but Drake has a way of making the simplistic captivating. I played it again and again, stuck on the fact that Aubrey Graham has death on the mind. Drake's music is about ex-girlfriends, strippers, stripper ex-girlfriends, Toronto, Houston and stripper ex-girlfriends from Houston, but his music has never entertained the thought of death. He lives a life defined by carpe diem but "Legend" showed that mortality is weighing on his mind. Drake raps with sureness as if he's cemented in the game, but there's no way he can be sure about the moment after his last breath. Neither can I. Rapper, artist or construction worker, we all fear the day we can't predict. Maybe that's why Drake is taking blades to see women, celebrating so hard with his woes. He even said it on "Now & Forever," "I'm afraid I'mma die before I get where I'm going." It's unavoidable, no amount of money and celebrity will save you from an expiration date. Do not ask for whom the bell tolls Drake.

Biggie knew death, spoke of death, and slept with death. He dedicated both his album titles to the natural quietus. His lifestyle inspired his way of thinking, living and dying by the gun. If he goes, you gotta go. Even before Pac's death, it felt like he was riding shotgun with the reaper. Pac was ready, welcoming the mortal surprise around the corner. He had heart and guts; a man that didn't fear the scythe. We glorify these two, they're our heroes that left too soon. When they died, we mourned like the loss of family members. Both spent their careers with death next to them in the studio, shouting her out with their middle fingers up.

I've been writing full-time for a few years, supporting up-and-coming artists, but in my short history, I've only known one artist to pass away. He went by Avionadramida, an artist from Maryland who was in the Kool Klux Klan. We never met, barely tweeted each other, but I thought he had immense talent. I remember the day I saw the news on Twitter, I remember thinking it was a joke, and I remember the feeling of emptiness once I realized it was true. He had just turned 18 a few months before, too young to drink, old enough to die. I never thought there would be a day that I wouldn't get a submission for a new mixtape, that I wouldn't be posting his new single. He wasn't killed in a drive by or stabbed in a bar fight, his life was taken by an epileptic seizure. It still feels unbelievable.

If I die I'm a...I wish I could answer that question. I've been in love with the idea of immortality since I started writing, that I would pen something that would outlive my limitations. Lately, I feel that I'm writing too much, that the pieces are paper cuts and not stab wounds. I want to lunge these words into your heart so that my sentences are repeated, regurgitated, and passed down like sacred scriptures.

I want to be to writing what Mona Lisa is to art, what Pac is to rap, what Steve Jobs is to technology. Drake wants the same, success in the form of eternity. I'm almost certain the brown skin stripper with the lime green stilettos will outlive us both. She was a true artist. I should've tipped her more.

Embracing Art In A Sea
of Dying Seconds

Fireworks detonated in the sky, gunshots boomed from the streets, liquor drained from the bottles — we bid 2016 a farewell worthy of a year that consisted of beautiful wins and tragic losses. As the numbers descended, as the voices enthusiastically counted down, as the peach fell indicating the birth of a new year, I thought of time and how we all swam in a sea of dying seconds. I thought of all the buried minutes and hours lost throughout my years; a metaphorical skeleton reminding me not to commit the sin that Chuck Noland realized while stranded on a deserted island.

What is the value of a second? What is the worth of a minute? What is an adequate price for an hour? These are questions I never asked myself but sat at the center of my soul as the sky was filled with color, as another bullet fell from the heavens, as another shot was taken.

I've always found it a bit humorous how Jay-Z tried to resist being defined by age and time. When he became old by rap standards, far removed from the days of his youth, Hov insisted that 30 had magically become the new 20 — an attempt to rebrand the inevitable, an attempt to be more aged wine than expired Heineken. Jay wanted age to be defined by his own terms, a master of his universe, but with each year his body continues to reveal how age catches us all. We see it with our favorite rappers, our favorite entertainers, and of course our parents and grandparents — the graying hair, the slowing movement, the beautiful transformation into their final form; a form that reminds us that youth isn't eternal.

Old is something I never desired to be, I wanted nothing more than to swim in a fountain that would keep me from the cancer of Father Time, but Pharrell refuses to share the secret location. Childish Gambino rapped, "I'm here for a good, not a long time" on the grand finale of his *Culdesac* mixtape, and the words resonated with my inner desire to be a momentary blaze of glory. But watching his transformation, and seeing how time has aged him into an incredible artist, I now want to be a phoenix that continues to burn for an eternity. I'm stepping into this year no longer stuck on the idea of being young forever, no longer associating getting older with staring down the barrel, but embracing the fact that I need to cherish this life of mine, and understand the value of the one thing that money cannot buy.

Nas once rapped, "I switched my motto, instead of saying, 'Fuck Tomorrow,' that buck that bought a bottle could've struck the lotto." Even if I disagree with the sentiment of spending money on lottery tickets, the bigger message of making an investment for your future instead of living in the present hit home. It's easy to fall into the "YOLO" mindset, to simply be a spirit who drifts in the moment without believing in tomorrow's sunrise. Death hovered over most of 2016, taking the lives of living legends and acclaimed heroes; each burial was a constant reminder of mortality, and how our little time here will never be enough. I look at the lives of Prince, Muhammad Ali, David Bowie, and Phife as figures of impact, soldiers of art who left an immortal mark on this world. Losing them is tragic, theirs were irreplaceable spirits, but now we must bear the weight of their legacies and continue progressing forward.

We all have an expiration date, so our lives should be measured by all that we accomplish before reaching that unknown day or night. Tomorrow isn't promised, but within tomorrow is another chance to be here forever.

I don't want to waste any time this year, nor do I plan on wasting anyone else's. I don't want to fall into an idle state, or in commitments that aren't soul-stirring. Time is precious, and how we spend our time is equally as important to how we spend our money. Mastering the management of both is how you avoid regret and accomplish all that you can. Passion is the only leader I plan to follow, and I hope it continues to lead me somewhere that is more paradise than purgatory. Within learning the worth of my time, I'm discovering my worth as a man and as a writer. Knowing your value is necessary in this business, but especially in life. It's something you don't want to discover too late or allow someone to bestow upon you.

I look around at my family, friends and peers coming to terms that we won't always be together. Last year, rather abruptly, former DJBooth writers Nathan and Lucas both departed from DJBooth. Like any other business, co-workers find other ventures, explore new jobs, and are replaced by new employees. I realized some months after, how I took their presence for granted. Subconsciously, I fell into a place of comfort, and their leaving stirred me awake. It was a reminder that nothing lasts, even a great editorial team can be broken up like the Lakers without Shaq, Miami without LeBron, and the Spurs without Tim Duncan.

When things end, you have the memories as a reminder of when they were great, and a reason to believe they will be great again. As I cherish every second, I'm doing my best to cherish people, from my oldest friends to my latest Twitter followers. It's like being retaught the value of a dollar, the value of good people, and the value of time.

I need to make time for albums again, to live with the very music that once motivated me to write. The whirlwind of releases is easy to get lost in, but great art shouldn't be tossed in the microwave, rather hung on the walls of our mental museums. I'm making time for better food, better drinks (better water), and better company to keep my spirit nourished and filled. But also making time for solitude, meditation, and self-care—finding the ultimate balance between being selfish and generous with my time.

I think every artist needs to be constantly lost within them-

167

selves and others — too much of either can be disastrous, another lesson I learned from 2016. There's a form of insanity that you discover when trying to make everyone happy. And there's a form of madness that's connected to an overindulgence of narcissism. I'm making time for sleep, the mistress I neglect the most. But after a year of feeling the crash that comes after long nights of writing and energy drinks, I have a newfound appreciation for the cousin of death. Being a better son, being a better friend, being a better writer, and just being the best version of myself is motivating all of my decisions in this new year. This is not the year to settle for good enough, but to go above and beyond limitations.

I Am Wale:
Learning to Live Without Recognition

I stare at my canvas, a blank document, running my fingers across the letters like keys on a piano. The familiar feeling of anxiety greets me. He's the ghost that haunts my writing, a constant reminder that banal words and stale sentences are unacceptable. I felt this strain before DJBooth, before RefinedHype, back when I was writing rap reviews for a rock website. Even back then I wanted my name to be synonymous with great writing more than anything. I wanted to be remembered for being someone that brought something memorable with each article. With each release I thought Complex would hunt me down, shower me with praise and a job. They didn't. Where was Fader? Where was The Source? I was Kanye on "Touch The Sky," dealing with an internal crisis, wondering, 'Damn, are these writers really that much better than me?'

Bukowski once said, "Baby, I'm a genius, but nobody knows it but me." Summing up the feelings of every creative person to ever live. I've never met an artist that didn't see his expression as something God-given, something meant to be shared and acknowledged by the world. Everyone from trap rappers to acrylic painters wants to be recognized, wants to be adored for their craft, but few will openly admit this natural emotion. I care too much, a confession that I wouldn't share with a preacher or Pope. "Stop bitching, stop moaning," is what they would say. Yelling how great and talented you are will only attract a mob holding up "be humble" and "be patient" banners; and those will be the nice banners. Your confidence, this seemingly uncontrollable passion to get your work out into the world, will be perceived as egotistical and arrogant, you'll be labeled as conceited. You will be labeled as Wale.

169

Lil Wayne on the "Nike Boots (Remix)" was my introduction to Wale. That's back when a new Wayne feature was hitting blogs every week, a voracious streak of verses, but I was stuck on this one specifically. Even though Wayne's heads and tails double entendre is immaculate, it was Wale's wordplay that really caught my attention. You can tell when rappers care about each bar, making sure each line hits listeners like a locomotive. I can imagine Wale sitting down filling notebooks full of lyrics. Writing is an art, and that song introduced an emcee that cared about what he was saying.

Lyricism isn't the only thing Wale cared about. As the years have flipped by, it's become inescapably clear that he also wants everything that the best deserves: accolades on accolades, platinum plaques, 5 mics in The Source, the top of every list, universal respect from critics, peers and the people in general. I never thought Wale was the best rapper, but he was one of the most passionate. He has the competitive spirit of a gladiator. The same publications I hoped would some day hire me to write for them were the same publications he wanted to deem him elite after every album.

"I was depressed not being where I wanna be in my career when I've put the work in. I wasn't sleeping. I was drinking all day and didn't have anyone to go to. I couldn't fight it." —Wale, Billboard interview[34]

It wasn't until I read his interview with Billboard that I realized Wale is simply Kanye without the critical acclaim. Not neccesarily in the sense of talent, but desire. What kind of monster would Ye be if *College Dropout* and *Late Registration* weren't successful? If the pink Polo and soul samples fell to deaf ears and he got dropped from The Roc, where would Ye be? Kanye needs the recognition, the applause, in some ways he even needs the hate; it feeds that creative beast. And now that he's largely conquered music, Kanye now seems intent on prying some respect out of the fashion world's hands; any world not recognizing his greatness is the world he most wants recognition from. Shades of Wale at every turn.

I now realize how much of Wale is in me. If we're being honest, how much of Wale is in all of us? We can call him a prick, egotistical, but ultimately he wants what we all want: to be recognized. There was a time when I was releasing articles that I felt deserved millions of views. Anything less, I completely failed. I would be up from sunrise to sunset writing, believing I had something the world needed to read. I needed to believe in myself that strongly to even create in the first place, but that also meant a life of regular disappointment when reality fell short of my own expectations.

Success is a rare word that's uniquely defined. To some it's simply happiness (another word not easily defined). To others it's some sort of grand achievement, a GRAMMY award or a college diploma. Every person has their own vision, and I find myself wondering how Wale defines success. In a way he seems completely dissatisfied by his current accomplishments. But as far as rappers go, he's in a position other up-and-coming artists would give anything for. Loyal fans, prosperous tours, turning a mixtape series into a studio album with Jerry Seinfeld. What else could you seek to achieve? He still wants more though. Our minds create these elaborate scenarios, we believe wholeheartedly that the outcome will resemble this image. When it doesn't, the spirit is crushed. There's no pity party you can throw that will alleviate the disappointment. It's like suffocating under the weight of your own supersized ambitions.

Wale is one of the most openly vulnerable artists in hip hop. It's not just the music; on social media and interviews he shows a side of himself that most would keep private. He walks through the world stark naked, bearing his soul, and the hecklers continue to chew into him. He said that the outside world has always meant the most to him. He values the opinions of others. Ironically, he wants to please the people, which makes him a huge target for shade throwing. He's constantly at war with the jokes. *The Album About Nothing* going number one or the Toronto TV announcer calling him "No Drake" — which does he care about more? For Wale, it's deeper than just making an album better than the last, it's about overcoming the memes and jokes and slights. To an extent, that resonates with me. There are some people that will only see me as the writer that Kid Cudi called a "sideline nigga," someone whose words don't hold weight anywhere on this planet.[35] I might never write an article that will make some readers see past how much they hated me for that *Illmatic* piece.

What, exactly, do you want Wale? And then what would happen if you ever obtained it? The fans are supporting, the critics are raving, yet he's still not pleased. It's like he has this elusive goal that's completely unreachable, or maybe he's disappointed that he's reached his goals and still feels the same void. Success is looked upon as a finish line, but life continues once you reach it. Nothing ever finishes. I wanted to be a paid writer, and I've been that for the last four months. It's been great, it's been stressful, it's been confusing. The celebratory phase has ended and I don't know what's next. Would being my favorite rapper's favorite writer give me new-found fulfillment? Getting a book deal? I've already learned that I can be crowned the greatest of all-time today and beheaded tomorrow.

During these moments of absolute confusion, I think about David Carr, the renowned journalist from the New York Times who recently passed away. After a long battle with cancer, Carr collapsed in his office at the New York Times. Something about him being at work the day he died that astounds me. He was a writer until his very last breath. Death is the finish line. Success is spending your life doing something you love. I'm trying to learn that I'm already successful.

Notes & References

32 Taylor, Trey, "Tyler, the Creator has been doing it better since 2011," Dazed (July 11, 2017) http://www.dazeddigital.com/music/article/36700/1/tyler-the-creator-has-been-doing-it-better-since-2011

33 Lewis, Miles Marshall, "Read Mos Def's First-Ever Cover Story From 2000," Fader (September 9, 2014) http://www.thefader.com/2015/09/14/mos-def-cover-story-issue-3.

34 Wete, Brad, "Wale Opens Up About Drugs, Depression & Seeking Respect: 'I've Been Through Shit'," Billboard (March 30, 2015) http://www.billboard.com/articles/columns/the-juice/6516931/wale-drugs-depression-the-album-about-nothing-interview.

35 Yoh, "Kid Cudi Said My Writing is Worthless, So I Wrote About It," DJ Booth (November 25, 2014) http://djbooth.net/news/entry/kid-cudi-twitter-response.

Part 5
FRESH PERSPECTIVES

You Need to Do This Independently: Brent Faiyaz's Manager, Ty Baisden, Rips Apart the Major Label Business Model

Brent Faiyaz is on fire. Over the past 10 months, the 22-year-old has melted hearts as the frontman of Sonder, burned up charts as the hook-man on GoldLink's platinum single "Crew," and his newly-released solo debut, *Sonder Son*, is being received with admiration.

It's an impressive feat when a fairly unknown artist begins to make noise in January and consistently remains the subject of praise all year long. Faiyaz is about to hit the road for a second time this year, this time as a solo headliner. This will be his show and people will be coming to hear his voice. And tickets are selling fast; there's a tweet on his timeline congratulating the young star on selling out his LA show in 12 minutes. To say he's blowing up would understate the surge of excitement burning in the underground's underbelly.

With accomplishments and accolades come questions: How is Brent doing it all? Is he an industry plant? Is he a mindie artist, posing as an independent act while a major label is funding the entire operation? In an era of secret signings and uncertain indie claims, everyone is under suspicion.

For insight on his current label situation, I reached out to Ty Baisden, Brent's manager and the man credited with turning around his career. Ty confirmed Brent and he are 100% independent.

That's not all he said, though.

Born and raised in Atlanta, Ty has worked behind the scenes for years as an artist manager, but prior to connecting with Brent all of his previous acts were based in rap. After reaching a point of exhaustion with that side of the game, his sights turned to R&B and his thoughts turned to action when he discovered Brent's SoundCloud in 2014.

In the three years since the two connected and began mapping out how they would approach the music industry, a lot has occurred: label meetings, proposals, letdowns, and hours of studying hip hop's greatest businessmen like Master P, Jay-Z, Diddy, and more.

Ty saw Bad Boy and Roc-A-Fella as empires that were forced into independence because no one initially cared. "We weren't forced into independence because everyone wanted to be in business with us. But their terms forced us to be independent," Ty told me during our hour-long conversation.

Ty was transparent, candid, and blunt about the entire major label system, the idea of independence in 2017, ownership of black art, and treating the music business like any other business. He was also clear about his mission: the desire to educate and inform those who have career ambitions in music.

This interview has been lightly edited for content and clarity.

Yoh: Is being 100% independent the plan or have you been waiting for the right record deal?

Ty Baisden: We had a whole plan for year one. Year one was basically August 2015 to August 2016. The second year was when we were going to do the album. We were going to drop the EP, get a deal, get the label to fund it, and do the album on an island somewhere or some shit. The label will fund it, boom boom. That was the year two plan, from August 2016 to August 2017. It wasn't until we started the process and hit these milestones that the labels started coming. When the labels started coming, the conversations weren't real exciting conversations. When I say not exciting, I mean, I started asking questions they couldn't give me honest answers to. I was like, "Hmm, this shit not making sense now that I'm thinking about it." When I sat down with Troy Carter over at Spotify, he was the beginning of the nail in the coffin [of trying to get a deal]. He was like, "You need to do this independently."

Yoh: What were those conversations with the labels like?
Ty Baisden: When we started to have these conversations with the labels, it was like, these niggas are trying to pay me 11% out of 100%. Just because you motherfuckers give me some money early? Fuck that. You crazy. That shit don't make sense.

We had some really great meetings. We met with L.A. Reid, and L.A. said he loved Brent. That was the only meeting we took and actually allowed Brent to sing in an office setting in front of someone. Me and Brent respect what L.A. and LaFace did for R&B music. That's why we decided to do it. Taking the whole team up there and doing the little performance. It is what it is, I already knew how it would end. We went and we did it. L.A. was saying how special Brent was, how he was going to be so big, and how he hadn't been excited about an artist like this in a while. All these different things. I'm just listening and paying attention. Then I get the deal proposal and I'm like, "Wait a minute, my nigga. This is not a special deal." That's the problem. Those types of interactions are what led us to decide on being independent. People will say that's how it goes in the business, they send you over the contract and you gotta negotiate. Nah, my nigga, there are principles in life. If you sit down and tell [Brent] he's a special artist, you better make sure that fucking deal is special. If not, your word isn't as solid as what you just told me. I kept seeing a lot of that in these conversations about a deal. That was the first strike. Mind you, we had amazing meetings with everyone. No bad meetings. Everyone was excited, they were fans, and were really passionate about the music. But when those contracts came in…

Yoh: First strike? What else was in the contracts?
Ty Baisden: Like I said, I'm a principled guy, [so I had] sent out a proposal of what I wanted [to the labels]. Once I met with Troy [from Spotify], we were talking about Spotify's support and Troy was like, "I wouldn't do anything because this is real music. There's a big resurgence of people who like this type of music. If you guys just wait, this is going to work. I'm not saying don't do any business with a major label, but make it so the terms are favorable to you guys." I'm like, "Damn, you're right." But since I had already sent out the proposals before the meeting, I told Brent's lawyer, if any of the labels that we sent the proposals to give us exactly what that proposal asks for, I'll do the deal. Like I said, principles are principles, they don't change because you're in a different arena or business. My principles would be the same if I was a school teacher or if I was selling pencils. So, I was like, if they give us exactly what it says, we will do the deals. So we started having conversations [with the labels] and we're not getting exactly what the proposals say. Interscope, they were one of the conversations I had on the phone about the actual contract. I was speaking with [Interscope EVP] Joie [Manda], and I've known Joie for a while, he's been very supportive of me in general. When I say support, I mean always responding to emails, taking meetings, and things of that nature. The moment I was on the phone with Joie, and I told him about speaking with my lawyer and the terms I didn't agree upon that I wanted to talk out. The terms were — Yoh, you aren't a lawyer, but when I say this to you you'll know it doesn't make sense — about royalties. A major label only pays you one way: through your royalty. Now, industry standards — make note of the fact that I hate the word "industry standards," I hate it — from what my lawyer told me are that generally a recording

artist who is new and gets signed to a deal is going to get a 14% to 16% royalty payout from the label. My proposal had an 18% royalty payout from the label.

Yoh: 18% is far from unreasonable.

Ty Baisden: I told Joie I didn't understand how if Brent has an album [already] out that's probably going to be a digital-only release that's never going to stores or [being released physically], and the label is going to acquire this body of work through a deal we will potentially do, you are saying that is too high. That's high for a new artist, but we'll do it anyway because we really believe in it. His response was, 'We invest a lot of money early. Being that we invested so early, that's why we give a [smaller] percentage. We don't want to scale it because that's not how it works.' That's the last real conversation I had with a major label. I was like we going to do this shit ourselves. This was in November 2016, [Brent's *A.M. Paradox EP*] was already out. I'll commend Joie and Interscope, they were on it early. Joie was trying to sign Brent before I even put out the *A.M. Paradox EP*. I really believed in putting out this project independently first, though. I felt like I would jeopardize what Brent could become if I did any official, long-term business before the music was out. Joie was in the studio in August 2016 trying to sign the kid, before any projects were out. The project *A.M. Paradox* dropped in September. [Senior VP of A&R at RCA Records] Tunji was early as well because he had already signed GoldLink, and Brent and GoldLink worked on the "Crew" record back in early April or May of 2016. So Tunji was already hip, I was sending him demos and things of that nature, but Tunji wasn't putting too much pressure on it because he had so much going on and there wasn't a body of work out at that point. I was just putting out singles here and there. Everyone was paying attention but nobody was putting a bid out. Interscope, Atlantic, and Epic were all trying to get in bed, but Interscope was there super early. The year ends, we're getting ready to drop the Sonder album, and we have to pay for this solo Brent album. He wanted to go to the Dominican Republic and I had to figure out how to pay for that shit. [*A.M. Paradox*] picked up, Brent's "Poison" record is growing, the Sonder single "Too Fast" is out by now and that record is growing, so now the labels are on my head even harder to do something. So I said, I'll tell you what: one album for $150,000, all in.

Yoh: Just one album? For that amount?
Ty Baisden: One album, that's it. I'll do that if someone wants to do it. LA Reid said fuck that, I'm not doing it. I was cool. Mike Caren and Jeff Vaughn over at Atlantic/APG were like, 'Nah, Mike Caren wants five albums, he wants to be involved with the deal as it grows.' Okay cool, I was good. Speaking with Tim Glover at Interscope, I said, "Listen, this is what I want: We can do this one album, see how we like each other and then keep it moving. Cut me that check for $150k, I get you the album, and we work it together." Tim said he would talk to Joie and he came back and said that they had something better. I'm like, "Listen, my G, there's nothing better than what I offered. If he can't do this, I'm not the meeting type, I'm not trying to have a bunch of meetings. You guys came to the studio, we've chopped it up, this is what we want to do and we not meeting again about it." That was the last talk. They weren't trying to give us one album for $150,000. It's a preconception that black artists only want money. The motherfuckers will not say it in public, but with urban artists, there is a misconception that all we want is money. So I was like, okay then, I'll take it away from the money. Give me $150k all in, distribution and license deal, whatever you want to call it. They didn't want to do it. We decided to keep it moving. The major labels have padded the numbers to make it seem unrealistic to do this shit yourself.

Yoh: With no label, how have you been able to fund all the projects and tours?

Ty Baisden: Brent started to study Master P. He started to look at all these videos of P. By the time we were at the end of January and put the Sonder project out, and it started growing, he had already begun to see the thought process. He was like, "Man, Master P sold this many records? He was getting 85% of everything? Shit, I want to be like Master P." Me and Brent were funding a lot of the early Sonder shit. When Sonder started making money, it paid the company back. Then the money that Sonder is making now is funding [future] Sonder work. Literally two different companies. Sonder Global LLC is a completely different company. Brent is a partner in Sonder Global and he used the company that he and I started to fund Sonder until Sonder was able to self-fund themselves.

Yoh: What's the company you and Brent started?

Ty Baisden: Lost Kids LLC. Completely self-funded. Sonder is a Lost Kids investment. Being that Brent is a partner in Lost Kids, he funneled the money to make sure that Sonder had rehearsals, all the small shit that it takes. All the different things until that money started to generate from Sonder's merch, tours, screens and all that. Sonder is funding itself and it hasn't even been a year. We self-funded both of the shows in New York and LA. We self-funded the Sonder tour for 11 cities. All the marketing and promo was self-funded. The "Too Fast" video, we funded a percentage of it. Noah Lee, the director, was so passionate about it that he and his team raised the capital to finish shooting the "Too Fast" video. This shit has been a community thing. Even the trip to the Dominican Republic, me and Brent invested $25,000 into that trip. We flew 10 people there, not including myself. The only person who couldn't go was [Sonder producer] Atu, but everybody else who Brent has worked with flew out to work on the *Sonder Son* album. We're not rich, we had to figure out how we would fund it. I called everybody who was involved as far as the Airbnb people, the flights, and I was able to pay off everything in three installments.

Yoh: Do you think your method and process will work in the long run? Funding everything yourself?

Ty Baisden: Yes. The reason is smart investing and having great products. The amount of money we need to build a company is not the amount of money people think you need to build a company when you have a product that's working. Now, if Brent wanted to have a Range Rover and have all the jewels and get the crazy mansion, it won't be sustainable. But there's an understanding of what it takes to be independent and investing in yourself more and more as you see things work. I want to build this up how Facebook built it up, and how Spotify built it up. If I build it up and own the content, the venture capitalist world will be knocking on our door. There is a boom in the business sector that deals with music. We'll surpass the five billion, six billion, seven billion, and eight billion revenue stream on recorded music over these next few years. And now, all of a sudden, the music business starts a trajectory back toward that 11, 12, 13 billion dollar revenue stream from back in '98 & '99. Now, it's not about who got the masters, it's about who got equity, who got shares, who got stakes in the company. That's the only business I want to be in. I don't want to be in the "I own your masters" business. That's the business the labels been pitching and they will continue to pitch until people like myself or anybody else decides their ownership is not worth what they're trying to sell you. Especially in this era. This is the motherfucking gold rush, especially for black art.

Yoh: It's the music business, but you want to run it as an "actual business."

Ty Baisden: I'm going to be honest with you: I told you I would talk my shit. I feel like the numbers are padded. The major labels have padded the numbers to make it seem unrealistic to do this shit yourself. I called Fly, the CEO from T.I.G. Records. As an independent label, they have had four or five No. 1 records at urban radio. I think out of those records, they've been Platinum or double-Platinum. I was just picking his brain, "Bro, how much you paying for radio?" He said his radio campaign was $100k and could get up to $200k. I was like, "That's it? That's a nation-wide campaign?" He's like, "Yeah." I was always told from record labels that if you trying to go to radio you needed a half-million dollars. You're telling me that when urban music is the pinnacle of consumption, it only takes [a few hundred-thousand dollars] to have a nationwide urban music campaign? Obviously, we talking about a record that's working and successful online. If you got a good product and you're investing in a street team, traveling, marketing, and advertising costs, everything you have to spend to market a record outside of it just being online where you identify it. When you do that radio campaign, that includes college radio and your internet radio, it's a campaign across the board. It's either the people who are putting together these campaigns are overcharging the label because the label got it, or the label is padding the numbers because you in debt and they want to keep you in debt, because as long as you're in debt you don't see the light. You gonna stay in the debt, and they'll continue to collect their percentage of their royalty. They not even taking the whole 100% of what's made as a recoup, they're taking their percentage off the top and then taking the rest of it and saying we'll put this toward the debt. Man, it's hard to get out of debt when you only making an 18% royalty.

Yoh: And they don't even want you to have 18%...

Ty Baisden: Check it, this is another thing that trips me out about the music business. Let's say all the money they advance you is a loan. In any other sector of business, once you pay the loan back, you own whatever the product is. You either have no balance and you can leave, or you own what you paid for. Imagine you finance a house for 100 racks, you pay it off in three years, and the bank still owns the house. And you're still paying the mortgage?!? That's what the major label does to the artist. Y'all gave me the money to create this body of work. Y'all gave me the money to sign with y'all 'cause I got this body of work. But when it's all said and done, after I pay you back all the money you loaned me and you took your percentage off top, you still own me. That's crazy, B! One thing I will agree upon, though, is a situation where you sign an artist and no one knows who that artist is and you develop [the artist] and you pay for everything. Every situation is different. It's like having bad credit and good credit. Niggas with good credit don't gotta put [down] a sizable down payment. Hell, they probably give you all kinds of bonuses because you got good credit. That's what life teaches us, do good in life and you get rewarded. You do bad, you don't get rewarded.

Yoh: Why do you believe so strongly in sharing all of this information with young creatives?

Ty Baisden: I don't believe in charging people for information. I don't believe in being a middleman for information. The only reason why I decided to do this — I'm not trying to be no superstar or in the scene — is because I believe the information I'm gathering and learning is very important for young black men. I want to inspire the way I was inspired. If it grows outside of that, that's just God's blessing. I think it's very important for us, in this position, to try not to block young kids from getting that knowledge so they can be successful. It's not progressive for the culture to withhold information when you know you can help. You don't have to get paid for every single thing that you do. This interview is very important to give that knowledge for anyone who wants it. It may be a woman who feels like she's not getting the right information. It may be someone who is disabled, who maybe can't walk but is really good with numbers and they've always dreamed of managing somebody, but they feel like they can't do it because of their disability. I feel like information is king in this world, especially in an industry full of dumbass people. That's your leverage.

Daring to Go Beyond:
The Impact of The Neptunes and
Pharrell on Music Culture

What I always found fascinating about The Neptunes is how they went beyond just one genre. Hip-hop, R&B, rock, pop, soul, they made it all, and they made it with everyone. You could tell by the chords, the drum patterns, sounds that seemed both old and new, strange and alluring, weird but cool, they blurred the lines, and rewrote the rules.

Pharrell and Chad were the living, breathing embodiment that creativity has no rules, no walls, no barriers or prisons. Being an artist meant freedom, boundless possibilities if your mind could take you there. Digging into their discography is like attending a restaurant that will serve you 12 different courses throughout the meal. The same minds who got their start writing on "Rumpshaker" in '92 and gave us the lunch-room table classic "Grindin" with the Clipse also presented Gwen Stefani with a hit song ("Hollaback Girl"), Beyoncé with an anthem ("Work It Out") Britney Spears with edge ("I'm A Slave 4 U"), and were a crucial part of Justin Timberlake's transition from boy-band member to superstar. From dope boys to pop stars, they could morph to fit any world.

What made them special is how it could all mingle into one big musical world. Through them the Clipse worked with Justin Timberlake, Snoop Dogg worked with Mariah; Kelis with ODB. Genre-fusing and blending was natural since the foundation they used to create was pulled from a range of sources. They were the offspring of the music from yesteryear's, making the sound of tomorrow, leaving the biggest impression on the kid of the present. Part of the reason why The Neptunes cult was such a large group

186

was due to it being a collection of fans whose interest was in various genres. The benefits of being outside the box, attracting everyone else who refuses to be caged in.

Fashion, music, skating, jewelry — Pharrell was the poster child for daring to be different. He cites Kelis as the one who upped his taste in fashion, making her a huge influence that sparked a future trendsetter. But Pharrell was on his own pedestal, especially with Billionaire Boys Club — a brand that rivaled Sean John and Roc-A-Fella. Without Kelis, who knows where Pharrell would stand as a fashion icon. But without Pharrell, does the world get Kelis? You have an artsy, creative, rocker black woman that was unlike anyone out at the time. I wasn't really aware of Kelis beyond "Milkshake," but after talking to countless women, her importance goes much deeper than Billboard charts. She was a figure, a symbol of representation that impacted women to be different the same way Pharrell did to men.

What he saw in Kelis made a world of difference in people's lives, and the same can be said for the Thornton brothers. Under their Star Trak umbrella, the Clipse were able to go beyond Virginia. *Outside of In Search Of and Clones*, Clipse's *Lord Willin* and Kelis's *Tasty* were the first projects to be released through Star Trak's Arista deal. Slim Thug, Robin Thicke, The High Speed Scene and Kenna all released albums through Star Trak. Even Snoop Dogg was able to resurge with *R&G: The Masterpiece*. Of course, the label ran into issues that slowly brought its demise, but they rarely get credit for daring to take on new acts, try and push new talent.

They also used the label to step into the spotlight in another way. N.E.R.D's three albums created something like a cult fol-lowing. Another great example of how they dared to be different and it paid off. The offspring of the rock band is everywhere - even though Pharrell was a good vocalist, a decent rapper, it was the rock band that assisted in transcending him. Fader published an

187

article in 2015, about how the N.E.R.D forum invented the rap internet. I don't agree with the headline, the points are far too vague, but everyone from Tyler, The Creator to M.I.A was part of that community. It truly was a cult of kids who admired and looked up to Pharrell, Chad, and the music that they continued to create. Those very kids have grown up, they're artists now, trying to carry the same ethos that they found so alluring. I feel like that's what has kept Pharrell so young. If punk-rock captured the angst of being a teenager, Pharrell and company breathed being different into the lungs of everyone who watched them from afar.

Nelly and Mystikal, Noreaga and T.I., 2 Chainz and A$AP Rocky, Kenna and The Cool Kids, Earl Sweatshirt and Mos Def, Future and Wale, even after the rise of Auto-Tune and the end of The Neptunes, the desire to work with Pharrell and Chad has yet to wane. Pharrell's a star, he's always had the charisma, he was destined to be more than a background producer. Before Metro Boomin blew himself up, Pharrell had reached a completely different level of fame and notoriety. He did the band, solo albums, even the gangster grill — the DJ Drama and Pharrell tape was one of the gems that came out in 2006. Everything from hearing him rap alongside T.I. and Young Dro, freestyling over "Liquid Swords" and having models in the hood made Pharrell the definition of cool. The nerd that was bigger than the jocks, Pharrell would have all kids wanting to ride skateboards and throw up the Vulcan salute when rappers were known more for gang signs and expensive Hummers. His very essence was cool, and somehow that spirit has continued to captivate despite his age. That's longevity. Long after he's dead, people will hope to be half as innovative and cool.

Tyler, The Creator rapped on his new album, "In Search of... did more for me than Illmatic." Out of all his lyrics, it was one of the most shocking to hear. Knowing Tyler, knowing the influence of Pharrell, The Neptunes, and N.E.R.D, it shouldn't come as a surprise, but it's still a statement. One that really captures what that music means. When "Happy" was the biggest song in the world, I wondered what that meant for Pharrell's legacy. He's getting older, his music has changed a bit, but he's still able to dominate. The kids that watched *Despicable Me* may one day grow up and look back, discover *In Search Of* and never be the same, or maybe *Clones*, or maybe an Apple Music playlist of all The Neptunes classics that will spark the fire of who will carry his torch. When it's all said and done, he will be remembered as a genius who helped push music further.

It's been ten years since *In My Mind*, who knows what Pharrell will do in the next ten. Even if he did nothing but make shoes and chairs, his impact on music will never be erased. A legend living amongst us, silently innovating, inspiring, and making kids embrace their inner nerd, and hoping that with each new song that's played, you'll hear that familiar stutter from The Neptunes.

How Photographer Cam Kirk
Is Making A Difference In Atlanta,
Rap Music, and Beyond

Upon entering Cam Kirk's cozy Atlanta loft, your attention is drawn to a fairly grandiose framed photo of Gucci Mane lying against the wall. On a counter in the living room rests a huge stack of 5 x 7 prints that might take over an hour to flip through fully, with a snapshot of Rae Sremmurd sitting at the very top. To even get a glass of water from the refrigerator, you'd have to stare down a portrait of Lil Boosie posing on the door. His photography is all around, but you won't come across any landscapes, framed pictures of graduates, or even a street portrait of an eccentric stranger on the corner of Edgewood; Cam's subjects happen to be strictly rappers. Not the ones passing out mixtapes at McDonald's or sending unsolicited links on Twitter — his lens is pointed at the famous or soon-to-be. Cam will be the first to tell you he isn't a traditional photographer: "When I look at my life, it's amazing that I can even do this. I'm a rap photographer. I don't shoot weddings, I don't shoot proms, I don't have a gig shooting clubs. I shoot rappers as my full-time job."

Cam is unlike the big, bold, and colorful subjects he shoots. He's rather reserved, laid-back, and fairly shy; these qualities were an insecurity back in high-school, but he's since turned them into strengths. He is able to capture candid shots of rap stars because of his personality: the fly on the wall, the invisible man, the photographer who doesn't disrupt the vibe, but always gets the shot. "I'm not the forceful photographer, I'm not the one to make my moment happen. I let things naturally happen," explains Cam. "Natural movement. If Gucci [Mane] did something with his hands, it's a natural movement. If Future wants the lights off in the studio, then fuck it, I'll make it work. I'm not going to have a flash, I'm going to figure it out."

One rapper he has fond memories of is the late Bankroll Fresh. On the day of his passing, under three different photos that he took of Trentavious White, Cam Kirk wrote this caption on his Instagram: "Long live Bankroll Fresh the world lost more than a rapper." Rapper — that's what the media continued to call him when reporting the fatal shooting that took his life on March 5th. They weren't wrong. Bankroll Fresh was a rapper — Atlanta's very own Hot Boy — but he was also much more. If you ask Cam Kirk, he'll tell you about a young CEO who started his own label; a boss people could rely on; a father who was working toward a better life for his family; a friend who never treated him like some interchangeable "cameraman," but instead built a relationship that was deeper than rap. All these sides of him weren't being represented through the news, lost in the story of a homicide at a studio.

Not only did he lose a friend, at the time, Cam Kirk wasn't in Atlanta to mourn and celebrate his life. "The passing of Bankroll happened when I was on tour. Metro was out of town, we weren't here, we weren't home. We didn't get a chance to all come together and pay our respects to a friend. I wanted to come back to the city and do something special for him." So Cam reached out to a few friends to help bring a dream into fruition. Metro Boomin, Sonny Digital, and Southside (of 808 Mafia) — all prominent young Atlanta producers — chipped in to fund Cam's idea of putting Bankroll on a billboard. The location: the extremely busy intersection of 10th Street and Northside Drive in Atlanta's Midtown area, within walking distance of Georgia Tech. More importantly, the surrounding area is home to plenty of recording studios. What better place for an Atlanta rap artist than where Atlanta music is made? Up and down Midtown, going into the city or coming out, all those that pass 10th and Northside were to see Bankroll in the skyline — larger than they've ever seen him before. In many ways, it became a metaphor for how his passing has made him an even bigger giant, immortalized for what he did and what he had potential to do.

The untimely death of a friend revived a concept that Cam had but wasn't sure how to make into a reality: an idea for a gallery that would literally be bigger than anything he had done before. "I had the billboard exhibit idea for a minute — since I did Trap God. Thinking about what could I do next, [I thought], 'What if I put all these rappers on billboards?' I didn't know how, it seemed far-fetched at the time, but I knew who," Cam recalls. "Bankroll was one of them; when he was alive, I wanted to put him on a billboard."

The idea evolved into the Day 4 Billboard Photography Exhibit. On the 4th day in the book of Genesis, according to the Bible, God created all the stars and heavenly bodies. Cam's intention with his exhibit is to put stars in the Atlanta skies, hence the biblical title. Conceptually, Day 4 recalls a project that the illustrious photojournalist Chi Modu did with his Uncategorized series. An exhibition in which he placed iconic '90s-era photos of Biggie Smalls, Snoop Dogg, Method Man, and Tupac on exterior walls lining buildings in New York.

Chi considered his series a step out of the galleries, and a step forward into creating a kind of street art that can be considered "legal graffiti" — both qualities that Day 4 embodies. Not only does Day 4 bring art to people who might not normally visit a gallery or museum, it's amazing that Atlantans can drive by a place that went away from advertising some movie we might never see or a councilman not worth voting for. Now, there's actual art to take in. It also sheds light back to the art of photography in hip-hop. Unfortunately, paying for a billboard isn't cheap, which is why Cam's Kickstarter was in place. $6000 will allow him to put up 4 more billboards.

When I asked who else will be featured, Cam kept it a secret: a surprise to look forward to. What he did tell me: "A lot of what comes next depends on the Kickstarter. I have no intent of making money or pocketing mad bread off this situation... This is for the people, by the people. Whatever I raise will tell me the demand and determine how big it could be. This could be small, it could scale down. I paid for the first billboard along with Metro Boomin, Sonny Digital, and Southside, but even if I don't get enough money, I'm running this idea regardless. I don't care how it happens, if it doesn't get funded, this is an idea I feel so strongly about that it's going to get done." As of yesterday, Cam Kirk reached his $6000 goal.

It shouldn't come as a surprise to anyone that's familiar with Cam that his vision doesn't fall into the traditional. His way of thinking isn't conventional, which is why you never quite know what to expect from him. Last year's Trap God exhibit is a great example of how his mind works. He took an abandoned church and turned it into a gallery space — no, he turned it into a sanctuary that paid homage to Gucci Mane. Not only did he create an art-viewing space that correlated with the very essence of his subject, he delivered an unforgettable experience for those that came in attendance. What I found surprising was that the original idea wasn't to create a "trap house" atmosphere, but have it at an actual trap house. An idea that came to him while discussing his plans for the exhibit: instead of bringing the trap to a gallery, he wanted to bring the gallery into the trap. "A week before announcing the exhibit, the trap house we decided on in East Atlanta got raided. The police destroyed the whole crib," says Cam. "Soon as that happened, I didn't know how I would make it work." Luckily, he stumbled upon an abandoned church and made the interactive photo exhibition work. He turned a church into the kind of trap house Frank Lucas would applaud — a perfect home to showcase unseen portraits of Atlanta's most renowned trap deity.

All of this didn't happen overnight. It took many, many years for Cam to reach the point in his career for gallery exhibitions, world tours, and becoming a renowned name in the music industry. His story really begins with the decision to come to Atlanta from Maryland to escape the boring cycle of a predestined life: getting a government job, shopping at the local Saint Charles Mall, and finding the love of your life at Love Nightclub. Coming to Atlanta was a decision to change who he was and who he feared of becoming: no family, no friends, just an acceptance letter to Atlanta's prestigious Morehouse College.

During his summer visit to the college, there was something about the city that filled him with a sense of home (the girls from Spelman tend to have this effect on visitors). Cam chose Morehouse over the University of Maryland, but there was a catch. "The only way I could convince my parents to attend Morehouse is to tell them I wanted to be a doctor. Morehouse graduates the most blacks in medical school," Cam explains. "The plan wasn't to deceive them, but I [ended] up changing my major to Marketing after first semester. That was a big deal. They wanted me to come back... but I was determined to stay in Atlanta, so we worked out an ultimatum where I would take out student loans to help pay for the out-of-state fees."

So how does a shy, out-of-towner break into Atlanta's tight-knit music community? The answer is fairly simple. During his junior year of college, Cam booked Wiz Khalifa to perform in Atlanta during the 2010 Deal Or No Deal Tour. Originally, he contacted Wiz's manager for a possible meet-and-greet for the fashion organization Cam started at Morehouse, and it just so happened that Wiz was on a big countrywide tour with no dates in Atlanta. He was given an offer he couldn't refuse: "49 cities [booked], but we didn't have an Atlanta show booked. Wiz was my favorite rapper, I was into Wiz, and now I have the opportunity to book him. 4500 hundred to book Wiz, so I said fuck it, I'll just throw a concert. I took out a student loan to pay for Wiz, marketing, and my roommate put in half." The show was a sold-out success and on the flyer was the first time Cameron Kirkland used the name "Cam Kirk," a name a college friend always called him. He says, "It kind of just stuck with me." It was a night to remember — his favorite rapper, a sold-out show. It was only natural to immortalize the night with a photo — except Cam didn't have a camera. That moment inspired him to purchase his first.

The Wiz show and buying a camera were the two dominoes that fell and set off a life-changing chain reaction. He was recognized on campus as someone who was doing things, making moves. That kind of attention attracts others like moths to light bulbs. Outside circles started to embrace him. His next big opportunity was to shoot a day-in-the-life of ScHoolboy Q for his first headlining show in Atlanta. Even though he never shot anything like it before, Cam tackled the job. The next day, he was asked about following Estelle while she was in the city. On the last day with Estelle, he met Young Jeezy in the studio. Liking the vibe of Cam and the camera crew, Jeezy invited them to film him for All-Star Weekend. He went from filming no celebrities to filming 3 within 3 days. He wasn't a professional, he wasn't an expert; he was literally learning as he went along, but with enough bravery to try. That's what kept doors swinging open for him. "I chalk a lot of it up to me being a little more free-spirited than a lot of people. It goes back to my personality. I'm not a very stressful person, I move with the wind, I adapt to my environment. You get presented opportunities to do things outside your element. I've been able to adapt to situations and fit into situations."

Each job led to another job, each relationship led to another relationship, and shooting one rapper always led to another. Adapting, improving, and evolving — the grind made him better every step of the way. Cam turned his passion into a career behind the camera, capturing some of Atlanta's newest stars and some of hip-hop's brightest up-and-comers for a living. "I moved to Atlanta to change my life. Just to get away from the cycle. My father was in the military. My entire family works — no entrepreneurs, no one living off being creative. Atlanta made me… I say it, Maryland raised me, Atlanta made me. Every part of me, every aspect of me. I'm not the same person. My parents don't recognize me. I'm not the same. Atlanta is 100% of me. I still have D.C. pride, but I'm almost from Atlanta. It's that much of a home to me."

The Day 4 project represents home for Cam. It glorifies Atlanta's rap scene and the artists that fuel its music. Rappers are up there with our athletes as symbols of the city. Fitting, as it is that combination of place and culture that has changed Cam's life.

The Death of America's Most Dangerous Rappers: The Mainstream and What Happens to Rappers When They Become Safe

"I'm a rapper. And I am a gangsta. And I do what I want." Lil Wayne told that to Katie Couric in 2009, the footage would later be played during a CBS special for the GRAMMYs. Even with a nationwide smash single, this interview was the one that put a face to the voice for a lot of mainstream America. The man who had kids everywhere singing about lollipops spoke with the crude and outspoken tongue of a poetic sailor and the attitude of an outlaw and had more ink on his body than a Hell's Angel. That same year Wayne raised eyebrows for what was hidden in the secretive double cup and plead guilty to gun possession for a incident that occurred in 2007. Wayne was by all means famous, popular but with enough edge to make him seem a bit dangerous. To the outside world that viewed rap music from afar, he indeed appeared to be a gangster that did whatever he pleased.

As Couric later said, she was nervous about interviewing him. Wayne was the perfect cross between rap and rock star — the problems with drugs, a rebellious streak and a complete disdain for rules and authority. He was not the next mainstream darling but a rapper with two middle fingers and a million dollar smile sitting on a bank account fattened by teenagers eager to play music their parents didn't approve of.

Hip hop is an art form constantly under scrutiny. Mistakes can be dire; the wrong lyrics can disband brands and hurt the pockets

197

of rappers. Reebok swiftly cut ties with Rick Ross when unsolicited mollies started appearing in champagne glasses. Mountain Dew couldn't run fast enough from Tyler, The Creator when links were publicly made between his commercial and domestic violence. Public outrage doesn't allow for conversation, the people want action, a phenomenon Ludacris felt back in 2002 when Bill O'Reilly brought an end to his position as spokesman for Pepsi. He demanded that America boycott Pepsi while painting Luda as a terror who, "Degrades women, encourages substance abuse and does all things that particularly hurt the poor in society." Apparently raunchy rap lyrics are worse for kids' minds than sugary soda is for young obese bodies. Ludacris wasn't a menace to society, more like the crude uncle that slipped you booty magazines and told dirty jokes, but all it took was one man with a platform to tell the world he was ruining children for the big bosses to severe ties.

"However, Ludacris, like a cursing Pied Piper, can lead children into a lifestyle of defiance and destruction that could ruin them for many years — perhaps forever. And like the decadent mercenary he is, he'll laugh all the way to the bank doing it" - Bill O'Reilly

Fear brings discomfort, misunderstanding, angst and panic. Fear is what keeps many rappers from swimming in the mainstream. The right image could be the difference between boycotts and endorsement deals, the wrong image could forever sever ties with corporate America. Even an innocent snowman can be corrupted when aligned with a rap artist. With his snowman t-shirt, Young Jeezy had school systems across the country in a frenzy over a snowman with an attitude. Once parents learned of the tie to cocaine, he was the new public enemy number one. *USA Today* published an article about the shirt's nefarious ways,[36] and anti-drug organization National Families In Action considered it a "phenomena in which parents have no idea what their children are exposed to. There is a code that children are aware of but not parents." A wholesaler acknowledged that despite the controversy, the product was one of his biggest sellers across the country. Hated by parents, loved by the kids and the streets, Jeezy gained worldwide attention for having an incredible debut album and making Frosty frown. Now too dangerous for global brands, Jeezy would have to turn to his own corporate thuggin for his income.

Ice-T knows something about how controversy can be turned into profit. He put the fear of a revolutionary into the heart of the American government with his song, "Cop Killer." In 1992, Ice-T and his rock band Body Count put out their self-titled album right before the L.A. riots, his gritty, graphic protest song escalated in the aftermath. But Ice-T and his then-label, Warner Bros., came under fire from critics, the police, and even President George H.W. Bush and Vice President Dan Quayle chimed in with their distaste for the record and its message. This was no social media backlash — concerts were boycotted, death threats were made, local police in North Carolina threatened retail stores that their emergency calls would go unanswered if the *Body Count* album stayed on the shelves. With lyrics like, "I'm 'bout to bust some shots off, I'm 'bout to dust some cops off," it was bound to attract eyes from the biggest of bosses. While some argued that The First Amendment gave him freedom of speech and that the real issue was police brutality, those voices were the minority. Warner Bros. was accused of using the controversy to sell more records, and it was true that every protest only drew another curious ear to the album.

Sales of Ice-T's *Body Count* album surged dramatically last week in Texas and Southern California after law enforcement agencies and political candidates in those areas called for a ban of the rapper's controversial "Cop Killer" song. Ice-T's sales jumped an estimated 60% in Los Angeles, where Councilwoman Joan Milke Flores and the Los Angeles Police Protective League had urged Time Warner, the distributor, to stop selling the album. "We completely sold out of 'Body Count' this week," said Darrin

Mercado, store manager of Crain's Records on Pico Boulevard in Los Angeles. "I think the controversy over the album is really stirring things up. After all, the album has been out for a couple of months. Now, all of a sudden, everybody's asking for it."[37]

Looking back, it's incredible that Ice was able to transition from pointing blame at the badge to wearing one on television. It wasn't simply an event you could sweep under a rug, this man set the world on fire and thanks to the passage of time was able to escape with only a few bruises. Ice-T never lost a step, he just grew older, less controversial and was able to maneuver through the entertainment industry as if the government didn't once have him on their shit list.

Ice Cube is another rapper whose disruptive and daring days came at the beginning of his career. He was a strong, outspoken black man that was relentless on the microphone. There was no filter, no sugarcoating, no compromising, he rapped about race, his surroundings, and the world from the pit of his fiery gut and didn't care who felt offended. N.W.A.'s "Fuck The Police" came before Ice T's "Cop Killer" and received attention from the FBI. That was just the beginning of Ice Cube pushing buttons and stirring things up. Famously, when N.W.A. decided to play "Fuck the Police" despite the police's demands that it get left off their set list, "police rushed the stage and the group fled."

Cube's no holds barred approach came with it's own controversy. After the release of his album *Death Certificate*, any images of Ice Cube were banned from the state of Oregon. He was illegal in all retail stores, even the St. Ides Malt Liquor that he was endorsing. There was more to Cube than just being a rapper, other passions were pursued, and now there's an entire generation that will know the movie *Are We There Yet* before *Death Certificate*. He got older, less resistant to accommodation and was embraced by those in the mainstream. There's no way "No Vaseline" and *Ride Along* could come out during the same year but that doesn't discredit who he is. We can appreciate both sides of Ice Cube because they both are necessary as examples of how far hip hop can take you even when you don't play by their rules.

Once rappers are seen as safe, when they stop being "gangsters that do whatever they want," that's when they're embraced. It took Wayne seven years after his interview with Katie Couric to be featured in a Super Bowl commercial. It was the biggest night in advertisement, the deepest depths of the mainstream, and Lil Wayne was seen alongside George Washington in a scene for Apartments.com joking about The Jeffersons and apple pie.

He is no longer the rapper that spent a year at Rikers for gun possession or defending the substance in his styrofoam cup. When the big suits who only care about making money and protecting endorsements bring your name up in meetings and it doesn't leave the room in a state of awkward discomfort, you've made it. You have officially entered the safe zone.

It wasn't until 2011 that Eminem appeared in a commercial that played during the Super Bowl. 15 years ago, every time he opened his mouth there was outrage. He was foul-mouthed, graphic, and unapologetic. A bigger target than Jeezy's snowman. Now the world is accustomed to his offensive humor. There's very little about Eminem that is shocking now. In America's eyes he's about as dangerous as a can of Lipton ice tea.

The only other notable rapper that made an appearance in a Super Bowl commercial was Drake. Drake doesn't have a terrifying bone in his body, he embodies squeaky clean, the kale of rap. Even when he's in a heated "beef" he can release a diss song where profanity is scarce and hits on radio. If his career continues at this pace he will surely be performing "Hotline Bling" during Super Bowl 58. Pay attention to the ad, he teams up with T-Mobile to shoot a video for ""Hotline Bling." The company comes with changes, they practically butcher the entire song and Drake agrees willingly to do whatever will make them happy. He's the ideal rapper, the kind that will bow to their every whim, placing the company's vision over his artistic integrity. Popular with kids but safe enough to make the face of your product, he's the rapper of their dreams.

To gain entrance into the deepest depths of the mainstream media you have to be a rapper that simultaneously appeals to the young and be innocent enough to be tolerated by the old. By being endorsed by a company that's willing to pay millions to be viewed during the Super Bowl, Wayne has somehow joined the rankings of rappers who white people don't find frightening. In an age where album sales are down and label deals are worth less and less, endorsement deals are major for artists trying to do more than survive in this music industry. If Future and The Weeknd can team up with Apple after singing about their drugs for the last few years, there are opportunities that are possible without being Danny Tanner, but tellingly the only destruction Future and Abel have wrought is on themselves. You don't see them arrested, they don't make headlines for outrageous statements, despite their vices, they're thoroughly Apple-able.

With all the strides that hip hop has made in the last decade, it's still fighting some of the same battles to be accepted as an art form. There's still a big part of America that wouldn't be able to stomach Kendrick Lamar performing "Alright" even though he's one of the biggest artists of our age. Tyler, The Creator is being banned from entire countries for lyrics he rapped almost five years ago. There's always going to be a Bill O'Reilly, Tipper Gore, or someone who has a knee-jerk fear reaction when thinking of rappers. That's why we need balance — let Drake be Nelly if Kendrick can bare the weight of being Ice Cube. The mainstream isn't for everyone to swim in, some voices don't need that stage to reach the ears that need to hear them.

It's all about progress. The old become the landmarks for how far the culture has gone and the new arrive, ready to be adored by children who will hopefully grow into adults that won't be such pricks.

The Notorious B.I.G.,
Tupac Shakur,
and The Dark Side of Immortality

Suge Knight's black '96 BMW 750iL was nothing more than a luxury vehicle before the night of September 7, 1996. When the clock struck the hour of 11:15 p.m., the beautiful piece of man-made machinery was impaled by 14 scorching bullets from a late-model Cadillac. Four bullets traveled through the car and pierced the chest, arm and thigh of Tupac Shakur.

Imagine his blood pouring through the wounds, staining the passenger seat in crimson red. Imagine the screams of pain as his life began to flash before his eyes. Tupac may have died in the hospital six days later, but his murder took place in the BMW; the car is no longer a luxury vehicle, but a reminder of death on wheels.

Biggie Smalls sat in the passenger seat of a GMC Suburban believing he would be returning to his hotel room momentarily. He sat comfortably in the SUV, envisioning March 9th as just another night. Sadly, it would be the last night of his life. He didn't foresee the Chevrolet Impala SS sending five bullets into the Suburban's passenger side. Four of the bullets went on to strike his forearm, back, thigh and hip. From relaxing to facing death, from thoughts of home to meeting his maker, the vehicle is no longer a comfortable SUV but a reminder of a murder.

The fatal drive-by that took the life of Biggie happened just six months after Tupac's murder — both rappers shot four times, both rappers assassinated in cars.

To leave behind a legacy of art that continues living beyond your dying breath is the highest honor an artist can achieve, but we don't hear the voices of ghosts. This is the dark side of having a presence in the present without being here in the flesh, the artist risks becoming more merchandise than man. Immortality isn't meant to be exploited, but time and time again the dead are resurrected for profit.

It's been reported Suge's BMW is currently being auctioned away on Moments In Time for $1.5 million. The car has been restored back to its former glory and has had multiple owners throughout the years, but this is the first time it's being billed as "Tupac's Car — An Extraordinary Relic." This is selling one of the most gruesome items in Pac's legacy, a way of acquiring money for a dated item through his name, life, and death.

By some strange twist of fate, the GMC Suburban that Biggie was shot in has also been uploaded to Moments In Time for the same exact dollar amount. The current owners bought the vehicle in October of '97, they were simply in search of a bigger form of transportation for their family. The family claims they didn't know the vehicle's history until an L.A. detective reached out to them in 2005, explaining that the car was needed for trial. Knowing the SUV's history, they kept the car, but have now decided it's the perfect time to sell after 20 years of ownership. The owners are asking for a little over a million but also requested that the LAPD return the bullet-ridden doors that were removed while the case wasn't cold. I don't fault them for buying a vehicle and being unaware of the history, but I'm sickened by their desire to exploit Biggie's murder for money. Not only are they selling the car, but to sweeten the deal, they are offering the actual doors that the bullets went through before eating at his flesh like murderous ticks. Such an eerie object. Selling authenticity without considering that those bullet holes are from an assassination.

Real blood was spilled in these cars. Two men were gunned down, their lives taken, but now their names are simply used to sell a product that isn't worth the price tag. What is the value of these dated vehicles if you remove the names Tupac Shakur and

Biggie Smalls? Sadly, everything they touched while alive has worth now that they are dead. There should be a museum for these extraordinary relics; instead, everything is sold to the highest bidder. Their lives and legacies are to be sold, not cherished and treasured.

Look at how their old, unreleased music is still being packaged and sold to the public 20 years after being taken from this Earth. Is it not strange for Faith Evans to have a collaboration album with Biggie in 2016, especially one that packs in 25 tracks? To sell it as a collaboration with a soul who isn't here to collaborate? How thin is the line between homage and manipulation?

Can we champion the dead without turning them into marketing schemes and profitable puppets? It starts with posthumous albums and then it becomes holograms performing at festivals. I still cringe thinking back to seeing Tupac on stage, no longer with us, but rapping along to the Coachella crowd. I watched disgusted as Michael Jackson moonwalked across the stage at the 2014 Billboard Music Awards while his body was still resting below the earth. I understand fans want a second chance to witness their greatness, especially the many of us who couldn't fully appreciate them until after their passing, but holograms seem like a cheap, tacky experience compared to the real thing. Holograms are just another form of controlling the artist's legacy—exploitation of our beloved legends.

Celebrity culture has already created an exaggerated admiration for the famous, but it's amplified when it comes to those who are no longer with us. It's bad enough that you lose your life, but imagine watching from above or below as your art is used in ways you never wanted or imagined.

Someone is going to pay top dollar for both the BMW and the SUV. Someone is going to sit in the seat that Tupac sat in, and someone is going to recline where Biggie's body once rested, and they won't see it as strange or twisted. The items have been sensationalized, our immortals have become trophies, and it'll continue to happen in a world infatuated with the famous — alive and dead.

What's happening to Biggie and Tupac isn't new, I'm certain there are deceased rock stars, blues artists, and country singers who turn over every time an item of theirs is sold for top dollar. Prince will soon be greeted by a similar fate, beginning his transition from myth to dead man oversold to the public.

Art should be able to live beyond our time, especially when art has the power of influence that can impact the future. But the artist should be respected in death, able to rest in peace without becoming a commercialized object of affection. Admiration isn't evil, but it can affect how our eyes perceive people. I see the importance of having a will to protect your estate, but a will doesn't stop the next owner of the car you died in from trying to become a millionaire off of your name.

The sad truth is, artists are worth more dead than alive because of what they become. More than just an artist, but a relic without the protection of a museum; a memento people want as a souvenir. Death will immortalize an artist, but in death, they lose control of their art, their name, and their likeness.

Notes & References

36 AP, "Popular snowman T-shirt raises concerns," USA Today (November 5, 2005) http://usatoday30.usatoday.com/news/nation/2005-11-05-snowman-tshirt_x.htm.
37 Philips, Chuck, "'Cop Killer' Controversy Spurs Ice-T Album Sales," L.A. Times (June 18, 1992) http://articles.latimes.com/1992-06-18/entertainment/ca-913_1_cop-killer.

Part 6
ARTIST PROFILES

GoldLink in the Trenches:
The Complete Story Behind
GoldLink's *At What Cost*

People are dancing to my pain and they don't even know it. They get to dance and have fun while I'm still telling this story about how real...hectic [stuff] gets. —Goldlink[38]

On March 9th, GoldLink released "Meditation," the second single from his then-forthcoming album, *At What Cost*. The synths vibrate with the calming warmth of a baby's giggle, accompanied by sparse, tropical drums that swing with an infectious spirit. It's the kind of production that kindly asks your foot to tap, your legs to kick, your hips to wiggle, and by the time GoldLink arrives with his smooth, yet bouncy flow, it's hard to not slowly drift into a state of insouciance. The addition of Jazmine Sullivan's voice only adds to the elegance and soul of "Meditation"; "Shake, shake, shake the nerves off, in the name of dancehall shake the nerves off," she sweetly asks, a request that is hard to deny once the synths fade and the jaunty percussion possesses the body. You are in the moment, you are in the party, but it's only for a brief second. The beat slowly fades, voices are heard and, unexpectedly, the sound of gunfire erupts.

I ask GoldLink during our phone call how the song goes from a good time to such an escalation of violence. He pauses for only a moment before calmly responding, "It happens every weekend."

The night of the release for "Meditations," GoldLink had a club appearance at Rosebar in his hometown of Washington, DC. Nothing too special, another night with his friends, another night in his life. But the arrival of someone that was on bad terms with one of his friends brought tension in a realm of celebration. It didn't take long before a fight erupted, an inevitable clash. Just like on "Meditation," a night of fun swiftly turned into something more aggressive, life imitating art, or better yet, art captured by life. No shots were fired that night, but before he could enter the fray, GoldLink recalled, "A girl grabs me. She's in my ear saying, 'You have so much to live for. Look at your life, look at all these things, don't throw all this away for these niggas.' I don't know who she is, and she's holding me around my waist."

GoldLink, born D'Anthony Carlos, is a relatively famous rapper who is becoming bigger by the second. When he speaks, the way his words are pronounced and the heavy accent give away where he's from. Since the release of his 2014 debut mixtape, *The God Complex*, his "future bounce" signature sound has amassed a wildfire following that is only burning brighter by the day. "Crew," the lead single from *At What Cost*, recently crossed the 1-million-view threshold on YouTube. In April, GoldLink will be the first-ever rapper from DC to perform at Coachella, a huge win for him and his city.

The woman who held him that night was right, his future is too bright to be thrown away in a brawl, but that's the risk of being home: so many promising young kings fall at home before their castle can be fully built. Your status may change, but if your environment is a jungle, you'll always have lions, tigers, and bears baring their fangs. GoldLink's case is different, though. Home isn't just where his heart is, home is where a hero is needed, one that the people can see. The fight was just another slice of home, but the girl was another reminder of how much his city loves him. The love outweighs the hate.

"I didn't realize how much it meant to people until I was home more. Just walking around people will say, 'Why are you here!?' Surprised, but they respect that I live here. A nigga that sees me walking around all the time will stop me and tell me how much respect he has that I didn't leave and to keep going. Every time I go out someone is telling me something encouraging. The city needs a nigga they can see, a nigga that they can feel. They need to be able to look him in the eyes and see if that's who they want to represent them. Huey Newton was for the people by the people, that's how DC is. I gotta be at the go-gos, I gotta show my face, I gotta be in the hood — I have to." - GoldLink

Respect is important to GoldLink, seeing respect from those in the city that raised him is meaningful. His father is the one who advised him early on that when things started to get bigger, his home should be his return destination. LA was encouraged, an attempt to push him to the plastic wonderland that all rappers are sent to when it feels as if their time is coming. GoldLink resisted, fighting to make home the setting for his inspiration, and that became the backdrop for *At What Cost*.

Ciscero, a Maryland native, friend and frequent collaborator, said it best, "I get [that with] the internet, you can represent from a million miles away, but at the same time, you got to bask in the everyday life of it to really exude it. You are influenced by what you're constantly around"—a statement that reminded me of Future's account of living in LA with his then-fiancé Ciara. It was the era of his *Honest* album, and while some will vouch for Future's sophomore effort, calling it underrated, there are hardcore fans that look back on that album in disgust. It wasn't until Future returned to Atlanta, returned to the trenches, was he able to pull out his legendary mixtape trifecta: *Monster, Beast Mode, 56 Nights*. He found himself back at home and reemerged as a codeine-drenched phoenix.

"My personal thing was [that] I didn't know what I was doing until this album. GoldLink was just an enigma, just a nigga. Who am I really? I went back home, like where I was born and raised. I started remembering. I started reminiscing. Being in them trenches and understanding myself through all these people, through this city, it made me realize who I am. When I do music, I get immersed in it. If I was a journalist, if I was writing about animals in Africa, I would go to Africa and live. Live with zebras and shits. I came home. I stayed home. I got deep. I made sure. Niggas around me wanted me to go to LA, I wasn't going nowhere. There would be no album if I did." - GoldLink

Self-discovery and home came at once, and it's only natural that *At What Cost* would slowly morph into a project reflective of his environment. When you press play on the album, you hear of places in DC, you hear the language of DC, the swag of DC, the attitude of DC and the heartbeat of his city. Regional rap isn't dead, GoldLink is making sure DC is represented like how artists put on for Atlanta, New York and LA.

Obii Say, a fellow DC rapper, collaborator, and executive producer on *At What Cost*, explained all the intricate transitions that play a part in the album's pacing. "The transitions capture the spontaneity, the unpredictable pattern of DC," he points out. "Go-go is one aspect, significant because it's spontaneous. We wanted to translate that energy, capture the city's elements. Different aspects, different parts for people who are from here and for people who aren't. DC is best understood through experience, but the next best thing is to relate."

The abrupt, impromptu shifts happen swiftly and suddenly. The gunshots that happen on "Meditation," the stuttering self-destruction that plays out at the end of "Have You Seen That Girl," a vigorously vicious freestyle is interrupted by a soulful choir singing of heartless triggers, each of these moments are like lightning striking on a cloudless day, but each one is meant to evoke how calm can turn to chaos in the blink of an eye. The first listen is like boarding a roller coaster blindfolded, you don't see the loops coming but you feel each one — the thrill of not knowing when your world will be turned upside down.

Tone and atmosphere were a huge focus in making *At What Cost* feel alive. The album is meant to transport listeners into a storyline that's more broad than linear, but which can easily be followed. The "Opening Credits" sound like a sample from a movie clip, a haunting premonition of what's to come. Every song has significance, but one of the most notable to the story is the KAYTRANADA-produced "Hands On Your Knees." The beat is mesmerizing but there's no rapping, GoldLink is only mentioned in the narration of Kokayi, an OG DC sage who emulates the lead mic at a go-go show. Kokayi playing the lead mic and interacting with the crowd is reminiscent of stepping into any club, but this is a DC club.

The album's main character found a girl he's infatuated with on "Have You Seen That Girl?" but the problem is that she's from the opposite side of town, Obii confessed that in DC, "You need to worry about what street you're on more than what color you're wearing." That's why the first question GoldLink asks the woman he's pursuing is, "Shorty, where you from? Where your momma stay." Each song is a rising action to the shooting that occurs on "Meditation," a brewing beef between two sides over a woman, a modern day version of the Capulets and Montagues.

"We were thinking about the DMV as a whole, we were thinking about the history of DC music, it was almost like we strapped ourselves inside a time machine and transported ourselves back in the day to do some serious soul searching and some serious historical digging," says April George, Virgina—native, friend and frequent collaborator. "The greatest records are the ones that tell a story. Music that transports you to a place, it takes you away from whatever's going in your present, actual reality. That's why this project has so many analog notes to it, why it sounds so dusty. It sounds like a memory, because that's what we were trying to emulate, what [GoldLink] was trying to get across. Trying to transport you somewhere. Even if you aren't from here, it will conjure up something. That's why 'Hands On Your Knees' is so important to the storyline, it's the beginning of a memory and it takes you from there."

"Essence" is a word that recurred in all my conversations about the album. Both Link and Ciscero stressed that the goal was not to make a go-go album but to capture the essence of the go-go they grew up on. Instead of just acquiring the sound, the instruments and the BPM, the vision was also to capture a feeling of going to a go-go — the fun and joy, along with the dread and darkness. The original go-go bands sprung into the DC area in the mid-'60s to late '70s, a style of music that never peaked in the mainstream but has evolved and is still relevant to DMV residents.

The violence that came along with go-go juxtaposed with the beauty of people coming together to celebrate the music they created was thrilling, but it turned problematic with city officials. Go-gos were deemed unpredictable; a place where you could go to hang with the homies, but it was uncertain how each night would turn out. While the community loved the culture, clubs were being shut down and would refuse to allow go-go bands to perform.

"I became so afraid of death that I'm no longer afraid of it."

"When they said, 'R.I.P. Lukey Luke on the mic' — there's a video on YouTube — everybody started jumping, losing their minds," Link reminisced, talking about how a young man hit by a car was celebrated by throwing a go-go in his honor. "They're celebrating this dude's death because that's what they think he would want them to do. So there's a positive aspect to it and a negative aspect to it. I wanted to blend both of them. That's why 'Meditation' is so light and so fun but ends so fucked up."

He also recalled how the stabbing of a 17-year-old boy was the last straw for his era of go-go (surprisingly, something similar happened in 1987). The city implemented a ban that took away a piece of the city's culture. It was like taking away their identity in their own backyard.

"There's a thing called go-go parking here, it's really just when you back into a space. We call it go-go parking because you can never go to a go-go or a party in DC — in the DMV — and not reverse your car. At the let out, if some shots rang out, you need to get the fuck out of there quick as possible. So if you're stuck with all the other cars and your car is facing the wall you might not get out. It became a term." - Kazz (GoldLink management)

What happens when a piece of beautiful culture and community is also the cause of death and dread? "As an area, we suffer from a form of PTSD from that era alone. That's where the darkness comes from," Link states, referring to some of the darker undertones that can be heard on the album. Along with a case of PTSD, Link is coming to terms with the fact that he's been dealing with a mountain survivor's guilt. For most of our conversation, his voice is calm, but there was a lot of weight attached to his words when he confesses, "I lost a lot of niggas, and I'm way too young to say that," adding, "I lost a lot of good people. You don't know how many niggas died just making this album. Niggas die so much around here we can't be afraid of that motherfucker no more. I became so afraid of death that I'm no longer afraid of it." Eerie, yet profound, his views of death can only come by way of too many funerals for men and women who were too young to go.

"Do you know what happens in the summertime?" Obii asked me during our conversation. "It's the most beautiful time of the year, and the rise of shootings and murders." As his words cut through me, I couldn't help but think of Chicago, New York and all the other cities that get hot as soon as summer arrives. "It starts early," he said, "So early that you don't know what happens." Over 600 miles away in Atlanta, I could feel death in the air.

You can't have the light without the darkness, which is why *At What Cost* doesn't pick a side. It gives listeners a dose of feeling the most alive and the feeling that life can be taken away at any moment.

216

There's a line on "Crew" that I only recently caught, one that's far darker than the song: "Niggas got killed for the boy living dreams in the hills." This is his lead single, one of the more radio-friendly songs on the album. He doesn't dive in too deep, but if DC is a *m.A.A.d city,* GoldLink wasn't a good kid — he's a troublemaker who was once more Vince Staples than Kendrick Lamar. *At What Cost* reminds me of Vince's *Summertime '06,* both albums are glimpses into the dark sides of two artists who escaped from the madness but haven't entirely left it behind them.

"That's supposed to be the devil talking to me."

There's an internal struggle Link is still coming to terms with on this album, regarding how he went from bullshitting around the city to attending pep rallies because kids at the school wanted him in attendance; being embraced in places where he was once kicked out of, and receiving blessings while seeing the ghosts of all the friends who didn't make it here to stand alongside him.

A slice of GoldLink's past can be heard on "The Parable of the Rich Man." I originally confused the woman's voice for a girl, and he candidly corrected my mistake. "These are real stories. That's not a female, that's supposed to be the devil talking to me." This is his version of DMX's "Damien," or better yet, Kendrick Lamar's Lucy on "For Sale?" For all the times he's escaped death, for every time he's dodged a bullet, for every time he survived when there was no way to survive, she claims to be the reason and now she wants him to pay.

"One of my favorite albums is Snoop Dogg's Doggystyle. That "G-Funk Intro" started out with The Lady Of Rage. Everybody but Snoop Dogg started that album and it sets the tone for the album. When Ciscero was like, "I show these niggas what I'm worth every day, I thank Jesus 'cause he keeps me blessed man, niggas get murked every day,' that shit sets the whole mood for the entire album." - GoldLink

The heaviness of confronting the melancholy side of DC life doesn't drown the songs in sorrow, it's actually the DC guest features that assist in keeping the album bright and full of soul. This communion of artists connects with go-go's idea of people coming together to celebrate black music. Kokayi is a highlight, without spitting a bar he is a shining example of all the club DJs who make you feel like you're in the liveliest of parties.

Wale, another DC OG, floats on the springy "Summatime." He's still the slick wordsmith who will find a way to intertwine references of Prince and Cinderella. Link admitted that he wasn't aware of Brent Faiyaz prior to "Crew," but the fact that he was from back home was reason enough to gamble on his voice—a gamble that paid off. I'm still in awe that Link was able to find Mya, but the famous DC native also delivered. Jefe (formerly Shy Glizzy), Ciscero, Lil Dude, and April George all hail from the DMV and all appear on *At What Cost*.

The only features that aren't homegrown are Steve Lacey (of The Internet) and Jazmine Sullivan — both who delivered noteworthy performances. There's also the little nuances, all the streets, buildings, parks and slang used. The music video for "Crews" takes place not far from Link's father's house, and those that know the area will appreciate the significance of its appearance. Even a title like "Kokamoe Freestyle" has DC relevance, paying homage and immortalizing the Southeast freestyle legend. *At What Cost* is truly an album made at home, by those at home, that just happens to reach ears beyond the DC limits.

"[My manager] Henny linked [Brent Faiyaz and I]. Told me he was from the DMV and could sing, all I needed to hear was DMV, I'll give him a chance. We end up going to the session, I played him the 'Crew' jont and this other one that Craig David wants. We did both them jonts, we were just playing around. Really random. He's vicious. Before Mya, we was looking at Amerie, and she was definitely down and then Mya came and we were sold. I had crushes on Mya and Amerie, those two were my girlfriends [laughs]. Lowkey, we didn't try to only get DMV features and then it kind of happened. The Mya thing, we needed a girl from back home, but everyone else naturally happened." - GoldLink

After the pictures with André 3000 surfaced, there was speculation that the elusive OutKast member would be appearing on the album. When asked about Dré, Link said honestly, "Fuck a verse, the fact he gave me his time is a blessing. I just appreciate that shit so much." I got a bit more out of Obii, who went with Link to New York and was in the studio that night. "It was surreal," he recalls. "[André] showed up, kicked it, and laughed with us. He gave us advice on maintaining and longevity. [It was] one of the most enlightening experiences. The whole time I kept thinking, 'If I suddenly wake up from this dream, I'm going to be hot.'"

"The original song that was supposed to be 'Herside Story' was actually a KAYTRANADA beat that was called 'Big Pimpin Video Vibes,' but I couldn't get it. His brother already had it. The original version of the song had a girl with a DC accent talking about, 'what the fuck you niggas got me fucked up,' like a clip of her just wilding out. The inspiration behind 'Herside' is a typical DMV girl who is mad at you so you got to talk with her. So I pull up to the Rita spot—the Rita spot is like the shit for ice cream in the DMV, like everybody go there. [It's] where the girls be at. Basically trying to get back right with your shorty." - GoldLink

Compared to GoldLink's previous projects, *At What Cost* is a conceptual body of work that doesn't give you a straightforward look at the man behind the mask, but it does give a transparent look into DC culture, and to know GoldLink is to know DC. There are a lot of different ways the album cover and title can be broken down, but I love the question that it poses: At What Cost? On the cover, he has the money, the gold, the girls and the car, but everything is burning all around him.

Speaking with Kazz, one of GoldLink's managers, he gives an interesting, abstract perspective:

"Think about the album title, 'At What Cost.' We're doing all this stuff. In a weird way, the girl dying isn't DC culture, she isn't go-go culture, but it kind of was. This is a real abstraction that I kind of pulled myself, it's like a metaphor for what we did to our own culture even though we didn't do it by ourselves. So in the story, these dudes shot somebody and they don't really care. Karma came to bite the main character in the ass, for all that this shit happened for. It all happens for this girl, she's gone at the end of it. If you look back, DC had this genre of music that was our own. We created something that only we truly understood. We killed it, we didn't kill it by ourselves, gentrification and the city officials had impact but the violence played a part. At the time we didn't see it that way, people were just going for their hoods but at the end of the day what do we have left? 'At What Cost?'" - Kazz

GoldLink discovered himself while making this project. He brought in strangers from home and close friends who lived around the block. It takes friends and family to make an authentic piece of art that's meant to represent more than yourself. *At What Cost* isn't meant to be the crown jewel of DC, but rather the beginning of genuine preservation.

"I'm a walking testimony, but then imagine if that nigga start giving?" he asks, rhetorically. "You start feeling what that nigga doing. He's not just taking from us, creating a story for us, but then he's creating opportunity for us. That's what it really is." It's not just about expanding home but bringing something back. It's about being the guiding light so that eyes outside the city can see there's culture and talent being uncovered, ignored and overlooked.

The making of this album was a meticulous process, it went through constant changes and transformation before settling on a final version. The flow is still slick enough to impress a pimp in Port Arthur, Texas, and the production has the bounce that has made each GoldLink album a fulfilling listen. He's gotten deeper into musicality and textures, but the biggest difference this time around is a focus; a desire to present a side of DC that hasn't had a chance to share its story. Not the prettiest story, not the most glamorous, but one that listeners should be able to relate to easily.

We've all been foolish for love, spent time with the crew, and had to bury friends soon. We all know about parties that turn into shootouts and the thrill of going back next week. Universal experiences delivered through a DC lens, one that truly takes you into the city where the White House stands, where go-go flourished, and where life greets death the way day greets night. By following one man's mission to get the girl, we're introduced to an area and culture that comes with the narrative.

At What Cost is fun, reflective and honest — a John Singleton coming-of-age gangster blockbuster meets Shakespearean romanticism. An album about what happens when you go back home to find the story you were always meant to tell.

It's Dark and Hell Is Hot:
A Close Look At DMX

Happily Ever After - the ending that fairy tales promised would be the reward when catastrophes are conquered, when good triumphs over evil, that once you beat the odds all would be well until the end of days. From naïve children to hardened adults we silently cling to this belief, the simple idea that if we can overcome the obstacles that lay before our path an eternal paradise awaits. Isn't that what the lottery is? A gamble for the chance to escape the gravity of financial worry and truly fly. In 1998, DMX won the lottery and flew to prosperity, becoming only the second rapper to ever net two platinum selling albums in the same calendar year. DMX had seemingly reached the promised land.

He entered the game bearing the fangs of a Cerberus with a bark from the depths of Hades, he was unlike anyone hip hop had ever heard before. Rampaging passion coated his tortured poetry, mixed with an explosive energy of pure rage that could be compared to a bull, one born seeing only red. His voice had a distinctive, intense gruff that perfectly matched the raw imagery he illustrated. He made New York into this dog-eat-dog underworld where you could live and die by your gun. It was both brutal and brilliant. X wasn't a rapper who wore a shiny suit, he came dressed for war. No one saw him arriving with such swift dominance and no one foresaw his painful fall.

Fairy tales end when the books are closed. Lottery winners are forgotten after the news reports their victory; we don't get to witness them lose all their winnings and eventually fall back to Earth. Sadly, we never stopped watching DMX, a troubled man that never could escape to paradise, a man that never received his happy ending. His path led only to more darkness, more despair and more obstacles.

My memories of Dark Man X are vague due to being so young at the time. His reign over hip hop was witnessed through the ears of a seven-year-old who couldn't help but get rowdy in car rides as "Ruff Ryders' Anthem" played. It was one of those songs Dad would cue up at the highest volume and the car would vibrate like a Nintendo 64 controller with Rumble Pak. The energy surged into my soul like a sugar rush. I didn't know what kind of shops he was opening or what shops he was shutting down, but I mouthed the words without hesitation. I would watch my little brother some years later have a similar reaction to "Party Up," he barely had a mind old enough to lose, but visions of a five-year-old acting an absolute fool in the backseat comes to mind every time the song plays.

A decade later I was 17 with a soul weighed down by my teenage doubt and stress. I was a young man drifting in this world very worried about my present and future, so I searched for music that captured the feeling of fear and failure that haunted me. Discovering "Slippin" was like being enveloped in a darkness that surpassed my own. This is where light didn't enter, what rock bottom sounds like, a voice singing from the pit of despair. There's a very real anguish that makes the song so absorbing, but what stunned me after hearing him spill so much sadness is that DMX wasn't without hope. In the chorus, he acknowledges the slip, the fall, but also that he has to get back up. It's not blind optimism because the song doesn't end with him standing on the mountain top, and it's not self-absorbed loathing for pity, but a man who knows his demons better than his angels. I return to his darkness when I need a reminder that we aren't defined by our slips or falls, but if we have the strength to get back up. Sadly, DMX has spent a lifetime slipping, falling, and searching for the strength to stand.

"See, to live is to suffer but to survive, that's to find meaning in the suffering" —DMX

Suffering is what DMX knows. It greeted him very early, as if from the womb darkness was waiting with open arms to adopt him. It followed him in his mother's home where he was introduced to poverty, torment, abuse and hunger. He was so hungry he once swallowed her perfume because it smelt good, good enough to eat. The emptiness of his stomach is what led him to the world that awaited outside. That was the beginning of his misfortune, the start of years of group homes and juvenile institutions, cold streets and stray dogs, prison cells and rap music, God and faith, alcohol and cocaine.

There was addiction, alcoholism, and violence, but very little love or compassion, until he met Tashera Simmons, but by then the trials and tribulations had turned the boy to a man. He found God and rap music while locked away but even when he started pursuing music as his priority, trouble was never far. The day before he signed to Def Jam, he was beaten nearly to death for a crime he didn't commit. Karma found the perfect day to come for all the times he did wrong. Briefly being hospitalized with a mouth wired shut didn't stop him from going to the studio where Lyor Cohen awaited. Lyor arrived as a favor to his newest Def Jam employee, Irv Gotti. Lyor swears when DMX began to rap he could hear the wires breaking in his jaw as the aggressive lines flowed from this aggressive man. He was signed on the spot.

DMX met his demons before becoming the industry's top dog. You could say they assisted in making him a successful rap star. It took seeing hell and living in that inferno to burn down booths and create the kind of music that pours out from deep within. The very flame people gravitated toward was born from what was burning him internally, he was a man on fire. The reason his music took off and so swiftly is because people either related to the world he saw — felt his passion, or were simply allured by the man. You never knew what X would say next. It didn't matter if he was lyrically holding his own with greats, describing brutal acts of violence with Damien or having a sincere moment with God, people wanted more.

It's a bit crazy thinking back on how being a dog was his brand, it would be interesting to see an artist attempt to pull that off in this meme era. The music sold and continued to sell well until his fifth album, making him the first artist to ever achieve five consecutive number one albums. If he would have retired like he planned, it would have been a flawless career in terms of number ones. Beyoncé joined him last year when her self-titled surprise album made her the first woman to achieve the five album feat.

It took 13 years for him to receive any recognition made for a sharp emcee. But it wasn't just his rapping capabilities that appealed to everyone, DMX was known for putting on a great show. Several years back, Jay Z credited X as the rapper that made him step up his performance. They co-headlined a tour together in '98/'99, and Jay humbly admits that X tore him to shreds onstage. There's a clip going around Twitter with the caption, "DMX performs for a continent." It's actually a couple of seconds from his set during Woodstock '99 but by the vastness of the crowd it looks to be a miniature country. It's insane to watch, to witness how these songs impacted such a boundless amount of people at the height of their novelty. One of the most important performances of his career can't be found online but it's mentioned in his VH1 Behind The Music. During the prayer that ended his shows sometime in '98, after the release of both his Platinum albums, he breaks down in tears and fans in the crowd begin to cry with him. Irv Gotti says that, backstage, X was on his knees crying, asking God, "Why me?" "I didn't know how to interpret the love," DMX would say. Even at his highest height, he was still low. Even with hundreds of thousands of fans, he still felt alone. You can escape your environment but you can't escape yourself.

Even after the sales began to drop, the movies tanked, and a new arrest was present with each MediaTakeOut refresh, you hoped that he would clean up his act and get himself together. He was one of a kind, the wave he brought didn't last long but it had impact, from breaking Swizz Beatz and the Ruff Ryders to the horrible but iconic movie *Belly*. Even before breaking out big, DMX was a part of some great hip hop moments. He rapped on "4, 3, 2, 1" with LL and Canibus; cyphered with Mos Def and Big Pun and predicted that he would go Platinum; and rapped alongside Jay-Z and Ja Rule as a group that crumbled before it could begin. It's easy to forget once someone fades to the back.

In an old interview that he did with Sway after the success of *…And Then There Was X*, you can tell from the conversation he was focused.[39] He had his loving family, had a new label, his career was striving, his faith was strong, he bought and was fixing up an old church in Yonkers and had big plans to build a shelter for teen mothers. Reading the transcript, you just imagine his happy ending was near, that he would continue to do great things with this gift that grew where the sun didn't shine. Fast-forward to today and X is a completely different man.

Sway: I understand that you might be building a shelter and a kitchen?

DMX: Yeah. That's the foundation. My wife is in charge of it. It's called the Mary Ella House, after my grandmother. It won't be for the homeless. It would be for teenage mothers. We'll take them in. Rather than give them a job, we will put them back in school. Give them knowledge. Get a GED, and then send them off to college. Then they'll feel a lot better about themselves. They're in there for the kids, and they'll stay there, but they have to stay in school. You leave school, you leave here. We only help those who want to help themselves. I know it's hard out there. A lot of teenage mothers, man.

"Loving you is complicated." Looking at the line, it could easily be something from one of DMX's old notebooks. Not a big surprise, Kendrick said *It's Dark And Hell Is Hot* is the album that inspired him to start rapping. They both carry a pain and guilt that can only be fully expressed on the microphone. I also believe both came to the same conclusion, that the meaning of their suffering was to voice their plight and hope it could help anyone that listens. Even knowing about Kendrick's *.good kid, m.A.A.d city*, there are very few artists that have continued to go into the bleak abyss as often as X. Maybe that's why his music has never had a successor, in this new generation of artists no one is crowned as "The new DMX." His first few years are truly something rare, I can't think of an artist that broke out as big and as fast. In this current climate, a new dog using his old tricks would likely be overlooked.

When I heard about X recently collapsing and being rushed to the hospital, I saw tweets that seemed to believe that this would be it, that he went to the edge of no return. I thought about his recent years - the Zimmerman fight; his son attempting to sell his plaques on eBay; desires to be a Pastor; all the headlines; and his scene in Chris Rock's Top 5. Unfortunate, so unfortunate. But it wasn't until I threw my headphones on and listened to the music, listened to those first four albums, that I was truly saddened. I knew if he died, then all around the world headphones everywhere would be listening to him bark once more. That's what happens when great artists die, we remember them in mourning, celebrate their classics and miss them dearly for the good times they brought. His time on top might have been over a decade ago, and he certainly hasn't been a perfect role model, but when he does leave, it's going to sting.

Frank Ocean and the Biggest Heist the Music Industry Has Ever Seen

"If your house is on fire, you need to get out of the house" —Frank Ocean

$1,000 dollars isn't enough to fund a dream in music, let alone a nice enough mattress to have dreams upon. A lack of sufficient funds didn't discourage a young Frank Ocean, though, who, at the time, was singing under his government name of Lonny Breaux. Frank decided to live the life of an artist and departed from his home in New Orleans to the unknown of Los Angeles. The demo tapes he took with him were worth more than the money in his pocket. They were the lottery tickets he gambled upon; the keys to unbolt locked industry doors. He was chasing after quality, planning on using the money for recording those demos in LA studios.

What was supposed to be a trip lasting only six weeks became a new life on the West Coast. The beauty of a dreamer is his or her ability to contain the naive innocence of children, to believe beyond the reality of logic and twist faith in their favor. The story of Lonny Breaux is the story of a dreamer.

Six weeks turned into four years before Frank Ocean (born Lonny Breaux) was able to sign a record deal, while odd jobs and songwriting allowed him to make a living. The demo tapes didn't turn him into a star, but they allowed him access to rooms where stars were already born. That's where he met Tricky Stewart, producer and A&R for Island/Def Jam. Stewart was well-known in the industry for working with songwriters like The-Dream,

Rihanna, and Justin Bieber. He was the man Lonny needed to take his career from songwriter to artist. In his 2016 interview with *Fader*, Tricky recalls how impressed he was by both Ocean's singing and songwriting; astounded to the point of wanting nothing more than to sign Breaux as an artist, a solo singer who would pen for no one else.

It was the dream come true, discovering someone who has the keys to the kingdom, not a seller of fantasy but a gatekeeper willing to let you in. Just before the wheels could turn, though, Tricky left Def Jam without getting Frank's career in motion. Frank was left on the label and left on the shelf:

"The label wasn't motivated by the signing. They didn't give him the respect that I thought he deserved. I couldn't really get Def Jam to respond to him the way that I wanted them to respond to him. At the time, with every record I was doing for Def Jam, we were on fire, whether it was Justin Bieber or Rihanna. I'd worked with The-Dream at Def Jam, and he had done extremely well, with 'Love/Hate' and 'Love vs. Money.' So I'm thinking it's going to be gravy bringing my next guy through. The truth is, if it wasn't for Chris Clancy and the Odd Future team embracing Frank, we may not even know who Frank is today. On the Def Jam side, I couldn't get nobody to pay attention to him. In that moment, we lost Frank Ocean — as a major record company, and from this industry as we knew it. When the label rebuked him and he found himself, the label lost it for everybody involved."[40]

Positions are in constant flux in the music industry. The old guard shifting can leave an artist unattended, ignored and forgotten. The door opened and closed for Frank, and he was in a contracted confinement with no assistance and no way out. Frank signed to Def Jam in 2009; the following year he connected with Tyler, The Creator and Odd Future — and everything changed.

He was older, more mature than the collective of outspoken misfits, but he found them to be what he needed. They were a source of inspiration to break the rules and continue pursuing a career in music. The group reminded him that it was possible to do it himself, bringing new life to an old goal. He changed his name from Christopher Edwin Breaux to Christopher Francis Ocean; from Lonny Breaux to Frank Ocean. He did everything the label was supposed to do. His self-sufficiency is the only reason his debut mixtape saw the light of day.

There's a great breakdown in Frank's interview with *Waxpoetics*: "I didn't want it to sound like a mixtape. It wasn't a mixtape to me; it was an album just as much as any other release was — it just wasn't in the major-label system. So I treated it like that, I A&R'd it like that, I recorded it and mixed it like that. I spent time and money on the mixes. I didn't have a lot of money to be spending racks on mixing it. So it was definitely a labor of love and passion. It just had to get done, as far as I was concerned. It was the only way that I could be heard in the way that I wanted to be heard."[41]

The drive to create was an act of defiance against the shelf as a final resting place. Frank Ocean took his destiny into his own hands and self-released *Nostalgia, Ultra* in 2011. Complex wrote an article just after the releases of *Endless* and *Blonde* which included a quote from Frank's (now deleted) Twitter account. Frank wrote the tweet after the release of Nostalgia, Ultra:

"i. did. this. not ISLAND DEF JAM. that's why you see no label logo on the artwork that I DID. guess it's my fault for trusting my dumbass lawyer and signing my career over to a failing company. fuck Def Jam & any company that goes the length of signing a kid with dreams & talent w/ no intention of following through. fuck em. now back to my day. i want some oatmeal and toast. brunch swag."

Not only was the album an internet success, Frank was able to send the biggest middle finger toward the label who left him without a rope to climb up from the abyss. The first win was executing a release underneath their nose, but the true victory would come when Def Jam came running to sign Ocean, again. Based on Tricky's 2016 testimony, three weeks after *Nostalgia's* wildfire the label would attempt to court Frank like a kid from Atlanta with the latest viral trap hit. They didn't even know about the name change and were the last label to the party; they were simply chasing after the noise, pulling out their checkbook for whoever was making all the ruckus.

I can't help but wonder if this was all a part of Frank's calculations, using their brash ignorance as leverage for more money, or more resources. He couldn't wait to publicly denounce the label, but when the option came to sign with any label, he once again chose Def Jam.

In the 2012 interview with *GQ*, Frank broke down his demand:

Frank Ocean: "Give me $1 million if you want the next album."
GQ: "Is the label more hands-on with this project? Do you still have the space to function as independently as you did with the first album?"
Frank Ocean: "I function as independently as I did — it's in better studios. My recording conditions are a little bit more posh, but it's the same. I still don't have an A&R; I'm holding all the creative control. I'm making the record that I want to make."[42]

It took Frank six years before the $1,000 he brought to LA turned into $1 million from a major label. When Lonny Breaux became Frank Ocean and decided upon a path without assistance, something more than a name changed. The very idea of a traditional career and being under the thumb of a label was thrown away. He knew what it was like to be shelved, tasted the life of an artist trapped, and also saw the power in being an artist who does it alone, independently. Def Jam was able to get *Channel Orange* in 2012, the album they paid for, but Frank Ocean didn't belong to them. Tricky said Def Jam created a monster with Frank — no, they awakened the dreamer who didn't accept the terms and conditions of a broken industry.

Four years after *Channel Orange*, the visual album *Endless* was released. A few days after that, *Blonde* was released. One album under Def Jam, one album completely independent. As with *Nostalgia, Ultra*, the internet was in a complete frenzy over the unexpected second project. I don't know how much revenue Def Jam made from *Endless*, but as it was released only as a visual and not an album that could be streamed or bought, I have to assume it was very little. *Blonde*, on the other hand, would chart at No. 1, selling 275,000 copies in its first week. It was later reported that Frank would potentially make $1 million in profit from that first week.[43] The same amount that Def Jam paid for *Channel Orange* was made back in the first 7 days of Blonde. For the second time in Frank's career, the label was left staring at a fully erect middle finger. One can draw a cool parallel to Dave Chappelle, who turned down $50 million dollars from Comedy Central to eventually make $60 million from Netflix years later on his own terms.

"'A seven-year chess game' is how he described the process of buying himself out of his contract and purchasing back all of his master recordings — using his own money, he said."[44] This quote comes from Frank's lone interview since the release of *Blonde*. If Frank truly has been planning this checkmate on Def Jam for seven years, the Ocean's 11-esque plot dates back to *Nostalgia, Ultra*. Ironically, his name change was inspired by Frank Sinatra and the Steven Soderbergh heist film. Quietly, the change of his name foreshadowed one of the biggest heists the music industry has ever seen.

During his four-year absence, Frank's time away was spent crafting all the content he released in 2016 but also allowed him four years to reset: new management, a new lawyer and a new publicist replaced his former team. If his goal was to remove Def

Jam from his pockets, it would have been counterproductive to release music for them to reap benefits, or to tour with them seeing a percentage. Like any great heist, you need the proper team to ensure the highest level of success. Frank's robbery was *Reservoir Dogs* without Mr. Orange to foil the plans.

The reason we are now seeing new music from Frank on such a regular basis is due, very simply, to his newfound artistic freedom. He stated in his *New York Times* interview that he is free from a label, free from operating through the outdated laws that have been accepted as the norm.[45] No one can voice disdain for dropping a single on Apple Music and an alternative version on SoundCloud. There's no labelhead to melt down due to a lack of promotion behind the singles; the old guard would have screamed to the heavens as "Biking" dropped while "Chanel" was still scorching the internet. In an industry going through the biggest change since Napster, Frank is able to navigate the industry's ocean without being held down by the weight of outside opinion. The independence he sought was earned, the fruits of his war are finally starting to blossom, and the popularity around his name continues to grow without sacrificing anonymity.

"After an interminable wait (in music industry standards, at least), Ocean fulfilled his contractual obligations, sources tell Billboard, and increased his potential profit share from 14 percent to 70 percent of total revenues from *Blonde* within a 24-hour period, seemingly pulling a fast one on the biggest music company in the world in the process. Def Jam and its parent Universal, stuck with an overshadowed visual album that isn't for sale, and cut out of any revenue from the "proper" album that's headed to the top of the charts on the strength of 225,000 to 250,000 equivalent album units earned in the week ending Aug. 25, were left with what amounts

to a very long music video and without one of their marquee artists." —Dan Rys[46]

The label wasn't able to claim *Blonde*. They lost an album, but more importantly, they missed out on all the content after it. Ideally, the *Blonde* rollout should still be ongoing, but the system doesn't rule everything around Ocean. He is a rule-bender, a master of his own universe, and before a second video could surface from *Blonde*, new music has been released. "Chanel," "Biking," "Lens" — fantastic, album-worthy singles with star-studded features and second volumes.

Blonded Radio is presenting new music on a medium where Frank can reach fans and still stay reclusive from the spotlight. He's able to utilize and benefit from new forms of connection without sacrificing an ounce of his mystique. Fans have access to his favorite oldies and the new school artists he's breaking through his curated playlists, a kaleidoscope of genres and eras that take new ears from OutKast to Céline Dion to Biggie to Pixies to Aphex Twin — and that's just in the first episode. When Jay-Z appeared on the show's debut episode, the surprise guest was only further incentive to tune in. Each broadcast is unlike the last; no one expected Young Thug on a remix for a song from *Endless* when Episode 005 surfaced (early on a Monday morning, of course). It was suspected that Frank had abandoned *Endless*, his final tie to Def Jam, but once again, he's thinking differently than the rest of us.

Other than Drake and Chance, no other artist has Frank's pull with Apple Music. Attention for his radio show grows by the day, his singles are taking over the internet one by one, and that's not even mentioning a potential summer smash hit ("Slide") with Calvin Harris and Migos. After taking four years off — four years of absolute silence — Frank Ocean has had a near-flawless start to 2017, and he's doing it all while playing by his own set of rules.

The story of Frank Ocean is the story of control; one man's mission to walk in the shadows and take all he lost in the light. He waged war against the labels, leaving victorious and still able to captivate the world. Instead of going the route of traditional radio, he is becoming one of the biggest winners through the digital medium. Frank rejected the rules, fought against tradition, and is taking full advantage of this hyper content age without drowning listeners with his presence. He has his masters, he's making all his money, and he isn't showing any signs of slowing down.

There's no telling what is next, and that's the beauty of independence: anything is possible. I don't even think Frank is planning a new album, not when he just escaped the album format. When Frank ceased being the starry-eyed dreamer expecting the industry to do right by him, he started living a dream few artists will ever get to see. He has done it again and again, and there's still no label on his album art.

From Boy to Beast:
How Paranoia Transformed Drake's Persona

Trust and betrayal, paranoia and skepticism, fake love and scheming peers — Drake is all too familiar with these concepts as if he was more mob boss than rapper. He believes in keeping the family close and keeping away from new friends, but these thoughts stem from the many blades being lunged into his spinal column. Think back on the confrontation with Meek Mill, how it began with a tweet exposing information that wasn't common knowledge, information sent from a former friend that took on the role of a foe. Meek wasn't a journalist who discovered a treasure chest of reference tracks, he was Nicki's boyfriend, an artist signed to Rick Ross, a frequent collaborator — but none of that mattered once he hit send.

Even if Meek was pissed at Drake, he did more than start a beef, he threw away an entire relationship. DJ Drama and Don Cannon were involved, friends who were like family to the Young Money label. Drake's beef with and victory over Meek can be likened to Caesar killing Brutus instead and surviving the Ides Of March, but what happens to Caesar after cutting down someone close who tried to bring him down?

To conquer is to risk being conquered, a risk that has constantly been a part of Drake's world since before fame. That's the significance of his mother's voicemail on *More Life*. She can hear it in his music, a change happening in her son; her sweet Aubrey went from boy to beast, a man devoured by his rise of celebrity and those conspiring to end his reign. Inside the ivory tower, King Drake is trying to protect all they want to take.

Certain rappers would call me to say 'What up, though?' / I used to brag about it to my friends / And now I'm feeling like all of these niggas cutthroat / And maybe that's all they do is just pretend / Damn, but I bought it though, I believed it —Drake, "Club Paradise" (2011)

On "Club Paradise," Drake admitted that his biggest fear was losing it all, he was coming to terms with fame and that the life he was living was more fantasy and fiction than reality. From the women to the rappers — just like Kendrick on *To Pimp A Butterfly* — he sought solace at home.

Six years later, he's still dealing with the pretending, a sign that his change in attitude is largely due to constant disappointment and paranoia. "Who's callin' my name? Who's involved now? Tell me who I gotta down, I'll do a song now," he raps on "Can't Have Everything," a song that howls of a rapper who is prepared to take the heads of any adversary.

On "Do Not Disturb," the final track on More Life, he confesses his inability to sleep knowing the risk of waking up to his private life being exposed to the public. I believe in this level of restlessness. What happened with Meek, Quentin Miller, and DJ Drama wasn't just rap beef, but rather being exposed by someone who was close to him, something that continues to gnaw away at him. Not only is he dealing with the woes of the music industry, the paranoia stays with him even when the music stops:

"Pistol by my bed, I'm sleep but I'm awake / For that one night when niggas try and reach inside my safe / Don't push me cause I'm way too uneasy nowadays / These guys move so greasy nowadays / I tell you my life and y'all don't believe me when I say it" — Drake, "4PM In Calabasas" (2016)

Young Thug recently released "Safe," a song stating how he spends more money on security than he makes, and what seems like a simple boast is more so transparency about a life surrounded

237

by landmines. Imagine Drake, the far bigger star, less of a thug and a larger target — there's more than one red dot on his head.

One of the most important lines regarding the change in Drake can be found near the end of "No Tellin'": "Please do not speak to me like I'm that Drake from four years ago, I'm at a higher place / Thinkin' they lions and tigers and bears, I go huntin'." The artist who is feeling uneasy about greasy guys isn't the same wordsmith that penned "Marvin's Room;" don't let the perception of his persona jade the reality of who he has become.

"How they go from not wantin' me at all / To wantin' to see me lose it all?" — Drake, "Lose You" (2017)

"I tell you my life and y'all don't believe me when I say it." It's important to highlight that last quoted bar in "4PM In Calabasas" — he makes a frank statement about the weight of his words because it's easy to dismiss such robust lyricism as tough talk and not realism. Don't see him just as Drake, but as an artist haunted by traitors, paranoid by the phony and only slipping deeper into distrust. Drake isn't a street guy, he isn't someone like 21 Savage who doesn't need assistance when it comes to street politics, but since *Take Care* he's voiced that there are people around who are prepared to come off the hip for his wellbeing — "No Long Talk" salutes enforcement like Chubbs and Baka. You can see this as tough talk or realize he's further surrounding himself with men who are about action as his star continues to rise.

Lately I just feel so out of character / The paranoia can start to turn into arrogance / Thoughts too deep to go work 'em out with a therapist —Drake, "Views" (2016)

Why would Drake, of all rappers, need this kind of protection? The answer lies in the past. In May of 2009, a 22-year-old Drake was robbed at gunpoint for $4,000 and a chain gifted by Lil Wayne. He was in Toronto on a date, a date that ended with staring down the barrel of a gun. Before *So Far Gone*, he was known more for being in a wheelchair than rapping, a grown child star and not yet a country's shining deity. The woman was unharmed, her purse unsnatched, a tiny detail that led Drake to believe he had been set up.

Drake walked away from the incident physically unscathed, but the event changed him. The good kid in a good city had encountered his own Master Splinter's daughter. You can hear it through his music how this one incident molded his mindset concerning women — like he mentions on "No Tellin'" he can't even find comfort in being invited to a hotel, feeling obligated to bring a knife with him years after the occurrence ("Yeah, she invite me to the telly, keep the blade with me / When I go to check a bitch, ain't no tellin'").

"The other day Lissa told me that she missed the old me / Which made me question when I went missing / And when I started treating my friends different / Maybe it was the fast paced switch up / Or the two guns in my face during the stick up / Maybe cause a girl I thought I trusted / Was who set the whole shit up" —Drake, "The Resistance" (2010)

Betrayed by a woman in his own city months before becoming the biggest newcomer on the blogosphere — imagine how that must affect the psyche? Set up in your beloved hometown before the claws of fame lift you into the public spotlight must blacken the soul a hue or two. This is an event that's been long forgotten but it's imperative in understanding the change in Drake's mentality. I believe the signs of paranoia started with the aptly-titled "Trust Issues." The first verse clearly states his growing mistrust of new women. He won't trust the mixing of his drink to just anyone in fear of being caught slipping, an experience he's felt before.

The second verse is a little bit more extreme and insightful into his mindstate:

"Certain people don't like me no more / New shit don't excite me no more / Guess that they don't really make them like me no more / You can look me in my eyes and see I ain't myself / Cause if y'all what I created then I hate myself / But still, let them girls in and tell 'em all / Leave their cell phones on the table where we see them" —Drake, "Trust Issues" (2011)

"Lord Knows" paints a more vivid picture of how the robbery impacted the way he moved: "And this girl right here, who knows what she knows? / So I'm going through her phone if she go to the bathroom / And her purse right there, I don't trust these hoes at all"—clearly a shining light on his nervous anxiousness. While deceitful, this is an attempt to calm an unwavering uneasiness that she might be the next one to put a knife in his back. The wound still burns, dating starts to feel like life or death even while Take Care-era Drake was considered softer than Young Thug's voice during interviews and more fragile than Iggy Azalea reading her Twitter mentions.

An old flame would bring Drake's second betrayal, Ericka Lee, the woman who is heard on "Marvin's Room." She used text messages from Drake — which reportedly read, "U basically made that song" and "It's shit without you" — against him as a way of getting co-writer credits along with other damages. She was offered a percentage of publishing but she wanted more. Ericka saw an opportunity and took it ("Ericka sued me and opened a business"). Another knife in Drake's back.

The after-effects of this incident can be found in the final verse on *Views'* "Redemption":

I'm a walkin' come-up, I'm a bank deposit / Sell my secrets and get top dollar / Sell my secrets for a Range Rover / Opportunity and temptation / They would sell my secrets for a tropical vacation / Sell my secrets back to me if I was payin' / Who's gonna save me when I need savin'?

"Redemption" represents a painful realization of who Drake is and what that means to people on the outside. Coming from a voice who constantly preaches keeping family close, to turn against a brother is a sin in the book of Drake. I believe this is what triggered his reaction to Kendrick's "Control" verse, he didn't see it as a competitive nod but another rapper he saw as a brother being disloyal. In a way, he reacted to "Control" in a similar fashion to T-Pain's reaction to "D.O.A.," he took Jay's assault on his signature effect personal. Too personal. Drake and Kendrick's beef never heated up because it didn't have a reason to escalate, but once again, like on "Club Paradise," Drake felt a blade from a hand he considered a friend's, or at least a good acquaintance's.

He would mention it on "Two Birds, One Stone," the lack of rappers who cared to stay in his good graces ("It seems like nobody wants to stay in my good graces / I'm like a real estate agent, putting you all in your places / Look what happens soon as you talk to me crazy"), almost exhausted waking up to new headlines with his name thrown in the mud by a new friend-turned-foe.

The paranoia and skepticism had only increased by the release of *Nothing Was The Same*, and one of the best examples can be found in the first verse of "Wu-Tang Forever":

"People like Mazin who was a best friend to me / Start to become a distant memory, things change in that life / And this life started lacking synergy / And fuckin' with me mentally, I think it's meant to be / Paranoid, always rolling with my mothafuckin' boys / But you gotta understand when it's yours / They don't really leave your ass with a mothafuckin' choice, man" —Drake, "Wu-Tang Forever" (2013)

Nothing Was The Same saw more creepin' and low moving, rap had finally overshadowed Degrassi and Toronto's most prominent star was on his worst behavior, but also introspective on all that was changing around him. Around this time is when we got the infamous *Rolling Stone* interview,[47] the one that would soil his relationship with the media (immortalized on "You & The 6" with: "Gotta be careful around Rolling Stone / Or anyone that's tryna

241

throw stones at me, momma"). The altercation with Diddy over the "0 to 100" beat occurred. He traded shots with his idols Jay-Z and Kanye. More friends turned to rivals or foes.

By the release of *If You're Reading This It's Too Late*, Drake has reached superstar status. He was the 6 God of Toronto, but there was such a strong sense of paranoia on the album that makes him seem more Achilles than Zeus. Just look at his conversation with Sandi:

"I got no friends in this, momma / I don't pretend with this, momma / I'on joke with this, momma / I pull the knife out my back and cut they throat with it, momma / I'm 'Game of Thrones' with it, momma / I'm 'Home Alone' with it, momma / I'm t- / I really hate using this tone with you, momma / I really hate getting aggressive on this phone with you, momma" —Drake, "You & The 6" (2015)

Songs about dying a legend and being worried about not making it to his destination, about taking a blade when invited to hotels by women, uncertain of where the night might lead; whispered accomplishments and screamed out failures; checks not in the mail and fighting with the label; energy-draining enemies and a brand new Beretta. On *More Life* he has a quote about being angry writing Views, but there is far more tension and animosity being spilled across *If You're Reading This It's Too Late*. The trap album signifies the death of Drake the soft, sensitive rapper and the birth of what the music industry made him. This is what it sounds like when fame and fortune are met with paranoia and anxiety — you become a different person.

What's most important is to remember that Drake is a man before a brand, only a robot would be unaffected by all that's been thrown at him in the industry. No matter how much he might mask it, with more knives in his back than Caesar, there's a reason why his raps sound so anti.

"Winnin' is problematic / People like you more when you

workin' towards somethin' / Not when you have it / Way less support from my peers / In recent years as I get established / Unforgivin' times, but fuck it, I manage" —Drake, "Lose You" (2017)

Old friends, the higher-ups, beloved idols, revered peers, former lovers — who hasn't tried to take Drake's head? Attacks on his authenticity, cultural appreciation being called cultural appropriation, distrust of media and critics, all while balancing being a rap star and a pop star. Who does Aubrey Graham become? Not the rapper, not the brand, but the man?

"Fake Love," despite being so sonically cheerful, epitomizes all his distrust; the feeling that everyone he encounters is hiding their true intentions. He's paranoid, ready for war against anyone who wants this spot he's worked so hard to earn. It takes me back to Jay Z's verse on "Light Up." Drake didn't take his advice, but he eventually became Jay:

"And since no good deed go unpunished / I'm not as cool with niggas as I once was / I once was cool as the Fonz was / But these bright lights turned me to a monster / Sorry, mama, I promised it wouldn't change me / But I would have went insane had I remained the same me" —Jay Z, "Light Up" (2010)

Acceptance is something Drake has always wanted, being embraced as an outsider never came to fruition the way he imagined. He once promised that when rap ceased to be fun that he would be done, and he even confessed last year that he doesn't love it like he used to (though he won't be leaving), but he has achieved too much and spent too much energy to not protect his position.

He's adapted to a new role, a lion dominating the animal kingdom. This isn't his natural habitat, and Drake isn't the aggressor, but the industry has a way of transforming nice guys into mob bosses. There are obviously unsaid and unknown events that also contributed to his metamorphosis, but I believe that more than fame, and more than fortune, it's paranoia that drove Drake to the place he is today.

Reaching Mount Olympus changes how the world sees you, the lonely top is the best position to watch those that want what you have. Who Drake is today isn't simply a tougher persona but the person he had to become, or else risk falling victim to the jungle. You either hang the bears or be the face atop a fireplace. Drake would make an interesting study of what happens if, say, Carlton had to survive the streets of Philly instead of Will being sent to Bel-Air.

Don't let the politician's image fool you, Drake may be Toronto's Harvey Dent but he's also Two-Face, the hero who lived long enough to see himself become the villain.

Donald Glover's 10-Year Growth as Childish Gambino

He creates and moves, builds and abandons, he's an artistic vagabond. Success doesn't satisfy whatever fuels him forward, he has a gluttonous appetite for the next endeavor. Almost a decade has evaporated since the release of his first rap project, Sick Boi. Almost 10 years since he put Donald Glover in a Wu-Tang name generator and received the moniker Childish Gambino. Donald is once again prepared to move forward, having recently announced one more album, a final goodbye. It's time to retire his rap persona.

Gambino has a line on the intro of his *Royalty* mixtape about how his mother wondered why he would leave a good job, a reference to his departure from the show "Community." She inquired a similar question when he left the writer's room of 30 Rock after three seasons, just as the NBC sitcom was beginning to truly flourish. Donald tends to time his retreats just as things are beginning to escalate, moments before mass acceptance. "Redbone" is currently rising like a Funkadelic Phoenix, sitting at No. 12 on Billboard's Hot 100, his highest-charting song ever. *"Awaken, My Love!"* debuted at No. 5 on the Billboard 200, Gambino's highest-charting album to date.

Just when it appeared Gambino would be embraced by the masses, inducted into the mainstream as a musician, the plug is being pulled.

"...I feel like there's gotta be a reason to do things and I always had a reason to be punk," he continued. "Being punk just always felt really good to me and we always looked at 'Atlanta' as a punk show and I feel like the direction I would go with Childish Gambino wouldn't

be punk anymore. As much as 'Redbone' is a punk song because it's a gospel song that's on the radio, I'm like there's only so far you can go before you just are the radio." —Donald Glover[48]

Rappers make retirement announcements like Apple announces new iPhones, but Donald is different. He has a history of leaving without looking back. When "Community" fans cried for a return of Troy Barnes, he didn't comply. It's safe to assume we are in the last days of Childish Gambino, the closing of a chapter I've followed closely since 2011 when EP was released. From watching the buoyant, bouncing red hoodie in the music video for "Freaks & Geeks" to viewing Earn's attempt to retrieve a blue jacket with a patch on the season finale of FX's "Atlanta," the years have flown by. As the 33-year-old closes this creative phase in his never-ending pursuit of creating, it provides us with an excellent opportunity to reflect on the various lessons learned from Glover's time as Childish Gambino.

Childish Gambino didn't begin as a social media darling. He was far from a favorite amongst bloggers and music critics. The disdain wasn't completely unwarranted, Donald wasn't the strongest rapper and far from the most endearing singer. Early comments and criticism surrounding his first few releases weren't entirely wrong about the nasal voice and his struggle with defining a style — he was a rough hybrid version of a quirky punchline Wayne meets a navel-gazing pink Polo Kanye who didn't drop out of college. He wasn't taken seriously, overlooked as a parody, and considered to be the actor-turned-rapper that wasn't Drake.

What makes Gambino's early offerings admirable is how he embraced what made him different. Critics were confronted on wax, he never fled from the criticism, and he continued to rap, sing, and create the music he desired. It wasn't always good but it was always Childish. When you're pegged as being different and not embraced by the world, it's an uphill battle to being accepted. Far more tomatoes thrown than roses gifted.

Childish Gambino deserved his tomatoes, even if Pitchfork's 1.6 rating of *Camp* still feels ridiculous, but the weight of the words never crushed him. Album after album he grew, teaching listeners lessons about growth and evolution. Sometimes you have to make "Do Ya Like" before reaching "Redbone," or "Not Going Back" before "Sober." It's okay to make *I AM JUST A RAPPER* before *Royalty* and *Culdesac* before *Because the Internet*. There are gems in his back catalog, honest music that created an early cult of fans who saw the promise. Everything happened in stages, development, and maturity as the music improved, and that crowd only grew larger.

Childish Gambino wasn't an overnight sensation or a musical genius that instantly captivated the world. His growth wasn't an isolated evolution, and he didn't enter the hyperbolic time chamber and come out in his final form. He was a never-ending work in progress.

Gambino had to discover his Noah "40" Shabib [Drake's long-time producer and one of the co-founders OVO] in composer Ludwig Göransson, the man behind the boards for every album since his debut project, *Camp*. Donald and Ludwig may be the most underrated duo since Lil Wayne and StreetRunner. It didn't stop with Ludwig, either. Donald surrounded himself with the Royalty conglomerate, trusted creatives to assist in building his vision. He didn't do it alone and he wasn't perfect. These are two key facts creatives must remember: greatness happens in groups and working toward being great will get you much further than being lazy with natural born talent.

After *Camp*, you can tell Donald began viewing the art of making music differently. He started to move into the mindset of selling an experience instead of just selling music. *Because the Internet* is arguably his best body of work musically, but it's also one of the best album rollouts of the digital era. The experience started by tweeting "Roscoe's Wetsuit," the beginning roll-out of not just a concept album but an entire world based around a character. From the way he dressed to the way he carried himself in interviews, music videos, and short films, Childish Gambino became the Boy that he wrote of in his screenplay. The screenplay didn't necessarily drive sales but it was another piece of art for fans to cherish. He found his voice as a storyteller and took that story beyond the recording studio. He stopped simply being a capable rapper making artistic progress and moved into his position as Kanye's creative heir.

Watching *Clapping For The Wrong Reasons*, the short film released before his sophomore album, the peculiar mood and bizarre tone is identical to what Atlanta became: a compelling story about nothing. The film wasn't just about previewing the music to come, he gave us a glimpse of the world he was building. Because the Internet was a reminder of how few limitations can be put on art. It was a performative piece more than just an album release. Pharos and *"Awaken, My Love!"* were world-building. He didn't just announce a festival, he created an application and festival to perform the music in the setting he desired. Gambino took the "build and they will come" ethos to a performative level, breaking the barrier of control that's hard to maintain in the digital era of album leaks and cell phone spoilers.

The best offer an artist can make in the digital era is an experience you can't download. If it can't be ripped, downloaded or pirated in some form, a new layer of value is created. Both *Because the Internet* and *"Awaken, My Love!"* went beyond the traditional release route to curate experiences. Virtual reality is the latest innovative way Gambino has grabbed the attention of his fans with the release of *"Awaken, My Love!"* on vinyl. Once again, he saw the promise in doing more, using today's technological resources to give an audience a way of experiencing the music that went beyond playing in their headphones. Gambino isn't the first to utilize the VR experience in his music, but by packaging the headset with the vinyl release, it puts him ahead of all the other artists likely to follow suit. What has always made Donald a fascinating artist is his ability not to become stagnant, always finding a new way to make the moment fresh and immersive.

After *Because the Internet*, Childish Gambino went on the Deep Web Tour, with an accompanying Deep Web Tour blog. The site was Tumblr-esque: infinite scroll-styled webpage, grainy disposable camera photos, and text posts from Donald and the team. Like all things associated with Gambino, the Deep Web Tour blog was taken down around the time that all of Donald's social media was deleted. There's something he wrote in the final blog post that I'll continue to carry as a personal mantra long after the days of Childish Gambino end:

"There's a reason 'bro rape' is still up on Youtube. i could take it down, but that's not real life. i also think the stuff in that video is still very relevant and worth talking about. but it's still up. because people should understand u don't have to be perfect. you can just learn."

Time, dedication, passion, and perseverance are what allowed Childish Gambino to prosper. He is the late bloomer that blossomed when the time was right. Artists tend to put pressure on themselves to be perfect, flawless, and beloved by all. He is a testament that if you truly trust the process and never stop growing, your time will come.

Notes & References

38 Younger, Brian, "GoldLink: 'People Are Dancing To My Pain, And They Don't Even Know It', WAMU 88.5 Bandwithfm (April 1, 2015) http://bandwidth.wamu.org/goldlink-people-are-dancing-to-my-pain-and-they-dont-even-know-it/

39 http://www.dmxworld.com/info/interview1.php.

40 Starling, Lakin, "Tricky Stewart Gave Frank Ocean His First Record Deal. Now He Says Labels Should 'Wake Up,'" Fader (August 26, 2016) http://www.thefader.com/2016/08/26/frank-ocean-album-def-jam-tricky-stewart-interview.

41 Trammell, Matthew, "The Frank Ocean Interview," Wax Poetics http://www.waxpoetics.com/blog/features/articles/frank-ocean-soul-caliber-cover-story/.

42 Wallace, Amy, "Frank Ocean: On Channel Orange, Meeting Odd Future, and His Tumblr Letter," GQ (November 20, 2012) https://www.gq.com/story/frank-ocean-interview-gq-december-2012.

43 Robehmed, Natalie, "Frank Ocean Already Made $1 Million By Going Independent," Forbes (April 30, 2016) https://www.forbes.com/sites/natalierobehmed/2016/08/30/frank-ocean-already-made-1-million-by-going-independent/#4a6d4981308f.

44 Caramanica, Jon, "Frank Ocean Is Finally Free, Mystery Intact, New York Times (November 15, 2016) https://www.nytimes.com/2016/11/20/arts/music/frank-ocean-blonde-interview.html.

45 Ibid.

46 Rys, Dan, "Frank Ocean's Album Is the Straw that Broke Universal Music's Back (and It May Get Him Sued)", Billboard (August 24, 2016) http://www.billboard.com/articles/business/7487032/frank-ocean-endless-album-straw-broke-universal-music-back-may-get-sued.

47 Weiner, Jonah, "Drake: High Times at the YOLO Estate," Rolling Stone (February 13, 2014) http://www.rollingstone.com/music/news/drake-high-times-at-the-yolo-estate-20140213.

48 Finley, Taryn, "Donald Glover Reveals Why He's Retiring Childish Gambino," (June 6, 2017) https://www.huffingtonpost.com/entry/donald-glover-retiring-childish-gambino_us_5936da0ce4b0099e7fafaaf3?ncid=engmodushpmg00000004.

Credits

All essays in this volume were written by Yoh and first published in different versions. Below is a list of the essays along with their previous titles and publication dates.

PART 1

"Hip Hop and the Spectrum of Summertime," first published as: "Chance The Rapper, The Fresh Prince & the Madness of Summertime," at DJBooth, June 15, 2017. Copyright © 2017 Travis Phillips.

"Kendrick Lamar Has Quietly Become Music's Biggest Christian Rapper," first published as: "Get God on the Phone: How Kendrick Lamar Quietly Became Music's Biggest Christian Rapper," at DJBooth, March 18, 2016. Copyright © 2016 Travis Phillips.

"LimeWire: The Wrong That Felt So Right," first published as: "Remembering Limewire, My Introduction to Downloading Music Online," at DJBooth, October 27, 2016. Copyright © 2016 Travis Phillips.

"From Queensbridge to Compton: Exploring the Duality of the Regional Hip Hop Perspective," first published as: "From Queensbridge to Compton, Exploring the Duality of the Regional Hip-Hop Perspective," at DJBooth, June 22, 2017. Copyright © 2017 Travis Phillips.

"J. Cole Was Signed by Jay-Z, then He Was Left Alone," first published as: "Nice Watch: The Overlooked, Astounding Story of Jay Z Signing J. Cole," at DJBooth, June 22, 2015. Copyright © 2015 Travis Phillips.

"Playlists and the Future of Lyrical Rap," first published as: "We Spoke to Apple Music's Hip-Hop Gatekeeper About the Future of Lyrical Rap," at DJBooth, August 28, 2017. Copyright © 2017 Travis Phillips.

"Even If It Destroys You: Lil Wayne and the Muse Called Drugs & Vice," first published as: "I Feel Like Dying: Lil Wayne & The Art of Self-Destruction," at DJBooth, March 26, 2015. Copyright © 2015 Travis Phillips.

PART 2

"Summertime '06: A Vince Staples Retrospective," first published as: "Vince Staples' 'Summertime '06' Album Will Lift Us Up," at DJBooth, June 24, 2015. Copyright © 2015 Travis Phillips.

PART 3

PART 4

PART 5

PART 6

Acknowledgments

Yoh acknowledges:

The pages that make up this book bare my name, but many men and women assisted in making them the best they can be. Thank you to my DJBooth editors Nathan Slavic, Brian Zisook, Lucas Garrison, Brendan Varan, and Dave Macli, without you I would still be at Olive Garden serving salads and breadsticks instead of living my best life as a writer. Thank you to Alina Nguyen and Kat Thompson of The Hundreds, and Benjamin Ingram of Mass Appeal, incredible editors. Thank you to Amir Ali Said and Amir Said (Said) of Superchamp Books, the reason the dream of this anthology was able to come true. Lastly, thank you to all the friends, family, readers, and colleagues who are not mentioned by name but know my gratitude is endless and eternal.
—Travis "Yoh" Phillips

Amir Ali Said acknowledges:

Thank you to my father, Amir Said, for presenting me with this challenge, and for offering his guidance and continued advice. I want to thank Yoh for aiming to write work that is daring and representative of our generation, and for his trust in this collaborative effort. Finally, thank you to Ferguson for his crucial assistance in copyediting and additional support.
—Amir Ali Said

Amir Said acknowledges:

Amir Ali Said, my son, best friend, and Superchamp co-founder, As always, thank you for your friendship, knowledge, courage, and curiosity. Your leadership in this endeavor was impressive and invaluable. Anna Zaborowska, thank you for your tireless commitment to Superchamp Books, your brilliance, and your timely proofreading. Jamie Claar, you are exceptional. Thank you very much for all that you do.
—Said

About the Author

Yoh (Travis Phillips) Travis "Yoh" Phillips is a writer from Atlanta, Georgia. His work has appeared in various online music publications, including DJBooth, Mass Appeal, The Hundreds, and Okayplayer. His book, *The Book of Yoh*, is the first book in the *Best Damn Hip Hop Writing* series.

About the Editor

Amir Ali Said is a writer, actor, and filmmaker from Brooklyn, New York. His first book, *Performance Day*, was published in 2013. His new book *Everyday Routine* will be published in the fall of 2017.

About the Series Editor

Amir Said is the creator and editor of the *Best Damn Writing* series. He is a writer, musician, and publisher from Brooklyn, New York, now living in Paris, France. He's written a number of books including *The BeatTips Manual*, *Ghetto Brother* (co-written with Benjy Melendez), *The Art of Sampling*, *Medium Speed in the City Called Paris (Poetry)*, and *The Truth About New York*. His new book, *Camouflage,* will be published in the spring of 2018.

CPSIA information can be obtained
at www.ICGtesting.com
Printed in the USA
FFOW02n0318191217
44093110-43379FF